Early and Middle Adulthood Second Edition

The Best Is Yet to Be—Maybe

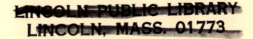

Life-Span Human Development Series

Series Editors: Lynn Dorman, Adolescent and Family Services, Washington, D.C., and Freda Rebelsky, Boston University

Late Adulthood: Perspectives on
Human Development, Second Edition
Richard A. Kalish

Early and Middle Adulthood, Second Edition
Lillian E. Troll, Rutgers University

Adolescence
Kathleen White and Joseph Speisman, Boston University

Perceptual Development
Richard Walk, George Washington University

The Cognitive Neuropsychology of Schizophrenia

Christopher D Frith

MRC Cognitive Neuropsychiatry
Project
MRC Cyclotron Unit
Hammersmith Hospital, London
and
Department of Psychology
University College, London

 LAWRENCE ERLBAUM ASSOCIATES, PUBLISHERS
Hove (UK)   Hillsdale (USA)

Copyright © 1992 by Lawrence Erlbaum Associates Ltd.

Reprinted 1993

Lawrence Erlbaum Associates Ltd., Publishers
27 Palmeira Mansions
Church Road
Hove
East Sussex, BN3 2FA
UK

British Library Cataloguing in Publication Data

Frith, Christopher D.
    Cognitive Neuropsychology of Schizophrenia.—
    (Essays in Cognitive Neuropsychology Series, ISSN 0959–4779)
    I. Title II. Series
    616.89

    ISBN 0-86377-224-2 (Hbk)
    ISBN 0-86377-334-6 (Pbk)

Printed and bound by BPCC Wheatons Ltd., Exeter

To Uta, Martin and Alex

Early and Middle Adulthood Second Edition

The Best Is Yet to Be—Maybe

Lillian E. Troll

Rutgers University

Brooks/Cole Publishing Company
Monterey, California

Brooks/Cole Publishing Company
A Division of Wadsworth, Inc.

Printed in the United States of America
10 9 8 7 6 5 4 3 2 1

Library of Congress Cataloging in Publication Data

Troll, Lillian E.
  Early and middle adulthood.

  Bibliography: p.
  Includes index.
  1. Adulthood.   2. Maturation (Psychology)
3. Middle age.   I. Title.
HQ799.95.T76   1984   305.2'4   84–15620
ISBN 0-534-03813-1

Series Editors: *Lynn Dorman and Freda Rebelsky;* Sponsoring Editor: *C. Deborah Laughton;*
Editorial Assistant: *Mary Tudor;* Production Editor: *David Hoyt;* Manuscript Editor: *Margaret
C. Tropp;* Permissions Editor: *Carline Haga;* Interior Design: *Linda Marcetti;* Cover Design:
John Edeen; Cover Photo: *Jim Pinckney;* Art Coordinator: *Rebecca Ann Tait and Michèle
Judge;* Interior Illustration: *Art by Ayxa;* Typesetting: *Graphic Typesetting Service, Los
Angeles, California;* Printing and Binding: *Malloy Lithographing, Inc., Ann Arbor, Michigan*
(credits continued on p. 225)

To my mother, Bertha H. Ellman,
and my children, Kathren, Jeanne, and Gregory

Preface

It is ten years since the first edition was finished. These years have seen impressive growth in both theory and research on development during early and middle adulthood, although this growth is minor compared to the expansion of comparable theory and research for the ends of the life span: infancy and old age. Most adult developmental theories still follow an early childhood model of step-by-step stages linked to chronological age or assume a universal downward regression in biological and intellectual functioning beginning after adolescence. Two prominent movements against this view are: first, the fitness and health-oriented research of biologists, and second, the "post-formal" theorizing of psychologists. Ten years from now, we might see the fruits of these efforts in more sophisticated ideas and in research focused upon the long years of adulthood—which are growing ever longer.

This edition retains the format of the first. The first chapter is concerned with relevant terms and theoretical issues. The next three chapters consider individual development: biological, cognitive/intellectual, and personality. The final two chapters look at individual development in social or interpersonal contexts: family and job. The epilogue provides a brief summary. This book is intended to be used either by itself or in conjunction with other volumes in the life-span series. It is particularly appropriate for use in tandem with Richard Kalish's *Late Adulthood* for the many courses that combine adulthood and old age into one unit, or in conjunction with life-span development texts that cover adult development only briefly. It is also suited for use by itself. Although there is now a variety of books that combine adult development and aging, there are still very few devoted to adult development alone, an approach that should appeal to teachers as well as nonacademic people. For academic use, it can be combined with several journalistic books.

The cautious optimism of the subtitle still reflects my perspective, based upon growing research attesting to possibilities for positive development over life as well as upon my own development over these years. In arenas where opportunities are available, adults' growth can be as evident as that of children. Life is not set at the age of four; changes in behavior to adjust to changes in circumstances are continuous. Some people still deteriorate, it is true, but it seems ever clearer that much deterioration is attributable to environmental restrictions. The new swing toward a functionalist perspective on development brings with it corollaries for change—positive change—where it is "permitted."

It is customary at this point to acknowledge indebtedness to early mentors, colleagues, and assistants. In both the first edition of this volume and my subsequent larger volume entitled *Continuations: Adult Development and Aging,* from which I borrowed many passages for this edition, I expressed appreciation for the model of continuous adult development provided by my mother, Bertha Holland Ellman, and for the ongoing intellectual stimulation provided by Bernice Neugarten. Many colleagues have broadened or recharged my thinking over the years; to mention one now would be to slight others. My students, both graduate and undergraduate, still challenge confusions and misconceptions and point out errors large and small. I also wish to thank C. Deborah Laughton, editor at Brooks/Cole, who prodded my often weary efforts to complete this work.

I remain grateful to those who reviewed the manuscript of the First Edition: Paul Baltes, Max Planck Institute; Vern Bengtson, University of Southern California; and Richard Kalish.

My special thanks go to those who reviewed the manuscript of the present edition: Ellen Beck, Sinclair Community College; James A. Booth, Community College of Philadelphia; Patricia Blumenthal; Nancy Datan, West Virginia University; Joseph Lyons, University of California at Davis; Paul E. Panek, Eastern Illinois University; Clara Pratt, Oregon State University; and Robert F. Rycek, Kearney State College.

Finally, the continuing development of my three children, Kathren, Jeanne, and Gregory, during their adult years affirms my optimism that "the best is yet to be."

Lillian E. Troll

Contents

Chapter One

Introduction

Although the adult years constitute one of the most stable periods of life, much change can and does occur during this time. These changes are usually so gradual, however, that we don't know they have happened until we look back. Sometimes these changes seem random, but sometimes they seem to form a pattern that we can call "development."

In eras or areas of short life expectancy—when the average age of death is between 30 and 40 rather than between 70 and 80—adulthood can be seen as the "end of the line," with everything that happened before meant to get us there and no place to go but down. Since most of us in the Western world can expect to live out at least the biblical three score years and ten, it is more appropriate to see adulthood as the middle of life, a long-lasting time that blends into an equally long old age. For those who have had and continue to have many options, it can be a time of promise and hope. When Browning (1864/1961) had Rabbi ben Ezra say "Grow old along with me! The best is yet to be," the future he had in mind was life after death, but for many adults today, this "best" can be on our side of heaven.

The Life-Span Point of View:
State or Process?

One way to study development throughout the entire life span is to focus on a series of **states** (stages). Another way is to focus on the **process** of change or development itself. The focus we choose determines the kinds of questions we ask. A focus on the state of adulthood, for example, means trying to find out what adults are like as a group—what distinguishes them from children or adolescents on the one end and from the aging and aged on the other. It does not direct attention to questions about how people get from adolescence to adulthood or from adulthood to old age.

A focus on the process of development, however, is concerned more with general patterns of change and continuity over the whole life than with any particular stage of life. This book favors a process approach. It compares periods of most rapid change (infancy, adolescence, and terminal old age, for example) with periods of slower change (late childhood and adulthood). Such comparisons could throw light on the nature of development—what starts it and stops it, what speeds it up or slows it down. Are there sequences or stages that everybody goes through? Are there critical turning points or crises associated with periods of significant change? If there are critical points, to what extent are they determined biologically and to what extent socially? In effect, can we establish some universal laws or principles of development that would be applicable at any point in life? Beyond this, is the process of developing associated with comfort or discomfort, with good or poor mental health, with improvement or deterioration in coping ability?

A focus on process influences the approach even when the examination is limited to one period in life, such as adulthood. Does development slow down during the adult years? Does it follow a sequence of stages set off by critical points? To what extent are changes induced biologically and to what extent socially? Finally, is the fact that people are now studying adulthood itself a consequence of historical changes that are altering the nature of this period of life, as well as that of the life span as a whole?

General Issues

Developmental theorists have long debated whether adulthood is essentially a stable period of life or whether change—developmental change—does occur or can occur. Not too long ago, Orville Brim and Jerome Kagan, two leading developmental psychologists, summed up the position congenial to this book:

> Humans have a capacity for change across the entire life span.
> . . . [we should question] the traditional idea that the experiences
> of the early years, which have a demonstrated contemporaneous
> effect, necessarily constrain the characteristics of adolescence and
> adulthood. . . . there are important growth changes across the life
> span from birth to death, many individuals retain a great capacity
> for change, and the consequences of the events of early childhood
> are continually transformed by later experiences, making the course
> of human development more open than many have believed [Brim
> & Kagan, 1980, p. 1].

Accumulating research has shown, in other words, that adulthood does not differ fundamentally from childhood in developmental possibilities. Constancy is impressive—individuals rarely change so much that they cannot be recognized—but not all characteristics are set in cement during the beginning years of life.

Following from a premise of both constancy and change are other general issues related to adult development. Six of these issues are described below.

Biological versus Social Determinism

Is biology destiny? To what extent can we attribute the psychological changes of adulthood to biological changes? The menopause, for example, is often said to produce a wide array of psychological changes that presumably would not occur otherwise. Is this true? During the years from 20 to 60, many people experience declines in strength, altered appearance, sensory deficits, or chronic diseases. Are there predictable psychological consequences—in feelings, in functional capacity, in social behavior—of such physical changes? Or is adult psychological development tied more to the social meanings of such changes than to the actual physical events?

Many developmental psychologists who are primarily interested in the early years of life have resolved this problem by means of an interactionist model (Freedman, 1965). They say that neither biology nor experience can be thought of apart from the other; both are intertwined from the moment of conception. As soon as the newly formed unicellular embryo changes to a two-cell organism, these two cells are no longer identical. Each one is influenced by its surrounding environment—just as this surrounding environment is reciprocally changed by the presence of the developing embryo.

Identical twins develop nonidentical personalities because of their differing roles in their family constellation. Both may be biologically programmed to be relatively aggressive, let us say, but one will become more aggressive than the other because it happened to win more skirmishes at an early point in time and thereafter was deferred to by other family members and implicitly encouraged along an aggressive path.

Chapters 2, 3, and 4 address this issue directly, although it underlies much of the content of other chapters as well.

Open versus Closed System

To what extent is human development "preprogrammed" or "built in"? Are we basically machines, computers, that once set on a course can be moved off that course only by outside intervention? Conversely, are we open, altering our paths in response to ongoing events and changing conditions of life?

It is possible to be more open at certain times of life than at others, or more open under certain conditions than under others. It is also possible to be either too open or too closed. People can shut off all outside influence and live in the closed world of autism or schizophrenia. Alternatively, they can be so open that they are overwhelmed. Some adults restrict the variety of their experiences, become less open, and even develop "backward" instead of "forward." (This idea is discussed further in the following section.) More adults, perhaps, regulate the input of new experience in a way that enables them to remain essentially stable over most of the rest of their lives, or they may regulate new experiences in some areas while they remain open in others. It is also possible that some people are always more open to new experiences than others.

Chapters 3 and 4 deal with this issue.

Quantitative versus Qualitative Change

Are changes during adulthood just additions to or subtractions from what was there before, or are they basic changes in structure, creating something new and different? Are they generally positive, leading to improvement, or negative, leading to deterioration? Are they reversible and responsive, like those of chameleons, perhaps, or are they irreversible and fixed metamorphoses, more like those of frogs?

It is possible to have change that is not development. The definition of development, in fact, is a problem. Neugarten (1973) has defined it as processes "in which the organism is irreversibly changed or transformed . . . and which vary in an orderly way with age regardless of the direction of change" (pp. 312–313). Notice that this definition encompasses negative changes as well as positive ones. A different kind of definition is derived from the theories of Piaget (1972), Flavell (1970), and Werner (1948). It involves a progression from simple to complex behavior, from undifferentiated to differentiated systems. A version of this latter concept is used in this book. It is based upon J.E. Anderson's (1957) concept of life as an open system—that is, one that is open to input from the outside.

Other things being equal, the more open people are to new experience, the more they are likely to change in response to changes in the environment—or, we might say, to develop. If people assimilate new information, they become more differentiated. The more differentiated they become, the more likely they are to reorganize these diverse elements into new categories— or, to use Piagetian terminology, to accommodate to them. It is the integration of these increasingly diverse elements into higher-order categories that produces greater overall complexity.

How many of the changes of adulthood are truly developmental, according to either definition above? This is one of the most controversial issues in the field of life-span development today. For one thing, development is probably more than accumulating—or discarding—information or experience. (See the concept of "crystallized intelligence" in Chapter 3.) If new information just elaborates on earlier information, the person does not have to change in any fundamental way. It is when new information seems to contradict old information that the person is forced to reconcile this contradiction by constructing new concepts that put all the information together into a more complex whole.[1]

Another controversial issue is whether to consider retrogression as development—that is, to include changes that move in the direction of decreasing complexity. As noted earlier, many adults restrict the variety of their experiences, become less open, and probably develop "backward" instead of "forward." It is because only some adults continue to remain open to new experience, and so to develop in a positive sense, that the word *maybe* was added to the subtitle of this book.

Chapters 3 and 4, again, deal with this issue.

Time

How do individuals' life times—where they are in their own life span—fit in with social time—where they are according to the expectations of the society in which they live? How do life time and social time relate to historical time—the period in which a life time or social time occurs?

Life time.   How old you are is measured most simply by counting the months and years since you were born. Chronological age, however, although useful in a statistical way to predict the incidence of particular diseases or the number of people born a certain year who are expected to be alive at some later date, is at best a crude measure. People born at the same time can differ widely in how long they may be "programmed" to live and in the rate at which different parts of their bodies may mature and age and die.

Anyone looking at a group of newborn infants in a nursery cannot help but be impressed by their differences in "maturity," alertness, and vigor. These differences increase with every passing moment, not only as a result of variations in biological characteristics but also as a result of variations in their life circumstances. In a seventh-grade classroom, populated primarily by 12-year-olds, some students look physically like adults, while others could "pass" as third-graders. Some girls have been menstruating for more than a year, while others have not even begun the body changes of puberty. Most— but not all—of the boys are still several years away from puberty.

What is true for physical appearance is also true for psychological characteristics—both intellect and personality. By the adult years, whatever predictive power chronological age had earlier virtually disappears.

---

[1]There is an alternative, which many people follow. They can ignore new information that contradicts previous information (producing "cognitive dissonance") and cling to their old concepts. This alternative is called **rigidity**.

After adolescence, in fact, prospective age of death would be a more meaningful index than age since birth. Consider a group of 40-year-olds. Some will reach the end of their natural lives in a year or two, while others will not die for another 60 or even 70 years. The difference is almost as long as an average life span! Because of these problems with chronological age, scientists have been trying for more than half a century to find a way of measuring "developmental age," looking for body changes that would predict how far along people are toward aging and death. While some success has been achieved in predicting how far children are along the path to maturity, efforts to achieve a comparable measure past maturity have so far been relatively unrewarding.

Social time.   All societies divide time into socially relevant units, transforming calendar time into social time. For example, a man in a simple society might pass from infancy to childhood to warrior-apprentice to warrior (and simultaneously to husband and father) and finally to elder. He would know what stage he was in because he would have experienced memorable "rites of passage" that marked each transition.

Age grades are found in all societies, not only simple ones, and are associated with particular duties, rights, and rewards. When the division of labor in a society is limited and social change is slow, a single age-grade system can regulate family, work, religious, and political roles. In a complex society like ours, more than one kind of age-status system is used. But even in our society, certain events are tied to chronological age: starting school, becoming eligible to vote, to drive a car, to drink. In general, there is more emphasis in our society on the events of entry into adulthood than on later markers. To use Neugarten's (1968) terms, there is more difficulty in being "age deviant" or "off time" in the early years than in the later ones.

Historical time.   Human development is influenced by long-term historical processes such as industrialization and urbanization as well as by short-term processes such as wars and economic depressions. People who were children during the Depression of the 1930s, for example, were affected differently from those who were adults at the time. Depression boys tended to become highly responsible adults who did not like their wives to work because they felt that their mothers' employment was shameful. Depression girls tended to overvalue conspicuous consumption. See Glen Elder's study of these effects in his book, *Children of the Great Depression* (1974). Those who experienced the Depression as adults often remained deeply concerned about security for the rest of their lives. But everybody who was alive during the Depression was affected by it in some way.

Although all these aspects of time are relevant to the study of development, time as such cannot be used as an explanation for development. It is what happens during those years, not the years themselves, that causes change. Chapters 4, 5, and 6 address this issue.

Variability versus Universality

In thinking about development, it seems to be easier to look at what is common among different people rather than what is not common. Most writing is of *the* life course, *the* midlife crisis, *the* effects of retirement rather than life-course differences, midlife differences, and the different consequences of retirement. But variety is at least as true as commonality. Some humans finish their life at 40 years of age, others at 100. Some experience one or more crises during their adult years, others do not. Some find retirement wonderful, others find it makes no difference, and others are devastated by it. Some women have to stop to think whether they are in their menopause, and others find their lives completely altered by it. All the chapters deal with this issue.

Turning Points

Does adult development occur in fits and starts, with disruptive crises and prominent turning points? This is one of the big unanswered questions today. Scholars are caught between two opposing points of view. At one end are those who see "development as a progression by qualitative leaps and structural reorganizations" (Riegel, 1975, p. 123). At the other end are those who see "development as a continuous accumulation of bits of experience or information" (Riegel, 1975, p. 123).

Ethologists, who study nonhuman species, point out that there may be particular points in the course of development when certain kinds of experiences have greater effect than at other times. They call these **critical periods.** For example, the events of early childhood may have more profound consequences in shaping personality and future behavior than those of adulthood or later life. Certain experiences, such as falling in love or having sexual intercourse, may have very different effects during adolescence than during the 40s and 60s. Becoming a parent can be a very different kind of event in the 20s than in the 30s or 40s. Widowhood in the 30s or 40s can be very different from widowhood in the 60s.

At some points in life, when biological events are abrupt, it is easier to take the side of the crisis theorists. A child's first walking or talking, for example, can seem to happen overnight and can have momentous consequences for that child's subsequent actions. The onset of puberty, although more drawn out, is a later example, as is, for some people, the first sexual experience.

Aside from these universals, biological events come about idiosyn-cratically—not "normally." For the woman, childbirth may be an exception, as may be menopause. Otherwise, it is only illness or disability that can have the kind of impact we are thinking of. In a broad sense, however, no illness or disability is universal, not even at the end of life.

Some turning points are given social significance by rituals that anthropologists call **rites of passage.** These turning points are important to the particular society in which people live. Most societies celebrate the onset of puberty. In our society, the turning points we celebrate are much more likely to be social changes than biological ones. It is graduation from school— elementary school, high school, or college—that is celebrated, not the onset of puberty. It is the social wedding, not the first sexual encounter. It is a new job, or a promotion, or retirement.

A number of life-span theories focus on "midlife crisis." Although each theory looks at it in a different way, they all maintain that "middle age" is a time of reversal, or at least a time of profound change and distress. Chapters 4, 5, and 6 address this very popular issue.

Models of Development

A proposition as to how development may occur, or at least what it may look like, can be useful in trying to study the process. Most models of development end with childhood. A few describe or attempt to explain changes during adolescence. Even fewer focus upon adulthood and later years.

Models of adult development are of two general kinds: open-ended and structured. Learning theories are examples of the former, stage theories of the latter. A few of the more popular current models are presented briefly below.

Open-Ended Theories

Some psychologists maintain that any commonalities we find at par-ticular ages or in particular sequences are accidental or are the result of com-mon experiences within a common culture, rather than being predetermined by inner maturational processes (Bandura, 1969). Social-learning theories stress the social determinants of adult behavior (Baltes, 1979; Brim, 1977) and the influence of important life events. They assume that learning one task or living through one kind of experience makes one ready for the next, pre-sumably more difficult, task or open to the next order of experience. Gagné (1968) sees the development of intelligence, for example, as proceeding from simple to complex through the learning of progressively more intricate sets of rules. He believes that stages of development are not related to age, except in the sense that learning takes time and that there is an "inherent logic" prescribing that certain abilities have to be acquired before others can be learned.

A different kind of open-ended developmental theory is that of Klaus Riegel (1975). His "dialectic theory" acknowledges many sources of influence for change: biological (including genetic), psychological, and historical. Following the 19th-century German philosopher Hegel and the German-American developmental theorist Heinz Werner, he sees human development as the result of opposition or contradiction between a preexisting state (thesis) and a new condition (antithesis). The resolution of this conflict is a new structure or function (synthesis), which incorporates both thesis and antithesis in a qualitatively different structure or function.

Not only do developmental models have to consider such issues as the openness of the developing organism and whether or not development is qualitative or quantitative, but they must also consider how passive or active an individual is and, according to Riegel (1975), how passive or active the environment is in which the individual develops. Riegel sees four possible juxtapositions of human beings and their environment.

These four positions are diagrammed in Figure 1–1. Box I represents the view that both the person and the environment are essentially passive, with change occurring in a random, or at least unsystematic, way. In this view, we are molded by the experiences we just happen to encounter as we go through life. Box II represents an active person in a passive environment. Piaget's (1972) theory and those derived from it, including Kohlberg's (1973) and Loevinger's (1976), generally fit this model. The individual actively seeks change when it is ready for it, assimilating those parts of the environment it wants. Box III represents a passive person in an active environment. In this view, development is simply the result of cohort or historical changes which mold people like blobs of clay. Box IV, finally, is the dialectic view, in which both individual and environment participate in complex interactions.

Individual	*Environment*	
	Passive	*Active*
Passive	I Behaviorists Social-learning theories	III Cohort or historical change
Active	II Piagetian theories	IV Dialectic theory

Figure 1-1. Theoretical views of cause of development

Stage Theories

Although current stage theories differ widely, almost all assume that:

1. Everybody goes through life in the same way (**universality**).
2. Everybody goes through the stages in the same order (**sequentiality**).
3. There is a predetermining end point to the sequence (**teleology**).
4. There is a good way, as well as a bad way, to go through the sequence (**adaptation**).

Many of these theories also make a fifth assumption:

5. The good way is in tune with current middle-class values (**class bias**).

Although many life-span developmental psychologists find one or more of these assumptions untenable and therefore any stage theory unsatisfactory, it is stage models of development that are most familiar, partly because they are easier to understand than open-ended models.

Current stage theories can be divided into three categories according to their basis: structure, life situations, and issues.

Stage theories based on structure.   Most stage theories of adult development come from theories of child development and thus tend to be either biologically or cognitively based. The influence of Jean Piaget (1972) has been strong over the past decades, although he himself believed only quantitative change was possible after adolescence. Kohlberg's (1973) moral-development stages and Loevinger's (1976) ego-development stages both are based upon Piaget's model but see continuing development possible during adulthood.

One characteristic of Piagetian-derived theories is that they stress the transformation of earlier structures into later ones. Rather than the image of a ladder, in which the person climbs from one state to the next, such models evoke that of metamorphosis, of drastic changes in form that result in essentially new individuals, even though the new individual is composed of parts of the former self.

Stage theories based on life situations.   Stage theories based on life situations generally present a sequence of developmental tasks. One of the simplest of these is Havighurst's (1972). Table 1–1 lists the tasks for his adulthood stages.

A variation of stage theory is proposed by Daniel Levinson (1978) on the basis of clinical studies of men. He sees three "gross" chronological periods in the adult life course—early, middle, and late adulthood—that are

Table 1-1. Havighurst's developmental tasks for adulthood

Early adulthood

Selecting a mate
Learning to live with a marriage partner
Starting a family
Rearing children
Managing a home
Getting started in an occupation
Taking on civic responsibility
Finding a congenial social group

Middle age

Achieving adult civic and social responsibility
Establishing and maintaining an economic standard of living
Assisting teenage children to become responsible and happy adults
Developing adult leisure-time activities
Relating to one's spouse as a person
Accepting and adjusting to the physiological changes of middle age
Adjusting to aging parents

Source: Havighurst, 1953.

connected by intervening transitions. The resulting sequence of stages is listed in Table 1–2. Levinson's model has captured the media. Gail Sheehy's best-seller *Passages* (1976) used it. Because it is closely linked to chronological age and the stages are described in detail, it is appealing for lay readers.

Stage theories based on issues. Erik Erikson (1950) bases his model on the developmental views of Sigmund Freud, probably the most influential

Table 1-2. Levinson's stages (for men)

Leaving the family (20–24): A transitional period from adolescence to early adulthood that involves moving out of the family home and establishing psychological distance from the family, analogous to Erikson's stage of identity versus role diffusion

Getting into the adult world (early 20s to 27–29): A time of exploration and provisional commitment to adult roles in occupational and interpersonal areas and of fashioning an initial "life structure"

Settling down (early 30s to early 40s): A period of deeper commitment, sometimes involving the expansion motif of Jung and Kuhlen

Becoming one's own man (35–39): The high point of early adulthood

The midlife transition (early 40s): A developmental transition involving a sense of bodily decline and a vivid recognition of one's mortality, as well as an integration of the feminine aspects of the self as postulated by Jung

Restabilization and the beginning of middle adulthood (middle 40s): A period in which some men make new creative strides but others lose their vitality

Source: Levinson, Darrow, Klein, Levinson, and McKee, 1976.

theorist of this century. Freud's stage sequence, presumed to have a biological base, ends with early adulthood. It was left to his followers, particularly Jung and Erikson, to map out a complete life development. Each of Erikson's eight stages starts with a new issue that involves a choice between two opposites— one good, the other bad. This choice influences all future life. The first stage starts in infancy, and the last is most characteristic of old age. Only three are designated as applicable to the years beyond adolescence: intimacy, generativity, and ego integrity. However, all stages are presumably operative to some extent throughout life. Gruen (1964) has redefined all eight stages to fit adult behavior. In Table 1–3, Gruen's definitions have been partially modified to apply to young and middle adulthood.

Like Erik Erikson, Carl Jung (1930/1971) followed Freud in developing a stage model for the progression of consciousness. He is probably most influential in his more general statement that the early years of adulthood are times of psychological expansion and the later years, from middle age on, are times of psychological constriction. This view has appealed particularly to those interested in the study of midlife crisis or transition.

The theories of adult development described here are only a few of those currently being considered. In Table 1–4, they are compared in terms of the six issues presented earlier in this chapter. With respect to the first issue, biological versus social determinism, for example, it can be seen that both Havighurst's stage model and the more open-ended learning theories favor social determinism. The two neo-Freudian theories, those of Erikson and Jung, include biology as an important determiner. In Levinson's model, this issue is not relevant.

Methodological Problems

The simplest way to approach questions about adult development is to compare people of different ages—say, 20-year-olds with 40-year-olds. If the 40-year-olds look and act differently from the 20-year-olds, it is easy to assume that this is because they are 20 years older. This kind of age comparison at one point in time is called **cross-sectional** research; it is shown graphically in Figure 1–2. In the right-hand column, three groups are being compared in 1980: Group 3 consists of 20-year-olds, Group 2b of 40-year-olds, and Group 1c of 60-year-olds. Let us say that they are all taking computer courses, and the measure of comparison is how quickly they are learning. If the 40-year-olds are slower than the 20-year-olds, and the 60-year-olds even slower than the 40-year-olds, it is tempting to assume that the older groups would have been as good as the 20-year-olds when they were 20 but that age has slowed them down.

The trouble with cross-sectional research is that although it gives us age *differences,* at least at the time of research, it cannot tell us whether the

Table 1-3.   Adaptation of Erikson's stages to young and middle adulthood

Stage	Positive resolution	Negative resolution
1. Basic trust versus basic mistrust	Person likes or trusts work associates, friends, relatives; feels essentially optimistic about people and their motives; has confidence in self and the world in general.	Person distrusts people; prefers to be alone because friends "get you into trouble"; dislikes confiding in anyone; distrusts self and the world in general.
2. Autonomy versus shame and doubt	Has own attitudes and ways of doing things, not because others expect them; is not afraid to hold own opinions or do what he or she wants.	Is self-conscious about own ideas and ways of doing things and prefers to stay with tried and trusted ways; avoids asserting self in group; emphasizes how much like others he or she acts and feels.
3. Initiative versus guilt	Takes pleasure in planning and initiating action; plans ahead and de- signs own schedule.	Lets others initiate action; plays down success or accomplishment.
4. Industry versus inferiority	Likes to make things and carry them to comple- tion; strives for skill mastery; has pride in production.	Is passive; leaves things undone; feels inadequate about ability to do things or produce work.
5. Ego identity versus role diffusion	Has strongly defined social roles; feels at home in work, family, affiliations, sex role; enjoys carrying out role behavior; has sense of belonging; takes comfort in style of life and daily activities; is definite about self and who he or she is; feels continuity with past and present.	Is ill at ease in roles, lost in groups and affiliations; does not enter into required role behavior with much conviction; may make radical switches in work or residence without meaning or purpose.

Table 1-3 continues on p. 14

Table 1-3, continued

6. Intimacy versus isolation	Has close, intimate relationship with spouse, children, and friends, sharing thoughts, spending time with them, expressing warm feelings for them.	Lives relatively isolated from friends, spouse, children; avoids contact with others on an intimate basis; is either absorbed in self or indiscriminately sociable; relations with people are stereotyped or formal.
7. Generativity versus stagnation	Has plans for future that require sustained application and utilization of skills and abilities; invests energy and ideas into something new; has sense of continuity with future generations.	Seems to be vegetating; does nothing more than routines of work and necessary daily activities; is preoccupied with self.
8. Integrity versus despair	Feels satisfied and happy with life, work, accomplishments; accepts responsibility for life; maximizes successes.	Feels depressed and unhappy about life, emphasizing failures; would change life or career if had another chance; does not accept present age and mode of life, emphasizing past; fears getting older; fears death.

20-year-olds will slow down as they get older and become like the 40-year-olds in 20 years. To find out about age *changes,* we need to follow the same people over the years. This second kind of study is called **longitudinal** research; it is shown graphically in the diagonal of Figure 1–2. A group of 20-year-olds (Group 1a) were tested in 1940, reexamined in 1960 (Group 1b) when they were 40, and reexamined again in 1980 (Group 1c) when they were 60. By comparing the performance of the same people at different ages, researchers can control extraneous factors resulting from different times of growing up, such as economic conditions, education, and whether or not computers were a fact of life. As mentioned earlier, the varying conditions of early life can have lasting consequences: the life path of one age group may not be equivalent to the life path of a later or earlier age group. Thus the development of Group 2a would not be the same as the development of Group 1a.

Table 1-4. Comparing some developmental theories on six issues

Issue	Havighurst	Levinson	Erikson	Jung	Learning theories
Biological versus social determinism	Social	Not relevant	Partly biological	Mostly biological	Social
Open versus closed system	Open to normative demands	Relatively closed	Selectively open	More open at some periods than others	Open
Quantitative versus qualitative change	Quantitative change	Qualitative development	Qualitative development	Qualitative development	Quantitative change
Time	Implicit chronological age	Explicit chronological age	Social time	Biological time	Not relevant
Variability versus universality	Universality	Universality	Universality	Universality	Variability
Turning points	Implicit	Universal and prominent	Universal and prominent	Universal and prominent	No

Warner Schaie (1970), who first pointed out these methodological hazards, suggested that it would be better to use **cross-sequential** research. By combining the information from both cross-sectional and longitudinal approaches, it is possible to correct for historical and **cohort**[2] variations. Putting together Group 1, Group 2, and Group 3 in 1940, 1960, and 1980 gives a better estimate of developmental change itself. Furthermore, by comparing people of the same age across time, it is possible to get an estimate of the effect of cultural change. This would apply, in Figure 1–2, to Groups 1a, 2a, and 3a and to Groups 1b and 2b.

Another serious problem of longitudinal research will not be so easy to overcome, however. That problem is "survivor bias." Because, in general, more advantaged and more vigorous individuals tend to survive longer than those who are less advantaged and healthy, the groups of subjects in the last round of testing or observation are not really the same groups as those who began in the first round. The people at the low end of the distribution—on almost any measurement, in fact—are probably no longer alive, and therefore the group average seems better than it would have been if the complete original group had survived (Riegel, Riegel, & Meyer, 1967). Because of this effect, it is important to under-interpret curves of change from longitudinal studies. Abilities may seem to stay the same or improve over time, but they may not have changed at all, or even have deteriorated, for the people in the last round of testing—the survivors.

The Generation Effect

To understand the development of American adults, we must account for the effect of cultural change: the generation effect. To illustrate, consider the different circumstances in the past lives of the various age groups of people who are adults in the mid-1980s. The examples given here are applicable more to middle-class whites than to working-class, poor, or non-white people.

The *60-year-olds,* born in the 1920s, were young children during the Depression, surrounded by needy relatives flocking together from rural areas. They were highly involved in World War II: the men in the armed forces, the women in jobs formerly held by men. After the war, many men went to college on GI loans and on to middle-class bureaucratic "organization-man" positions. Their wives returned as soon as possible to the traditional roles of mother and housewife and to the conspicuous consumption associated with suburban affluence and many children. Their indulgence in the "feminine mystique" thus complemented their husbands' occupational conformity. Their children, born in the late 1940s and 1950s, were ripe fodder for the drug-imbued counter-

[2]A cohort consists of people born at the same time and brought up under the same conditions.

1940 *First Round*	*1960* *Second Round*	*1980* *Third Round*
		Group 1c, Survivors of 1a, who are now 60-year-olds
	Group 1b Survivors of 1a, who are now 40-year-olds	Group 2b, Survivors of 2a, who are now 40-year-olds
Group 1a 20-year-olds	Group 2a 20-year-olds	Group 3 20-year-olds

Cross-sectional comparisons: Groups 2a and 1b; Groups 3, 2b, and 1c
Longitudinal comparisons: Groups 1a, 1b, and 1c; Groups 2a and 2b
Cultural-change comparisons: Groups 1a, 2a, and 3; Groups 1b and 2b

Figure 1-2.   Hypothetical cross-sequential research model. (Adapted from Schaie, 1970.)

culture, rejecting the security that comforted their parents. If the 60-year-olds' parents are still living—and some still are, mostly their mothers—they are probably a burden to their children, wherever they may be living. The people in this cohort, therefore, may be burdened with prolonged responsibilities to both parents and children. Nevertheless, many have been enjoying the comforts and even luxuries of economic affluence not available to them earlier.

The *50-year-olds,* born in the 1930s, were children during World War II and teenagers in the postwar period of affluence. A few were involved in the Korean conflict. They were expected to go to college, supported either by their parents or by readily found employment or stipends. They married early, had children early, and went in for even larger families than did the age group ahead of them. They took suburban affluence as a matter of course; it was easy for them to have confidence in themselves, their future, and their world. They may not have been as involved with their children as the previous group. Because most of their parents are in poor health or dying, the 50-year-olds are heavily involved with their care or with decisions for their care, particularly in the case of daughters.

The *40-year-olds,* born in the 1940s, were part of the postwar baby boom. They were scared by the atom bomb, blasé about space travel, and heard about corruption in high places on television. They were young children during the postwar period of affluence, and they expected M.A.s, Ph.D.s, or high-level jobs to come naturally—so naturally that many disdained them and "dropped out." They went in for early marriage and early childbearing, but few children. Self-actualization is their goal, and the worthwhile life their value. They can welcome changes in marriage or in lifestyle because they grew up in security.

The *30-year-olds,* born in the 1950s, were also part of the postwar baby boom and grew up in a denser, more highly populated world than that experienced by any previous generation. Their world has been one of constant anxieties—Vietnam, nuclear weapons, rising prices, crime, violence, and drugs—rather than immediate crises such as war and depression. They married late, if at all, divorced readily, and had children later than previous age groups, often raising them in single-parent households.

The *20-year-olds,* born in the 1960s after the peak of the baby boom, grew up in smaller households. Even more than those ten years older, they are given to hard rock, their fantasies split between nostalgia for the not-too-distant past and future wars in outer space. They have been indifferent about school, lived in single-parent or reconstituted families, and had multiple kinship allegiances. Where they are going it is too soon to know; many have been attracted by cults and fundamentalist religion and politics. They came of age in a country swinging to the right and struggling for economic existence.

Variation among Groups

There are pronounced variations in both timing and pattern of development according to sex, social class, and ethnic or cultural group, as well as age cohort or generation. On almost any dimension—cognitive, personality, family, or career—women show systematic differences from men, working-class people from middle-class people, Black people from White people, Italians from Jews, and those who grew up at one time in history from those who came of age in another. And these dimensions are themselves interrelated. For example, the difference between middle-class women and working-class women may itself be a function of placement in historical time. Their reactions to the "empty nest"—the time when the youngest child leaves home—might have been more alike in the 1930s than in the 1970s because both groups would have been socialized to more stereotyped sex roles and would have continued to bear and raise children until almost the end of their lives.

Gender Differences

Gender is one of the most important factors in development; women move through their adult years in a notably different fashion from men. In part, this difference is due to such biological factors as differential health and mortality. Table 1–5 shows that from the age of 35 on, more women are living than men of the same age—among Whites. Among Blacks, women start outnumbering men at the age of 20. The higher number of preadult males in

Table 1-5. Sex ratio in the United States population by age and race, 1981

	Women per 100 men	
Age	White	Black
Under 5 years	94.9	98.2
5–9	95.0	98.4
10–14	95.2	98.7
15–19	96.2	99.9
20–24	98.0	107.1
25–29	98.9	113.0
30–34	100.0	116.0
35–39	101.3	119.8
40–44	102.4	121.1
45–49	103.7	122.0
50–54	106.2	124.9
55–59	110.7	124.2
60–64	115.1	126.9
65–74	130.2	138.5
75 and over	184.5	168.8

Adapted from U.S. Department of Commerce (1983), Table 31.

both groups reflects the higher birthrate for boys. Even boys' higher death rates don't counter initial male oversupply until the adult years. But from then on, this ratio is reversed, in constantly increasing strength.

In addition to biological and numerical gender differences, differences in sex-role expectations affect how life events are interpreted, encouraged, or discouraged. In her discussion of age roles, Neugarten (1968) states that one should really speak of "age/sex roles," because men and women differ on every age expectation and age norm. Both men and women are generally expected to marry in their 20s, but women are expected to—and do—marry about two years earlier than men. Also, the implications of getting married or not getting married are different for men and women.

Societies often differ widely in what they consider proper feminine and masculine behavior, but all societies differentiate proper masculine from feminine behavior. The social clock and the developmental rhythm of a woman's life have very different timings from those of a man's life. And so far, in spite of the determination of many young—and older—adults of today to achieve a more uniform status and lifestyle, shifts in most sex-linked characteristics have been slow in coming.

All this does not necessarily mean that one sex is better off than the other. When all differences are balanced out by the end of life, the score may be more equal than might be judged at some earlier time of life. For example, early in life men seem to have more power than do women, and later women seem to have better health than do men.

Social-Class Differences

Almost as pervasive as sex differences are those of social class. The lives and life spans of middle-class men and women differ in many ways from those of working-class men and women. Class-linked variations in what people eat, where they live, what kinds of health care they can get, and how strenuous or stimulating their work is affect physical characteristics and life expectancy. Class differences in education and associated lifestyle, such as time spent in reading and other intellectual endeavors, can affect cognitive performance— initial levels as well as stability and decline over time. Class-linked values, such as conventionalism and traditionalism, can affect personality, family, and career patterns.

Ethnic and Cross-Cultural Differences

If the United States and Canada are compared with South America, Asia, and Africa, they may seem to be remarkably homogeneous in many ways. Within these countries, however, are subgroups with clearly divergent histories, sets of values, and living conditions that affect the course of human development. A Southern California study that compared Blacks, Mexican-Americans, and Whites, for example (Bengtson, Kasschau, & Ragan, 1977), found multiple effects in self-perceived health, self-identification as old, and self-predicted length of future life. Anglos (Whites) consistently tended to say they were in good health. Only 4% said their health was poor even when they were "old" (65–75). There were more reports of poor health by Blacks and Mexican-Americans between 45 and 54 than by Whites 20 years older.

In another study, involving five Israeli subcultures, Datan, Antonovsky, and Maoz (1981) found that it was not only the most "modern" or advantaged women who showed the best psychological adjustment to menopause. The most "traditional" women fared just as well. It was the women in the "transitional" groups who had the worst time, perhaps precisely because of their transitional status. This study is discussed further in the next chapter.

Some writers suggest that the important factors in explaining differences among societies are the ways in which people think about themselves and about the options available to them—options that may be associated with the complexity of their society. In a "simple" society—we are not talking about degree of mechanization or industrialization but rather about how much one has to learn before one can function independently—individuals can reach "maturity" at an early age. In a somewhat more complex society, individuals may not achieve the necessary competence before age 15 or 16 and may have to move out of the center of life by 70. In a very complex society such as ours, one might not reach "adulthood" before 35 and then might have to retreat at 45 as a wave of new more "up-to-date" specialists arrives. This is true today at least for some medical specialties and other occupations requiring a very high level of technical competence.

If a culture has had a long enough time to survive in its ecological niche, it is likely to have achieved a successful system of interrelationships, attitudes, and expectations for behavior. When this system is upset in any way, the members of the culture must establish a new one. This period of transition can be accompanied by acute distress, like that of the "transitional" Israeli women. This may be true even if, in the long run, they may end up "better off."

Mass migrations into industrialized centers over the past couple of centuries have put previously rural groups into profound transition and change. Rural people tend to maintain traditional, familistic, and intergenerational patterns of deference (Aldrich, 1974), while urban residents are more individuated and are not categorically deferential to elders. Adult development would be very different under these two conditions.

Summary

Adults can and do change and develop, although some psychologists believe that this change is quantitative rather than qualitative. There are diverse perspectives on adult development, depending partly upon how open adults are seen to be. It is important to consider the intersections between life time and social and historical time and thus to use research methods that combine both cross-sectional and longitudinal approaches. Some theorists see the adult years as a period of abrupt changes or turning points, whether these are brought on by biological events or social events or expectations. Some even see these turning points as common to all at particular ages, although others believe them to be more idiosyncratic, the result of each person's own life experiences. There are certainly marked differences in development by sex, generation, class, and ethnic group.

Chapter Two

Physical Development in the Adult Years

Adult Americans hope to look years younger than they actually are. They want to be physically fit and strong. Women probably care more about attractiveness and men more about strength and vigor—and sexual prowess—but both fear bodily deterioration. It is easy to sell cosmetics and fashions that promise youthful appearance. A new diet book can make its author rich. A new and simple prescription for vigor, from running to pushups, gets adopted overnight. Most people hesitate to speak the word menopause aloud, or the word impotence.

This chapter describes changes in the body during the adult years. It is not intended to be a comprehensive review of all physiological changes, but rather a review of what generally can be expected from the viewpoint of psychological importance. Unfortunately, there are many gaps in our knowledge.

Overall, adulthood is the time of peak physical status. Most body functions reach full growth and development by the middle 20s: height, strength, coordination, and speed of response, as well as health, efficiency, and endurance, are at maximum levels. For the next 20 or 30 years—and sometimes even longer—declines from this peak are so gradual as to make them seem like a long plateau. By about the age of 50, however, there is usually enough bodily change to justify using this age as a rough biological marker.

Primary and Secondary Aging

Certain changes seem to be inevitable and universal—everybody who lives long enough will show them. Other changes—probably most that are to be described—are more frequent in the later years of life than in earlier years, but are not inevitable. The first kind of change could be considered **primary aging.** It would include the menopause in women and comparable hormonal changes in men, some chemical changes in cells, and gradual loss of adaptive reserve capacity. The second kind of change could be considered **secondary aging.** It can occur at any time of life but is found with greater frequency among older people. It may be the result of reduced reserve capacity and thus greater vulnerability, or perhaps of idiosyncratic reactions to other conditions. This kind of aging includes sensory loss, chronic diseases such as arteriosclerosis or diabetes, and brain deterioration, often called Alzheimer's disease. Few physical changes are primary, or inevitable and universal; in the human species, variation is the rule.

Developmental Age

As mentioned in the last chapter, much as it would be desirable to have a measure of **developmental age,** or progress along the **life time** dimension, research efforts to find such a measure are not much further along than they were in the 1930s, when Halstead's team of psychologists and biologists at the University of Chicago worked on the problem. When investigators at the Boston Veterans Administration Hospital (Fozard, Nuttall, & Waugh, 1972) correlated a battery of physiological and behavioral measures with chronological age, the only one that proved significant was graying of hair. In general, it has been more fruitful to measure distance from death than distance from birth. Palmore (1969), for example, using Duke University longitudinal data, and Libow (1974) with other longitudinal data report a number of behavioral and physiological indices associated with survival. In general, the more active and involved people are and the higher their scores on intelligence tests, the more likely they are to outlive other members of their **age cohort**—those born about the same time they were. Among the biomedical indices cited by Libow are lower systolic blood pressure, higher weight, lower serum cholesterol, and low serum albumin. More will be said about the relation with intelligence in the next chapter.

General Physical Attributes

Height

Most people reach their full height by their middle 20s; the average age at which all the skeleton is converted to bone is 18 (Timiras, 1972). Longitudinal studies show that these ages vary widely, however. Büchi (1950), for example, found increases in height into the 40s among men, mostly in sitting height. Gsell (1967) similarly reported that some people grow as much as 1 cm after their 25th birthdays.

Although cross-sectional studies consistently show decreases in height starting at about the age of 50, these decreases are due largely to *secular trends*. Successive generations are taller than earlier generations, at least over the few centuries since measurements have been recorded. Succeeding generations have not only been getting taller, they have also been getting heavier and maturing earlier. For example, puberty has occurred four months earlier each decade since 1840. Explanations for secular trends include better nutrition, improved environmental conditions, or evolutionary changes in the gene pool. The mingling and interbreeding of previously isolated populations resulting from widely increased mobility can lead to "hybrid vigor." Whatever the reason, older people who are shorter than their children may be thought to have shrunk with age, but in fact they never reached the taller heights of the later generation.

Longitudinal data do show some gradual decrease in height, on the average, starting at about the age of 55 (Kent, 1976). This decrease has been attributed to "settling" of the spinal column because of a decline in density of the long bones and vertebrae (Timiras, 1972). The lifetime loss in height of women is on the order of 4.9 cm (roughly 2 inches) and of men 2.0 cm (less than 1 inch) (Rossman, 1977). The greater shrinkage of women may be attributable to their greater longevity—they have more years to shrink.

Weight

Men in a Philadelphia Gerontology Research Center study continued to gain weight during their adult years until about the age of 55 and then began to lose (Kent, 1976). This agrees with the findings of cross-sectional studies, which have generally reported weight loss beginning in the 50s to the 70s. Secular trends toward increased weight have already been mentioned. The Metropolitan Life Insurance Company recently revised its "ideal weight" figures upward ("Ideal weight," 1983) to fit the new averages. Declines in old age may seem exaggerated because fat people may have less chance of surviving, leaving the leaner ones to skew the distribution in later years.

The average body fat in men increases from 11% at age 20 to 30% at age 65; in women, from 29% at age 20 to 30% at age 65. Apparently more women become fat earlier. In America, where the slim figure is valued, it is hard to find a woman who is not concerned about her weight. Most men do not become concerned until they are older. Since there is a decline in gastric juices after the age of 30 (Timiras, 1972), people who have not changed their diet by middle age may not only face obesity but also digestive upsets. Exercise is also beneficial, as noted in the next section on strength. It is easier to say that older adults should change their diet than to prescribe a good diet. Cross-cultural research has shown that what is good for one group of people with a common heredity, lifestyle, and climate can have no effect or even be harmful for other groups with different genes, different lifestyles, and different climates (Timiras, 1972).

Not only do people get heavier as they get older, but they also change shape. Arms and legs become thinner, waist and trunk thicker. This redistribution of fat causes the shifting profile by which we estimate age. Thin older people do not look like thin younger people.

Strength

Maximum strength follows maximum height, with a peak usually between the ages of 25 and 30. After this peak, there is a slight but steady loss of strength through the adult years, reaching a 10% loss by the age of 60.

Maximum strength in men declines about 42% from age 30 to age 80. Most weakening occurs in the back and leg muscles, less in the arm muscles. By middle age, it becomes more difficult to sustain great muscular effort. However, people who have been champions at the height of their power tend to maintain their relative prowess within their own age cohort, although new champions from younger cohorts will outdo them in time.

Appropriate exercise has been found to increase health and vigor at all ages (de Vries, 1975). This includes improvement in such factors as strength, work capacity, maximum oxygen uptake, muscle tone, heart rate, blood pressure, and body fat. The best exercises are aerobic, those that require oxygen, such as running, jogging, brisk walking, swimming, and bicycling. It is suggested that these be monitored by physicians or exercise physiologists, particularly for older adults, and regulated by the effects on heart rate.

Exercise can improve the strength and circulation of cardiac muscles and reduce the severity of arteriosclerotic lesions. Exercise of the leg muscles seems particularly effective in facilitating the flow of blood to the heart and thus indirectly maintaining body functioning in all areas, including the brain. Timiras (1972) quotes the saying "If you want to know how flabby your brain is, feel your leg muscles."

Optimum diet, climate, and exercise vary for different groups and individuals; what is ideal or at least good for one kind of person may be bad for another. As mentioned earlier, Americans are keenly interested in fitness. A 1975 survey of the population showed that half of all adults exercised regularly (Table 2–1).

As a rule, people who derive their feelings of worth from their bodies (for example, strong men, athletes, or beautiful women) are likely to be more sensitive to decreases in physical attributes than those who have other ways of assessing their value. Bühler (1972), who collected diverse biographical material about people's lives over centuries, found that what she calls the **biographical curve** of life is closest in timing to the **biological curve** for subjects whose self-image is most centered on their body. People who value themselves for their strength or physical prowess are going to show psychological patterns of aging as soon as their bodies start aging, whereas those

Table 2-1. Percent of population engaged in physical exercise, by type of exercise, sex, and age, 1975

	Exercise Regularly	Bicycle	Calisthenics	Jog	Lift Weights	Swim	Walk
Male							
20–44 years	53	15	17	11	10	19	31
45–64 years	42	7	10	4	3	8	31
65 & over	47	4	6	2	–	4	39
Female							
20–44 years	55	17	17	4	1	15	36
45–64 years	45	6	11	2	–	8	34
65 & over	39	2	6	–	–	2	33

Source: U.S. Department of Commerce (1981).

who value themselves for such nonphysical attributes as intelligence or interpersonal competence may continue to function and feel young for many years after their hair turns gray and their leg muscles weaken.

Skill

Manual dexterity declines regularly with age during the adult years. After about 33, hand and finger movements are progressively more clumsy. In later middle age it becomes harder to maintain a long series of highly coordinated manual tasks (such as those involved in banjo, guitar, or violin playing), although it is still possible to keep up with a short, rapid series (Fozard et al., 1972). However, these decreases in skill and dexterity are not usually reflected in job performance (Birren, 1964). Whether industrial-accident statistics and other indices used to measure job performance do not reflect skill changes because less competent workers move into jobs with less time pressure, are eliminated from their jobs by preferential hiring and firing, or are more vigilant and careful, we cannot say. See Chapter 6 for further discussion of this issue.

Health

Changes in health during adulthood are not all in the negative direction. For instance, the frequencies of illness and disability go up with the years, but the frequency of accidents goes down. Older adults tend to tire faster, have higher blood pressure and more dental problems, and need more time to recuperate from fatigue or illness. However, they are less susceptible to colds and allergies. Neither does middle age necessarily bring poor health. Many people live through all their adult years without ever knowing what it is to be sick or incapacitated in any way.

On the other hand, chronic diseases that are rare earlier in life become common in late adulthood. Diabetes reaches its peak between 50 and 60, particularly in men. Arthritis begins shortly after 40. After 40, the basal metabolic rate gradually declines, thereby decreasing the efficiency of oxygen consumption and making it harder to sustain great physical effort (such as long-distance running) for as long as in youth.

Appearance

Changes in health and appearance are probably the most salient clues for triggering changes in how old one feels, at least in modern American society. There is relatively little change in the way people look during early adulthood, but massive alterations in appearance in middle age. The increased tendency to gain weight and redistribution of fat in the body have already been mentioned. As Bischof (1969) points out, the middle-aged stop growing at both ends and grow in the middle. The bust or chest becomes smaller, and the abdomen and hips larger.

Perhaps the next most obvious change is in the hair. During the 40s, the hairline recedes—particularly in men—and the hair thins out. Again, mostly in men, baldness increases. Grayness increases at about the same time, so that by the 50s most men and women in our country are gray-haired, and some are even white-haired. There are other, less noticeable hair changes. Stiff hair appears in the nose, ears, and eyelashes of men, and on the upper lip and chin of women. Men need to shave less often while women need to start.

The skin loses elasticity. It becomes coarser on the face, neck, arms, and hands, and wrinkles appear. Some of these skin-associated changes result from muscle flabbiness under the skin. For example, bags and dark circles form under the eyes. These are particularly noticeable because the rest of the skin pales.

The critical area of the face is the lowest third. The distance between the bottom of the nose and the chin gets smaller as a result of changes in the teeth, bone, muscles, and connective tissue.

Posture and movements become less graceful because of such factors as stiffening of joints and loss of resiliency in muscles.

The voice slowly loses timbre and quality and becomes more high-pitched. By late middle age, most singers decide to retire.

The total effect of all these changes can be to make middle-aged people reluctant to look in the mirror. The reunion of old friends after several years' separation can be painful, for each is shocked at the change in the other and realizes that what is true for the other must also be true for the self.

Both sex and social class affect appearance, just as they do health in our society. Because counteractive measures take time, money, and effort, middle-class people can continue to look more attractive and youthful many years longer than working-class people. Similarly, because it is considered more important for women than men to look youthful and attractive (see Bell, 1970, for a discussion of the "double standard of aging"), women usually succeed in doing so—or at least they try harder. Diet, exercise, clothing, and cosmetics preoccupy many middle-class middle-aged American women. In an exploratory comparison of women's concerns with attractiveness and youthfulness, Nowak (1976) found the greatest concern with attractiveness among the middle-aged. Concern with youthfulness was progressively greater with each older group. Altogether, women of all ages tend to be more concerned with youthfulness than with attractiveness.

Body Systems

Endocrine System

Because the primary function of the hormonal system is adaptation to environmental changes, the major effect of degeneration in this system is a generalized decrement in adaptation. It is therefore more meaningful to look at general adaptive functioning rather than changes in any particular glands. In a healthy adult, defects in any one gland are quickly balanced by input from other glands. Even under disturbed conditions, repair of either the gland or the system is possible, and only with serious disease is there permanent disability.

During the years of adulthood, although there are likely to be progressive decrements in secretion of some glands, these defects are almost always compensated for. Fasting blood glucose is an example. Figure 2–1 shows that this remains remarkably stable throughout life, while maximum work rate declines by 50% from 30 to 65 years of age—unless, that is, one resorts to systematic vigorous exercise.

Cardiovascular System

Deaths from arteriosclerotic heart disease are noticeable from about the age of 35 in White men, 45 in White women. Black men and women are even more vulnerable. Kohn (1977) states bluntly that the cardiovascular system was not designed to last indefinitely, because it is composed of postmitotic cells, which do not renew themselves during life. These cells inevitably age, therefore, losing elasticity and undergoing other degenerative changes. By the age of 60, there has been, on the average, a 20% loss of resting cardiac function, as shown in Figure 2–1.

Cardiovascular failures account for an overwhelming majority of deaths after about the age of 50. Blood pressure begins to rise in childhood, and in

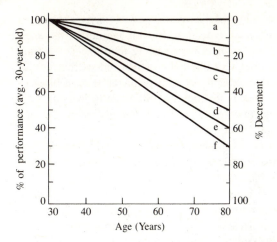

Figure 2 –1.   Age decrements in physiological functions in males. Mean values for 20- to 35-year-old subjects are taken as 100%. Decrements shown are schematic linear projections: (a) fasting blood glucose; (b) nerve conduction velocity and cellular enzymes; (c) resting cardiac index; (d) vital capacity and renal blood flow; (e) maximum breathing capacity; and (f) maximum work rate and maximum oxygen uptake. (Source: Shock, 1972).

Western countries elevates sharply in men during adolescence and again after age 50. In women, there is a more gradual rise during childhood, but a higher level than that for men is reached after 60. Perhaps this sex difference in later life can be explained by selective survival, because men with higher blood pressure will not have survived; women may be able to compensate better than men.

Hypertension, or elevated blood pressure, seems to be highly influenced by environmental conditions. It is also rather easily reversed. Less advantaged populations have significantly higher blood pressure all through life than do those more advantaged. Their life is harder in many ways, and they are consequently under greater stress. Stress, smoking, and diet all affect blood pressure; reducing stress, stopping smoking, and changing diet can all improve it. Libow (1974) reports that stopping smoking late in life, even after many years of smoking, can increase life expectancy.

Nervous System

The brain gets progressively smaller after about age 30, and there is an increase in moisture in the cerebral cortex at the expense of solids. However, what effects these changes have on behavior is hard to say. Both cross-sectional and longitudinal studies have found age changes in electroencephalographic (EEG) records (Obrist, Henry, & Justiss, 1961; Wang & Busse, 1969). These changes are particularly noticeable in alpha rhythms, which seem to be related to attentiveness. These rhythms decrease steadily with age during the adult years. However, this effect may be due less to aging than to diseases that increase with age—such as vascular pathology—which reduce the flow of blood to the brain (Thompson & Marsh, 1973). Treatment of such diseases might minimize deterioration in this function and therefore in its behavioral consequences. This is another example of the complicated interactions among body systems and between body systems and behavior.

Other EEG findings are even harder to interpret. For example, fast EEG activity is higher in the middle-aged, in psychiatric patients, and in women than it is in younger and older subjects, "normal" people, and men. Perhaps such findings reflect a complicated self-regulatory system in which changes in one part of the system set off compensatory changes in other parts.

In general, the chief behavioral effect of most nervous-system changes during adulthood may be a generalized slowing down of almost all functions and processes. If so, this could be the most significant behavioral change of the second half of life, and may be a major example of primary aging. If one reads more slowly and writes more slowly, walks more slowly and jumps away from danger more slowly, talks more slowly and follows what others are saying more slowly, one is literally "on another wavelength."

Senses

We communicate with the outer world through our senses. Blunting or losses in any sense can have profound psychological consequences, amounting in some cases to "sensory deprivation." Leon Pastalan, at the University of Michigan, developed several techniques for the use of students and young people in general to simulate the blunting of visual, auditory, and tactile stimulation (Thackrey & Pastalan, 1975). Putting on blurring lenses, ear plugs, and heavy mitts makes the sensory deficits of later years vivid. It is often hard for people who have good sensory acuity to realize the feelings of despair that can result from such blunting. See Figure 2–2 for an illustration of how different the world looks to people whose vision is less acute.

Vision

The lens of the eye starts aging from infancy; it becomes more opaque and less elastic each year. By age 50, almost everybody has at least one pair of reading glasses. The tendency to farsightedness increases about tenfold between the ages of 10 and 60. Watch, for example, how embarrassed people are when they have to hold a letter as far away from them as their hands can reach or grope frantically for their reading glasses to look at a photograph. Also, because the diameter of the pupil tends to decrease around age 50, less

Figure 2–2. The picture on the left shows a street scene as a young person with normal vision would see it. The picture on the right was taken through a coated lens, scientifically developed to record the image as it might be seen by an elderly person (late 70s) with normal age-related diminishment of visual acuity. Pairs of pictures such as these are a part of an audio-slide presentation prepared at the Institute of Gerontology. (Source: Thackrey and Pastalan, 1975.)

light comes into the eye and brighter lighting is needed. Dimmed lights of darkened theaters and restaurants can make middle-aged people functionally blind, even though they may be able to read without glasses on a sunlit park bench.

Recovery from glare and adaptation to the dark take longer in middle age, so that driving at night becomes more difficult. However, color vision seems to hold up through late middle age, even though more light may be needed to appreciate the colors.

Because retinal changes are rare before age 60, most adults have no trouble seeing, at least with glasses. Visual acuity is best at about age 20, remains relatively constant to age 40, and only then begins a slow decline (Timiras, 1972). It is possible to live to a ripe old age, however, without ever needing glasses or having any other visual problem. As illustrated in Figure 2–2, blunting of vision can markedly alter the quality of life. Studies by Palmer (1968) do, in fact, show that older adult men with high visual acuity tend to look for more stimulation in their experiences than those with poor vision. Poor vision, like other kinds of sensory deprivation, dulls many other aspects of life.

Hearing

Hearing seems to be best at about age 20. From then on, there is a gradual loss, more for high tones than for low, and, after 55, more for men than for women. Most hearing loss is not noticed, though, because it involves sounds that are not relevant to behavior (Timiras, 1972). Environmental differences, particularly exposure to loud noise, have marked influence on hearing acuity. The youth of the last few decades, therefore, should lose their hearing at much younger ages than older cohorts because of their addiction to very loud music.

Other Senses

There is no obvious change in taste sensitivity until about 50. After this age, although there may be no problem in discriminating the four basic tastes of sweet, sour, salt, and bitter, there may be less ability to distinguish finer nuances of taste. The number of taste buds diminishes after childhood, and those that remain tend to become less sensitive. A food that may seem too bland to the dulled taste sense of adults may be highly flavorful to children. The piquant spicing enjoyed by the gourmet is often unpleasant to the more sensitive child.

Sensitivity to touch appears to increase from birth to about 45 and then to decrease sharply. There is no evidence of a drop in sensitivity to heat or cold. Sensitivity to pain tends to remain steady to 50 and then to decline differentially for different parts of the body. To complicate matters, pain tolerance may decrease, so that less pain brings greater distress.

An interesting psychophysical cross-sectional study of sensitivity to smell (Rovee, Cohen, & Shlapek, 1975) found remarkable similarity across ages. The authors conclude that smell, which like touch is one of the earliest sensitivities, may be one of the last to decline under stress or in aging. What declines there are, though, are certain to affect sensitivity to taste. A good result, on the other hand, would be ability to tolerate pollution. Overall, sensory losses are secondary aging effects.

Sleep

While some aspects of sleep remain fairly stable during the adult years, others show clear age changes. Thompson and Marsh (1973), on reviewing the research in this area, believe that these changes are the result of central-nervous-system changes. Specifically, the total number of hours people sleep per night remains about the same, as does the amount of rapid-eye-movement (REM) sleep. However, as people get older—particularly after about 40—they wake up more during the night and have progressively less of the deepest kind of sleep (Stage 4). By late middle age, therefore, they spend more hours in bed—more and more of these lying awake—and end up feeling less rested in the morning.

Sex

Because of the enormous importance of sexual behavior to the survival of species or cultures, it is impossible to separate physiological from social factors in this area or to tell which age changes and differences might be inevitable. Most of our adult developmental information has come from three cross-sectional studies (Kinsey, Pomeroy, & Martin, 1948; Kinsey, Pomeroy, Martin, & Gebhard, 1953; Masters & Johnson, 1966) and one longitudinal study (Pfeiffer & Davis, 1972).

Every society overlays sexual activity with a gridwork of regulations and legends. In Western society, there has been rapid social change (period effects) in attitudes toward sex and in sexual behavior in recent years (Troll & Bengtson, 1979).

The widespread notion that men are more "sexual" than women—that men have strong sex drives while women are by nature passive receptacles—is prevalent among older cohorts but not among younger ones. So is the belief that sex is exclusively for procreation (held by older cohorts) instead of for recreation (held by younger cohorts). Such beliefs inevitably influence practices and interview responses.

It is important to distinguish among several sex-related variables that are frequently confused. Sexual **morphology** refers to physical sex differences, external as well as internal. Sex or gender **identity** refers to whether one *feels* like a man or a woman, irrespective of physical characteristics. Sexual **activity** refers to the frequency and manner of sexual behavior. This can vary from masturbation to coitus, from coitus with a same-sex partner to coitus with an opposite-sex partner. **Hormone** production is independent of both sexual identity and manner of sexual activity. Finally, **fertility** refers to the ability to produce children. Each variable shows its own developmental pattern, and, to complicate matters further, there are differences between men and women in each. A related topic, **sex-role** behavior, which refers to societal expectations for femininity and masculinity, is discussed in Chapter 4.

Whether one becomes a man or a woman is determined partly by one's genes, partly by one's hormones, and partly by the way one is raised. Practically every new embryo has either an XX genetic combination, if female, or an XY, if male. For the first six or seven weeks of prenatal existence, both genetic females and genetic males are alike, however. Only when the male hormones—the androgens—come into play are the genetic programs set in motion to make the potential males different from potential females. At that time, the basic female genitalia are changed to male genitalia, and other male structures appear. At the same time, females start acquiring female genitalia. Females thus have a more continuous gender development than males, who go through a sharp transformation from female morphology to male.

After birth, the hormones that played such an important part during the embryonic period "lie low" until puberty. From birth to puberty, the attitudes of parents and others become the important determiners of appropriate gender classification. A child may be genetically male and hormonally male (in utero) but may be raised female and, to all intents and purposes, may feel, act, and even look female. Hormones play a more important role again from puberty onward.

Sexual Development in Women

Puberty. Female adolescence begins with a sharp growth spurt and the gradual appearance of secondary sex characteristics such as axillary (underarm) and pubic hair and breasts, starting at about age 10 and ending at about age 18 or later, when maximum growth is reached (Timiras, 1972). The beginning of reproductive functioning in women is signaled at the time of **menarche** (puberty), generally between ages 10 and 13, by the first menstruation.

Over the past century or so, the average age of menarche has been gradually going down. It was about 16 in the early 1800s; now it is closer to 11. This kind of slow change is called a **secular trend.** The secular trend of menarchic age has been explained in various ways ranging from better nutrition to "hybrid vigor" from intermarriage among once isolated populations. There has been no significant further decrease in menarchic age for about 30 years now, however. Today's girls start to menstruate at about the same age as their mothers did.

Menstrual cycle and hormones. The menstrual cycle is controlled by the female sex hormones of estrogen and progesterone, which are in turn regulated by the pituitary. There are primarily two phases to the cycle: proliferative and secretory. Ovulation occurs at the midpoint of the menstrual cycle, depending on a complicated interplay of pituitary gland, hypothalamus, ovarian, and uterine products. Not all women have an invariant 28-day cycle— some menstruate as often as every two weeks and others as seldom as once in several months.

The coincidence of the menstrual cycle and the lunar cycle has intrigued people throughout human history. To many, there is a magical synchronism between the tides of the oceans, influenced by the moon, and the tides in a woman's body. Psychiatrists such as Theresa Benedek (1959) became curious about the relation between crises in female patients' disturbed behavior and the phases of the moon as early as the 1930s.

Subsequent research with women who were not seeking psychiatric help (Gottschalk, Kaplan, Gleser, & Winget, 1962; Ivey & Bardwick, 1968) found high self-esteem and low anxiety and hostility at the midpoint of the menstrual cycle (at ovulation, when the level of estrogen is at its peak) and significant increases in anxiety, depression, and hostility just before menstruation (at the low point of these hormones). Ivey and Bardwick, who interviewed college women at various times during the month, report dramatic differences in the content of their thoughts (Bardwick, 1971). For example, at ovulation, one woman said, "Well, we just went to Jamaica and it was fantastic, the island is so lush and green and the water is so blue. . . . The place is so fertile and the natives are just so friendly" (p. 32). At premenstruation, the same woman said, "I'll tell you about the death of my poor dog . . . my first contact with death and it was very traumatic for me. . . . Then my grandmother died" (p. 32).

Positive emotional feelings have been recorded at other times when hormone levels are high, as during pregnancy. When these hormones drop, we see postpartum depression (O'Leary, 1977) and menopausal depression. We should be wary of premature conclusions, however. It is impossible to separate physiological from socialization effects. As O'Leary (1977) points out, we are dealing with correlational data in all the studies, which tell us nothing about cause and effect. It is just as possible that behavior influences hormone levels as that hormone levels influence behavior—in fact, both probably occur. For example, McClintock (1971) observed that women who live together for a while or who are good friends come to have the same menstrual cycle and menstruate at the same time. Furthermore, people in our society are readier to attribute physiological causes to women's behavior than to men's; this is part of the sex-role stereotyping process, which will be discussed later. The rapid decline of estrogen level preceding menstruation is sometimes associated with physical symptoms such as water retention and pain or cramping as well as with the emotional symptoms mentioned. The term **premenstrual syndrome** is often used.

Not all women feel cyclic mood swings. In a study of more than 800 "normal young married women," Moos (1968) found that less than half—30% to 40%—reported such swings.

Pregnancy.   Estrogen and progesterone increase rapidly to very high levels after fertilization and stay high throughout pregnancy. During the second stage of labor, shortly before delivery, progesterone declines rapidly. Estrogen does not decline until just after the baby is born, returning to normal levels in 5 to 25 days after birth. These hormone levels have been associated with mood changes known as **postpartum depression.** However, depression has also been correlated with the length and difficulty of labor. And being pregnant and giving birth to a child have enormous consequences for a woman's social situation. Thus, it is almost impossible to separate biochemical effects from social effects.

There are wide individual differences at every point. Some women have no trouble conceiving, feel healthy and buoyant throughout pregnancy, and—particularly with natural childbirth practices that remove the helpless, institutionalized feelings from labor and birth—have short, easy deliveries and no observable postpartum depression. Such "lucky" women also are likely to find it easy to produce enough milk to nurse their children adequately. Other women have trouble at every point: They do not get pregnant when they wish or at all. They are ill throughout most of their pregnancy. They miscarry or have protracted, painful deliveries. And they cannot produce enough milk to nurse. Undoubtedly, both physical and psychological factors interact at all these points, as they do for ail biological processes.

Menopause.   Degenerative changes in the ovaries and other endocrine glands bring about a relatively dramatic stop to the menstrual cycle—menopause—in women around the age of 50. In part, this change is dramatic because of its association with sexuality and fertility in the minds of most social groups. In part, it is dramatic because it is noticeable. In part, however, it is dramatic because it occurs well before any other obvious physical changes associated with aging. Its association with sexuality and fertility is discussed later in this chapter. First, it is instructive to review what we know—or don't know—about the physiological events surrounding menopause.

Talbert's (1977) review of research on the aging of the reproductive system concluded that the menopause now occurs between 48 and 51 years of age for most human populations, but that the data are not consistent as to whether this age has changed over time, as the age of menarche has. There seems to be no relationship between age of menarche and age of menopause. If anything, early puberty may go together with later menopause (Timiras, 1972).

Menopause is followed by some atrophy in the vagina, the uterus, and the breasts, although much of this shrinking does not occur typically for 10 or 20 years after the menses stop and in fact may not be directly related to it. For example, the human uterus grows slowly from birth to puberty, then increases rapidly to the adult (nonpregnant) size of about $8 \times 4 \times .5$ cm. In very old women, it has been observed to be as little as 1 cm in length. Not only do the breasts shrink, but their glandular tissue becomes replaced by fat.

A wide variety of clinical symptoms have been associated with the hormone changes of menopause. Some medical texts, in fact, list as many as 50 such symptoms, taking half a page to present them in paragraph form. Such symptoms include everything from anxiety, depression, and tension to "involutional melancholia," from edema and backache to dizziness and headaches. Some people consider psychotic accompaniment of menopause inevitable. Families may attribute any complaint of women "going through the change" to this event. The one clear symptom that can be attributed to menopause, however, is the "hot flash." As the name implies, this is a flash sensation of heat. It is experienced to some degree by perhaps one-fourth to one-third of women at this time, and it varies widely in intensity. Some women may experience three or four "flashes" over a period of several years, and others half a dozen each day.

Although the degeneration of the ovaries leads to decreased estrogen production, other glands can continue to produce both estrogen and progesterone. Many postmenopausal women continue to have "female hormones" circulating in their blood for many years. This variability in estrogen content could explain the variation in "typical" menopausal symptoms, including "hot flashes." Even before the menses stop, irregularities in the menstrual cycle, menstrual cycles without ovulation, and premenopausal infertility can occur.

Many medical practitioners now prescribe supplementary hormones—estrogen and sometimes both estrogen and progesterone—when "natural" production decreases. Although there is considerable disagreement among both researchers and practitioners about the efficacy and safety of this treatment, the consensus seems to be that for the general run of women there is little, if any, generalized therapeutic value (Timiras, 1972).

Sexual Development in Men

Puberty.   The transition into reproductive maturity in boys begins later than in girls, starting at about age 12 and ending not before 20. Generally, the first signs following the growth spurt are the enlargement of the testes and penis and the growth of fine hair at the base of the penis. Hair in the armpits and on the face does not usually appear until about ages 15 and 18, respectively, and half the boys in the United States have not yet needed to shave at 17 or 18, usually to their embarrassment.

Many secondary sex differences in body size, shape, and tissue structure develop during the adolescent years. The most obvious, besides differences in hair and genitals, are men's greater height and strength, their wider shoulders, and women's breasts and wider hips. Most of these differences emerge during the prepubescent growth spurt, in which practically every muscle and skeletal dimension of the body changes (Tanner, 1962).

Many changes that boys experience in puberty, such as sudden erections in public places, acne, and "wet dreams," produce embarrassment and lowered self-concepts, particularly in our society where parents do not give much sex information. The importance of shared expectations is illustrated by the studies of Mussen and Jones (1957) on the effects of early and late maturing. Although early-maturing boys end up with enhanced self-esteem, late-maturing boys and both extra-early- and extra-late-maturing girls have long-lasting lowered self-esteem.

Male climacteric.   Some writers have been interested in the male climacteric. There can, of course, be no male "menopause." Unlike the relatively rapid changes of hormone level associated with ovarian involution, the decline in testosterone is gradual. In fact, some old men have testosterone levels as high as those of most younger men. There is a slight and steady drop in plasma testosterone between the ages of 20 and 90 (Doering, 1980), but no noticeable or functional change before the age of 60.

Fertility.   In the early formation of the embryo, an initial supply of germ cells migrates from the wall of the yolk sac to the newly formed male and female gonads. These immature ova and sperm develop differently in women and men. Females are born with about 500,000 ova, their total supply for life. After puberty, one is released at each menstruation. Since no more than 400 are released altogether, most ova degenerate over time. Studies by E. Block (1953) show that the number of oocytes (primitive ova) declines rapidly in the ovary from birth to 25 years or so, then stabilizes until about the age of 38, when a rapid decline is again seen. Nobody has systematically studied this subject in women over 45, although Novak (1970) saw an occasional follicle in women over 50.

Women become fertile at the time of menarche and lose fertility at the time of menopause. Both these processes are more gradual than one might think, however. It apparently takes several years for postpubertal women to reach their peak of fertility, just as it takes several years for menopausal women to reach bottom level.

Less is known about male development. Present information suggests that there is continual production of sperm following puberty, in contrast to the female's finite supply. The immature spermatozoa are converted to new sperm about every 74 days. Men seem to come to a more rapid peak of fertility than women, even though their puberty starts about two years later on the average. Men's fertility decreases much more gradually; some men have been known to father children when they were as old as 70 or 80.

There is a commonly held opinion that any mother over the age of 30 is putting herself or her child at risk. This has led to what could be called the "29-year-old syndrome," in which women at 29 rush into childbearing. If not yet married, they accept whatever marriage they can find—some even opt for pregnancy without marriage—because they think this is their last chance for motherhood. For the vast majority of women, this belief may be harmful. Most women in their 30s and many in their 40s can produce healthy children without risk, and many would make better mothers if they waited for more suitable conditions such as better marriages, more financial security, and the establishment of other life interests, such as jobs. In some cases, the technique of amniocentesis allows parents to discover the probability of abnormal offspring and gives them an option to terminate such pregnancies.

Sexual Behavior

Heterosexual sex.   Butler and Lewis (1976, p. 10) state that "the act of sex is complex, encompassing the body, the mind, and the emotions.

The physiology of sex includes nervous system and hormonal activity as well as specific organs." They delineate four phases in the heterosexual sex act: (1) excitement or erotic arousal; (2) intromission or plateau, in which the penis is placed in the vagina; (3) orgasm or climax; and (4) resolution or recovery. Essentially the same phases apply to both men and women. People are stimulated sexually in a number of ways—through sight, smell, touch, thoughts, and feelings. The pelvic area reacts. Muscle tension and congestion (filling of the blood vessels) occur, especially in the sexual or genital organs.

Men report the shortest arousal periods; the most insistent, frequent, and vigorous orgasms; and the quickest recovery periods during their late teen years, gradually decreasing in all these measures from then on—although not inevitably terminating at any time.

Women start out their sex life—if they start during their teens—with less enjoyment than men. During their 20s, though, women's arousal periods shorten, and their orgasms become deeper and more frequent.

The quality of a woman's marriage is related to her development of orgasmic capacity during the first five years of marriage (Clark & Wallin, 1965). Those who reported "good quality" marriages also said orgasmic frequency increased from 65% to 91%. Those who said their marriages were of "poor quality" reported few orgasms and no change over five years. Some women continue to grow more sexually proficient throughout their life. In fact, some women who have never experienced orgasms before start enjoying them in middle age—after the menopause and after their children are grown (Pfeiffer & Davis, 1972). This may be true more for current postmenopausal women than for future cohorts, who have not worried as much about unwanted pregnancies.

In spite of the many myths about women's reduced sexuality with menopause, there is no evidence that they decline in their physical capacity for sex, either then or later. Masters and Johnson (1968) found that while men gradually decreased in orgasmic capacity during their adult years, women showed no decrease, at least until their 60s. In late life, the clitoris may become slightly smaller, and the labia may become less firm as fatty tissue is lost. However, the clitoris "still remains the source of intense sexual sensation and orgasm, essentially as it was in earlier years. Women in good health who were able to have orgasms in their younger years can continue having orgasms until very late in life, well into the eighties" (Butler & Lewis, 1976, p. 14).

According to Butler and Lewis (1976, p. 19), "Most men begin to worry secretly about sexual aging some time in their thirties, when they compare their present level of sexual activity with their previous performance as teen-agers and very young adults. . . . Quite simply, their penises don't work in the same way," and they think they are becoming impotent (unable to have an erection sufficient to carry out the sexual act). Older men take longer to obtain an erection—a matter of minutes after stimulation instead of a matter of seconds—and the erection may not be as large, straight, and hard. Furthermore, they are more prone to premature ejaculation, although this can be controlled. Lubrication is reduced, and also the volume of seminal fluid, which diminishes the urge to ejaculate. "Younger men produce three to five ml. of semen (about one teaspoon) every twenty-four hours, while men past fifty produce two to three ml. Actually this can be a decided advantage in love-making since it means that the older man can delay ejaculation more easily and thus make love longer, extending his own enjoyment and enhancing the possibility of orgasm for his partner" (Butler & Lewis, 1976, p. 21). Butler and Lewis also say that "older men have a choice of an extended period of sexual pleasure with a milder orgasm or a briefer session with a more intense orgasm" (p. 22). On the other hand, younger men can have a second erection in a few minutes; older men may have to wait hours or even days.

Homosexuality. In spite of the political activity and publicity given the gay liberation movement in recent years, there is little research on the subject, either as to why some men and women prefer same-sexed instead of opposite-sexed partners or when in development these differences begin. So far, there is no convincing evidence for substantive physiological or psychological differences between "gays" and "straights." Men who prefer other men as partners can be very "masculine" in appearance, identity, attitudes, values, and lifestyles or, alternatively, close to the stereotypical woman in all these characteristics to the point of transvestism. The same can be said for women. Some theorists, such as John Money (Money & Erhardt, 1972), believe that such preferences have their origins prenatally in different hormonal development, although Money also points out that it is possible to raise genetically and hormonally male children so that they assume characteristics of the opposite sex. Social-learning theorists are more inclined to believe that such preferences are primarily a matter of early experiences with people of the same and opposite sex. Happier experiences with women than with men could lead either boys or girls to choose women as sex partners in adulthood—or vice versa.

Interest in sex. Not everybody who is interested in sex or aroused sexually engages in sexual activity. Not everybody who engages in sexual activity is either interested in sex or aroused sexually. Data on older people (for example, see Wilson, 1975) show no difference in interest between unmarried and no-longer-married women, although there are marked differences in activity. Married women continue to experience coitus, at least to the capability of their husbands, but no-longer-married women—widows or divorcees— may be restricted to masturbation, if they were not of a cohort brought up to believe it is "unnatural." Christenson and Gagnon (1965), in fact, found greater coital activity among women whose husbands were about their own age than among those whose husbands were older. They also found an increase in interest among older people, even though coital frequency dropped.

One way of measuring interest in sex is by asking people about their interest level. Another way is by asking them whether they dream about sex at night. Although there was a substantial interest among older women, more older men reported interest in sex than older women: 80% versus 30% (Verwoerdt, Pfeiffer, & Wang, 1969). Some of these sex and age differences may be cohort effects, as is suggested by findings that college students no longer show gender differences in sexual arousal by pictures (Sigusch, Schmidt, Reinfeld, & Wiedemann-Sutor, 1970).

Wide individual differences should make us cautious about attributing behavior of a 40-year-old woman to menopause or impotence in a 40-year-old man to body deterioration. What we don't have for the years of early and middle adulthood is the kind of longitudinal data that trace both physiological and behavioral changes. In an area of such acute interest, it is indeed surprising that until a few years ago, there was no such research even for puberty, and there still is none for the climacteric. Apparently, we prefer fantasies and myths.

Health

Health—or its opposite condition, illness—refers to the overall functional competence of a person rather than any specific body part or system. Thus, it is possible to be healthy even though many systems, such as the cardiovascular or digestive system, are not working as well as they used to, or as well as they should by normative standards. It is also possible to be ill even though one's body is in as good condition as that of most people, or in as good condition as might be required for survival or competent daily functioning.

Health has generally been measured by the presence or absence of illness or by functional capacity. Researchers at Duke University, for example, used the following six-point scale (Laurie, 1977, pp. 1–2):

1. **Excellent health:** engages in vigorous physical activity either regularly or at least from time to time
2. **Good health:** no significant illnesses or disabilities and only routine medical care such as annual checkups required
3. **Mildly impaired:** only minor illnesses and/or disabilities that might benefit from medical treatment or corrective measures
4. **Moderately impaired:** one or more diseases or disabilities that are either painful or that require substantial medical treatment
5. **Severely impaired:** one or more illnesses or disabilities that are either severely painful or life threatening or that require extensive medical treatment
6. **Totally impaired:** confined to bed and requiring full-time medical assistance or nursing care to maintain vital bodily functions

Using a similar criterion of activity limitation, the National Center for Health Statistics (U.S. Department of Commerce, 1981) reported that a majority of people of all ages have no limitations. As shown in Table 2–2, the percentage of people with some limitations increases with age, but even for those over 65 years of age the figure is only 46%. The biggest impact of age seems to be on heart conditions, arthritis, and hypertension. Sex differences are impressive only for arthritis and hypertension, with both conditions being more prevalent among women.

Table 2–3 shows an opposite age trend: a decrease in acute illnesses with age. Notice the large sex difference in injuries, which are much more frequent in males.

In physical development, as in other developmental processes, it is not possible to ignore cohort and period effects. The length of life, its style, what kinds of processes deteriorate or expand at what times, all have changed over the past century. Sex differences in life expectancy are one dramatic example: 100 years ago—and still today in countries that do not value women—many more men survived into old age than women. Figure 2–3 dramatizes another period effect: the decline in acute illnesses as a cause of death—

Table 2–2. Persons with activity limitations from chronic conditions, 1979, in millions

Age	Heart	Arthritis	Hypertension	Back	Legs	% no limitation
Under 45	4	5	3	14	10	93
45–64	21	20	12	10	7	76
65 & over	24	25	12	5	6	54
Sex						
Male	18	12	7	9	8	85
Female	15	22	11	10	7	85

Adapted from U.S. Department of Commerce, Bureau of the Census (1981). Covers civilian noninstitutionalized population.

Table 2–3. Acute conditions, rate per 100 population, 1970–1979

Age	Infections	Respiratory Upper	Respiratory Other	Digestive	Injuries
Under 6	60	133	63	12	39
6–16	39	88	60	15	38
17–44	21	56	51	12	40
45 & over	11	29	30	8	24
Sex					
Male	22	56	43	10	41
Female	26	64	51	12	28

Adapted from U.S. Department of Commerce, Bureau of the Census (1981). Covers civilian noninstitutionalized population.

1900

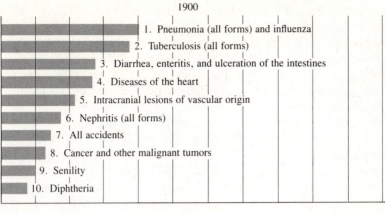

1. Pneumonia (all forms) and influenza
2. Tuberculosis (all forms)
3. Diarrhea, enteritis, and ulceration of the intestines
4. Diseases of the heart
5. Intracranial lesions of vascular origin
6. Nephritis (all forms)
7. All accidents
8. Cancer and other malignant tumors
9. Senility
10. Diphtheria

1940

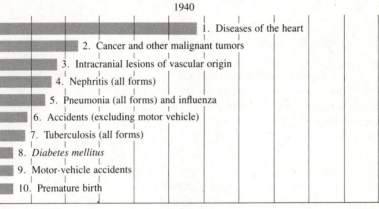

1. Diseases of the heart
2. Cancer and other malignant tumors
3. Intracranial lesions of vascular origin
4. Nephritis (all forms)
5. Pneumonia (all forms) and influenza
6. Accidents (excluding motor vehicle)
7. Tuberculosis (all forms)
8. *Diabetes mellitus*
9. Motor-vehicle accidents
10. Premature birth

1970

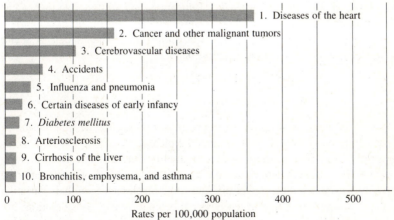

1. Diseases of the heart
2. Cancer and other malignant tumors
3. Cerebrovascular diseases
4. Accidents
5. Influenza and pneumonia
6. Certain diseases of early infancy
7. *Diabetes mellitus*
8. Arteriosclerosis
9. Cirrhosis of the liver
10. Bronchitis, emphysema, and asthma

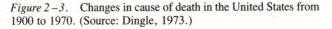

0   100   200   300   400   500

Rates per 100,000 population

Figure 2–3.   Changes in cause of death in the United States from 1900 to 1970. (Source: Dingle, 1973.)

regardless of age—and the consequent increase of chronic illnesses. Many adults whose great-grandparents and even grandparents, died young of pneumonia or other infectious diseases now are surrounded by old relatives who are pioneers in the realm of living long—who did not have models on whom to pattern their own later years. The adults of today are not likely to face old age with uncertainty to the same extent because their parents are showing them the way to do it, or not to do it.

It is worth noting, also, the significant changes in the two leading causes of death between 1970, when Figure 2–3 ends, and 1980. Deaths from coronary heart disease and cerebrovascular accidents (strokes) dropped dramatically, particularly among younger adults, while deaths from cancer increased. According to Weg (1982), a majority of cancers can be related to carcinogens and cancer-promoting substances in the environment as well as to aspects of lifestyle such as nutrition, smoking, and stress.

Social-Class and Ethnic Differences

Since poorer and more disadvantaged groups in our society are likely to have poorer nutrition and medical care throughout life, it is obvious that social class and ethnicity would be related to physical development throughout life. Less advantaged groups also have greater stress and less education in desirable health practices. In 1971, the National Center for Health Statistics reported that White middle-aged people had 19.5 days of restricted activity because of illness compared with 29.1 days for non-Whites. There was a linear relationship between income and restricted-activity days. Middle-aged people with annual incomes of less than $3,000 had 42.8 days of restricted activity, compared with only 14.1 days for those with annual incomes of more than $10,000 (U.S. Department of Health, Education, and Welfare, National Center for Health Statistics, 1971, p. 36). Unfortunately, most adult development and aging sources fail to report physical development and health data by social class, so that estimates are usually necessary.

Summary

The peak of physical development occurs during the first decade of early adulthood. This peak is followed by a plateau of varying length depending on the system or process, with a gradual decline through the remaining years of life. Most functions do not reach the threshold of importance to behavior before about the age of 50, and some much later than that. Variation is wide not only according to the physical behavior under consideration, but also by sex, social class, and ethnicity. By late middle age, most people are slightly shorter, somewhat fatter, somewhat blunted in their senses, and more prone to chronic diseases. Women have reached the end of their fertility, although the menopause is not as disastrous an occurrence as once believed. The most prevalent symptom is "hot flashes," and that is experienced by no more than one-third of women. There are marked differences between women and men in the development of sexual morphology, sexual interest, sexual behavior, and anything else having to do with sex.

In the past half-century, there has been a dramatic shift in the causes of death, from acute or infectious diseases to chronic diseases. Most diseases of middle age are "secondary aging," and many can be reversed or modified by appropriate diet, exercise, and medical treatment.

Chapter Three

Intellectual Development in the Adult Years

The common view, shared by many psychologists and the general public, is that people get smarter through childhood and dumber through adulthood. It is also believed that whatever influences can be brought to bear to improve intelligence must be brought to bear in early childhood. Our country, along with others, has poured enormous amounts of money into early childhood development. Access to college and jobs is often determined by policies that assume that applications past their 20s are riskier than younger ones. In fact, the only intellectual development attributed to adults is the attainment of wisdom.

This chapter reviews the research on cognition and ends up challenging many of the above preconceptions. People *can* get smarter during their adult years. Many older adults make better use of education and handle work problems better than people of 20. Furthermore, age differences are not necessarily equated with age changes, and it is important to consider the total person/environment situation because adults, like children, adapt to the requirements of their life situations. If they appear dumber than when they were younger, it may be because their situation in life demands that they be dumber, and they are smart enough to adapt. Factory workers on the line or traditional housewives would not fit in if they enjoyed reading history more than following baseball or consumer fashion.

The task of integrating research findings in the area of intellectual development is made difficult because there are two separate lines of investigation: experimental studies and intelligence tests. Investigators in these separate domains rarely read each other's papers. Furthermore, investigators of memory development rarely know what investigators of development in attention or learning are doing or finding. Another problem is the paucity of longitudinal or cross-sequential studies and the susceptibility of the predominantly cross-sectional findings to cohort and period effects, such as increasing years of schooling over the past century and increasing numbers of women in higher education and the labor market.

The issue of **competence versus performance** is central to theory in cognitive development in adulthood. It is allied to the issues of biological versus social determinism and open versus closed systems discussed in Chapter 1. Is the performance measured in cognitive experiments truly representative of the subjects' ability, or is it heavily contaminated by characteristics of the measurement situation or the life situation? Do women who return to school in their 30s improve in their basic cognitive competence as a result of studying and thinking in abstract modes, or do they just become more comfortable with the kind of thinking demanded by the experiments or tests? Conversely, do declines in some kinds of test performance in later years imply declines in underlying competence, or merely years of specialization in other kinds of problem solving?

There is not only an implicit model of the direction of intellectual change, but also one of the process of cognitive functioning. Generally, information is seen as recorded in a learning stage that involves attention and perception; it is then stored in memory; and finally it is retrieved—remembered—and put to use in thinking, problem solving, and creating. It is, of course, impossible in practice to separate the parts of this process. Learning, for example, can only be measured through memory.

The efficiency of learning and memory is affected both by how well the sense organs function and by the general state of the body. The profound consequences of sensory deficits have been discussed in Chapter 2. Not only does reduced acuity in vision, hearing, or touch, for example, close out a large part of potential information, but it has the secondary effect of lowering interest in the environment (Palmer, 1968). The kind and amount of new information taken in also depends upon existing capacity at the time of learning and the purpose of the learner.

Cognitive Functioning

Four general conditions of overall functioning have been studied: speed, arousal, attention, and caution. These are discussed below.

Speed

Research evidence suggests that everybody who lives long enough is destined to slow down, but there is enormous variation in what slows when. Thus, more complex cognitive functioning slows at an earlier age than simpler functioning, and healthier people slow down later than those less healthy. In general, there is relatively little change in speed of functioning during most of the adult years.

The pioneer research on slowing was done by Surwillo (1963). He reported that electroencephalogram (EEG) alpha periods, a generally accepted measure of speed of functioning, decreased about 4 milliseconds per decade of chronological age from 28 to 99 years. A review of studies of age changes in human motor performance by Welford (1977) concludes that simple motor times increased about 26% from about the age of 20 to the age of 60. A reanalysis of data for a wide variety of tasks involving speed, from reaction time to track and field events, showed that simple reaction time slowed only about 5% from the age of 20 to the age of 60, but reaction time tasks that required choice slowed about 15% in that time period, and the running events, which were more complex, slowed as much as 40% (Salthouse, 1976b). A longitudinal study by Schaie, Labouvie, and Buech (1973) found that the only function that decreased over a 14-year period was psychomotor speed. Finally, research with intelligence tests has long shown (Lorge, 1936) that older people have trouble with time limits.

But what really happens? Losses in sensory acuity or in neuromuscular efficiency accounted for only a small portion of the age differences found in response time (Botwinick, 1965). And slowing in speed of nerve conduction rarely accounts for more than 4 milliseconds per meter of nerve involved (Welford, 1977). Other factors that might be handicaps for older subjects also account for only a small proportion of the age differences in speed. These include unfamiliarity with the kinds of tasks assigned, lack of meaning of such tasks for noncollege populations—which older cohorts are more likely to be—and greater cautiousness.

Slowing is most noticeable in those tasks that are characteristic of central-nervous-system processes: discriminations leading to withholding of a response, responding to a series of stimuli, or matching stimuli. When Surwillo (1963) partialed out the alpha period scores from the correlation he obtained between reaction time and age, that correlation disappeared. Older subjects with equivalent alpha patterns acted as quickly as younger subjects did. Thus, general slowing could be attributed to central-nervous-system deterioration—to disease, not to "normal aging." It would be a secondary aging effect—more frequent in older people, but not an inevitable accompaniment of aging per se.

That increased response time may be neither inevitable nor irreversible is suggested by the fact that all research that shows average slowing also shows wide individual differences. Some older people are much faster than many younger people. Furthermore, age differences in speed scores have been wiped out by behavior modification techniques (Hoyer, Labouvie, & Baltes, 1973). Even physical activity showed up accidentally as a contributing factor. In a study at Duke University, where older people were being compared to college students on a variety of cognitive tasks, Botwinick and Thompson (1968) noticed, to their surprise, that as the year of testing went on, the college students' average reaction time improved. And while there were no clear age differences between older and college-age subjects tested at the beginning of the year, there were marked differences in those tested toward the end of the year.

What was even more curious was the difference between those college students who participated at the beginning of the year and those who participated later. The average scores of the students tested later in the year were much higher than those tested early in the year. In looking over their data, the investigators found that many college athletes, who had been busy in athletic activities early in the year, were volunteering as subjects after the athletic season was over. It was an easy way to fulfill their obligatory research credits for introductory psychology courses. Although the older subjects were clearly slower than the college athletes, they were not significantly different from those college students who were not athletes.

Following up on those Duke findings, Spirduso (1975) compared young and older adults who were or were not engaged in regular athletic activity. As expected, he found that those who did engage in vigorous physical activity regularly—young or old—showed faster reaction times than those who did not. Older athletes were faster than younger nonathletes. Unfortunately, because these studies are correlational, we cannot tell whether those people who do participate in sports, at any age, are those who have faster reaction times to begin with, or whether it is the participation that increases their speed. Longitudinal data on children show that newborn infants differ in general activity level and that these differences tend to persist (Bayley, 1968).

Diana Woodruff (1975) designed an ingenious experiment to test Surwillo's theory that the slowing of aging was related to slowing of EEG alpha waves. (Alpha rhythms in the EEG are in the range of 8 to 13 cycles per second and most apparent in relaxed states.) Woodruff trained both young and old subjects to modify their alpha rhythms by biofeedback. Those who increased their alpha speed also increased their reaction time, whether they were young or old. There was an enormous variability in amount of slowing among the older people. In a different study, Hicks and Birren (1970) found a range of slowing from 20% to 110%. Part of the time, older subjects were as fast as or even faster than younger ones. They were unable to keep it up, though—or they did not choose to expend the extra effort. Salthouse (1976a) raised the question of strategy as an explanation of many speed differences. Older people, that is, choose not to speed.

Arousal

Intellectual functioning is affected not only by the speed with which one processes information, but also, and perhaps even more fundamentally, by one's state of **arousal** or alertness. One can be highly alerted to the world

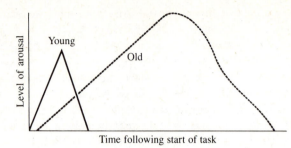

Figure 3-1. Arousal curves. (Source: Eisendorfer, 1968.)

or asleep, or something in between. Research with infants is exceedingly vulnerable to this **state** condition. There is no way to test a sleeping infant or a comatose adult. We all fluctuate during the course of a day in our degree of alertness. Some people are "morning people"; others, "night people." People do their best work at different times because they are differentially aroused at different times.

Psychologists have been wondering whether there are developmental patterns in arousal. Are adolescents more arousable than adults, for example? Are older adults less arousable than younger adults? Arousal, like speed of functioning, has been related to brain-wave frequencies. These frequencies are generally slower in older people. But the relation between arousal and performance is complex. Experiments by Eisdorfer (1968), for example, showed different arousal patterns for young and old subjects who had been asked to learn something new. Young subjects came quickly to a high state of arousal, performed the task, and then quickly returned to their base level. Older subjects took much longer to reach an adequately high arousal level and then, after they had finished their task, took much longer to return to base level. Older adults may even have a higher base level to begin with (Powell, D.A., Buchanan, S., & Milligan, W., 1975)—they may always be more aroused than they need be. Figure 3–1 diagrams arousal curves for young and old subjects.

Apparently there is an optimum level of arousal for efficient performance. People do not work well when underaroused, but they also do not work well when overaroused. Figure 3–1 suggests that older people not only have trouble returning to base level but also keep moving to higher and higher arousal levels (overarousal) before they drop back again. We all know that practice helps performance. This is particularly true for older people. One reason why practice may help older people perform better is that it decreases their tendency to become overaroused. They get used to the situation and are less anxious, and thus less tense or aroused. At least, this was found to be true in biochemical experiments by Froehling (1974).

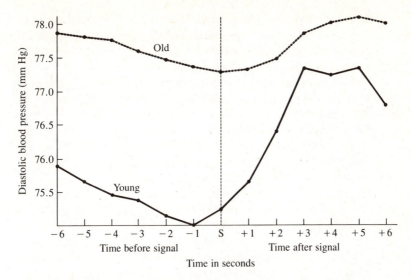

Figure 3–2. Beat-by-beat measures of diastolic pressure for young and old subjects before and after signal. (Source: Thompson and Nowlin, 1973.)

Eisdorfer (1968) measured arousal by analyzing the lipid (fat) content of the blood. Thompson and Nowlin (1973) reported analogous findings using measures of heartbeats. Generally, the process of focusing attention or becoming aroused is accompanied by slower heartbeats and by changes in blood pressure, particularly in diastolic pressure. Figure 3–2 shows the difference in diastolic pressure patterns found between young and old subjects who had been told that they were soon to be shown a stimulus to which they would have to respond. The different age patterns shown in Figure 3–2 correspond to those found by Eisdorfer, shown in Figure 3–1. During the preparatory interval before the stimulus (s) was actually given (6 seconds before), young subjects—starting at a somewhat lower base level of pressure, incidentally— dropped in diastolic pressure. After the stimulus was given and while they were responding, their blood pressure rose sharply. Then, following the response, it dropped sharply. Older subjects not only started at a higher level, but also their anticipatory change was shallow, as was their response change.

Attention

The term **attention** refers to the manner in which we focus on what we are doing, how "tuned in" we are to what is going on around us. Not only do people vary in the degree to which they focus their attention, but they also vary in how wide their focus is. Some people have a very narrow band: they can "take in" only a small amount of information at a time. Others have a very wide focus: they can "take in" a large amount of information in a unit of time. Furthermore, some information leaves a "deep trace," while other information leaves only a "shallow trace," which could presumably be "wiped out" more easily.

Birren and Renner (1977) pointed out that it might be as troublesome to have too narrow a focus as too wide a focus. If the span is too narrow, one loses a lot of information. If the span is too wide, one finds it harder to distinguish what is relevant. Such variation is influenced not only by intrinsic individual differences but also by state of alertness, general interest in what is going on, novelty of the surroundings, general mental and physical health, sensory acuity, and other factors.

People focus attention by selecting out those stimuli that are relevant to their current interests. As Birren (1969) stated, given the almost infinite amount of information available at any moment, the important process is to be able to ignore most of it. Most researchers on this topic present subjects with two or more tasks at the same time and measure how well the subjects can keep from being distracted. For example, Broadbent and Heron (1962) had young and older adults carry out a complex number-canceling task and simultaneously report which letters of the alphabet had been repeated during each minute. Young adults were able to perform both these unrelated tasks together fairly well, but older adults often had to drop one task in order to work on the other. Similar results have been found with color-naming (in which the name of the color appears in a different color) and card-sorting tasks (Comalli, Wapner & Werner, 1959; Rabbit, 1964).

Unfortunately, all this research is cross-sectional and may represent cohort differences at least as much as developmental ones. It has been undertaken in laboratory situations unfamiliar and uncomfortable to older adults and has been based on very small samples, generally unmatched for education, IQ, or other potentially relevant factors. We need much better research before we can come to any firm conclusions.

Cautiousness and Rigidity

The fourth characteristic of cognitive functioning—rigidity or cautiousness—is sometimes conceptualized as a style or personality variable and sometimes as an organic variable. Many studies—though far from all—have shown that older subjects, when compared with younger ones, tend to stick to previous solutions—to perseverate—even if changed circumstances make these solutions inappropriate. Is this because older people lose flexibility? Or is it because they have learned many coping strategies, including the advantage of not exerting energy unnecessarily? Is cautiousness a life-preserving quality or a handicap? So far, some research has found increased rigidity and cautiousness with age, but other research has not.

Supporting the hypothesis of increased rigidity are cross-sectional data reported by Schaie (1958), in which scores on the Primary Mental Abilities Test correlated with scores on rigidity tests, and both correlated with age. Chown (1961) found that those older adults who scored poorly on problem-solving tasks also tended to be more rigid. Granick and Friedman (1967) reported a persistent and rapid decline in general flexibility with age (again, cross-sectionally). Eisdorfer (1968) found that older subjects in learning experiments made more errors of omission, while younger subjects made more errors of commission. If they were not absolutely sure, the older subjects would not answer. Finally, Arenberg (1974) reported that older men did not devise problem-solving strategies as flexibly as they had six or seven years earlier (longitudinal data).

Other studies do *not* support a hypothesis of increasing rigidity with age. Birren (1969) reported that, although older humans *prefer* more time for problem solving, they do not *need* more time than younger people. Similarly, Botwinick (1966) found that if risk taking is necessary, older people do not seem to be more cautious than younger people. It is just as plausible to think of rigidity or cautiousness as adaptive behavior. Ready-made, stereotyped responses conserve energy and avoid trouble. Elias, Elias, and Elias (1977) point out that what is considered versatile and flexible by the young may be considered rash by older people and that what older people would consider well-thought-out, cautious approaches might be considered slow, ponderous, and indecisive by younger people. That is, we are talking about different, age-associated value systems rather than about fundamental personality or organic characteristics.

Perception

Perception is the process of selecting, out of all the mass of information around, that which is considered relevant. It is thus highly subject to the organic state conditions just discussed, as well as to past experience, present knowledge, and sensory acuity or other physiological conditions.

A central theme in Piaget's theory of cognitive development, as interpreted by Elkind (1970), is **egocentrism.** Egocentric people can only see from one perspective—their own. They usually cannot see themselves separately from their environment; they are embedded in it. According to Elkind, early development is characterized by a sequence of gradually achieved objectivity. Infants learn that objects exist separately from them—and that they themselves are separate from objects (including their mothers). Preschool children learn to differentiate objects from symbols. School-age children cannot tell the difference between facts and ideas, while adolescents have to learn to separate the viewpoints of other people from their own. Adults are presumably able to make all these distinctions and to see many possible points of view.

For example, subjects can be told at one point that they are to give directions to very young children and at another point that they are to give the instructions to their parents. The score is based on their ability to make the instructions very simple if they are supposedly talking to very young children or to be terse and concise if they are supposedly directing the parents. Subjects who cannot vary their directions to fit different audiences are judged egocentric. Those who are able to "get out of their own skin" into that of another are judged more objective. This theme appears in most of the perceptual research described below.

Visual Perception

Almost all research on visual perception has measured response to visual illusions. In the Müller-Lyer illusion, shown in Figure 3–3, the straight line is actually divided in half by the arrows, but the different directions of these arrows make the line segments look unequal. Egocentric subjects cannot "get rid of" the interfering effect of the arrows; objective subjects can "erase them mentally." A number of investigations (including Comalli, 1965) have all found the same age pattern of susceptibility to this illusion: a reversal in later life back to the level experienced by young children. Adults achieve objectivity but, if we can transform cross-sectional findings to processes, older people lose this ability to distance themselves and see other possibilities. In another experiment, younger and older adults were required to decide whether two two-dimensional drawings depicted the same geometric figure. Either the same drawing was shown in different positions, or mirror-image figures were used (Gaylord & Marsh, 1975). Older-adult subjects needed almost twice as much time as younger ones to rotate these figures mentally in order to answer the questions. A few other studies have used embedded-figures tests, which are another way of measuring ability to "get outside of" immediate contexts.

When Gajo (1966) used a more analytic research design, however, he found no perceptible increase in susceptibility to the Müller-Lyer illusion before the age of 60. And Eisner and Schaie (1971), using a cross-sequential design with a sample of men from 55 to 77 years of age, concluded that the increase in susceptibility to the Müller-Lyer illusion was partially a cohort effect and the decrease in susceptibility to the Titchener circles illusion was partially a test/retest effect. Schaie (e.g., 1970) has repeatedly challenged conclusions of age changes based on cross-sectional data.

When three age groups matched on education—college students and middle-aged and older professors—were asked to find the letters L, O, V, and E in an array of other letters, no significant age differences in final scores

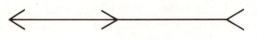

Figure 3–3.   The Müller-Lyer illusion.

were found. The oldest group missed more letters, however (Schonfield & Smith, 1976). Presumably they were more field dependent—more egocentric.

Auditory Perception

There is less research on auditory perception than on visual perception, and findings are also less consistent. A study of 156 community volunteers from 46 to 87 (Granick & Friedman, 1967), for example, found no significant age difference in discrimination of rhythm patterns. However, one longitudinal study of 282 New York adults between 20 and 80 found a noticeable decline in the ability to understand unclear speech signals after the age of 50 (Bergman et al., 1976).

Space Perception

Space perception seems to be one of the few characteristics that show persistent sex differences: from earliest childhood, boys seem to be better than girls (Maccoby & Jacklin, 1974). Yet, in one study, girls given special training to equalize experience, performed as well as boys (Goldstein & Chance, 1965).

Are there age differences in space perception? In one kind of experiment, subjects must judge whether a luminescent rod in a dark room is vertical or tilted. The chairs in which the subjects sit are themselves tilted, and the relationship between the subjects' tilt and the rod's tilt is examined. Six-year-olds say the rod is vertical when it is tilted the same way their bodies are. Twenty-year-olds, however, say the rod is vertical when it is tilted opposite to the tilt of their bodies. Earlier studies reported no change in adults until about the age of 60, when the perception of vertical was again in the direction of the body tilt (Comalli, Wapner, & Werner, 1959). Davies and Laytham (1964), however, did not find a regression in old age, nor did a study by Comalli himself (1970), using smaller age ranges.

It has long been hypothesized that the two hemispheres of the cerebral cortex do not work as a unit and that one hemisphere is likely to control the other. In right-handed individuals, the left hemisphere is dominant. Left-handed individuals, some think, are divided into those who have right-dominant brains and those who do not have any clearly established dominance. Developmental changes in dominance have recently been investigated, and the research findings reviewed by Woodruff (1978). For example, left-hemisphere dominance is set in both boys and girls by age 4. Clearer dominance is often associated with better performance on spatial-perception tasks, and men have clearer dominance than women.

Because there is less age-related loss in verbal abilities than in spatial abilities, some psychologists have considered the possibility that the two hemispheres of the brain age at different rates. However, there has been no empirical support for this theory. In general, biological indexes such as EEG wave patterns and hemisphere dominance may be related more to development in the first years of life than in later years. This is in accord with Birren's "discontinuity hypothesis," which states that there are different causes for age changes at the beginning of life and later in life (Birren & Renner, 1977).

Learning

Most learning studies derive from early association psychology. They typically require subjects seated in laboratories to form connections between two words or nonsense syllables—or any two or more stimuli presented together. These connections are tested by later presenting one of the stimuli and asking the subject to name the other. The factor of speed is central in most of these studies.

Most studies have shown that younger subjects (young or middle-aged) learn such lists more quickly than do old subjects, make fewer errors in the process of learning, and learn more difficult lists. Age differences are lessened and sometimes even obliterated when older subjects are allowed more time or can self-pace the tests. One of the most prominent of these studies is that of Canestrari (1963), who tested 30 men between ages 50 and 69 and 30 men between ages 17 and 35, all seeking work at a local employment agency. His two age groups were also matched on vocabulary (Wechsler Adult Intelligence Scale), education, and socioeconomic status. The younger subjects made fewer errors than the older under all three time conditions, but the difference between age groups was greatly reduced when they could pace themselves. The older group made 39 more errors than the younger when the time limit was 1.5 seconds, only 18 more errors when they had 3 seconds to work, and only 9 more when there was no time limit. (Note, however, that older subjects may expect age bias at an employment agency, and thus may be inhibited. Also, older subjects are used to controlling their own lives and thus may resist time controls.)

What is the effect of previous experience and previous learning on new learning? Does earlier experience facilitate new learning, perhaps by providing more meaningful categories into which new information can be grouped? Or, conversely, does it interfere with new learning by providing conflicting associations? Most experimental research in this area is based on tasks requiring the learning of one set of associations followed by the learning of a second, different, set of associations. Presumably, if there is positive transfer, better scores will be obtained on the second set. In an early study by Gladis and Braun (1958), three age groups were compared: 20–29, 40–49, and 60–72. The youngest group showed the greatest transfer effect—the most improvement. One possible explanation is that the older subjects encountered more interference.

A review of the research data led Arenberg and Robertson-Tchabo (1977) to conclude that "when well-established habits are beneficial for learning for the young, they are even more beneficial for the old; and when the well-established behavior interferes with learning for the young, it is even more interfering for the old" (p. 431). The frequent finding that meaningfulness of material is important to successful new learning in older adults is consistent with this generalization. In a large cross-sectional study, Botwinick and Storandt (1974) found no age difference from 20 to 70 in learning pairs of stimuli with high associative strength and progressively greater age differences as the pairs of stimuli became less meaningfully related to each other. In a comparison of reactions to tones versus meaningful spoken phrases, age differences in favor of young subjects were present for tones but not for spoken phrases (Shmavonian & Busse, 1963).

One explanation given for the beneficial effects of instruction is that instruction helps subjects "learn to learn." Older individuals presumably have less familiarity with the strange kind of learning required in experiments. Thus, when they are prepared ahead of time or equated for level of first learning, no age differences are found in transfer or retroactive studies.

Memory

A primary difference between living beings and machines is the living being's ability to make use of information to adapt to ongoing situations and circumstances. Survival is predicated on thinking out new solutions based on memory of earlier experiences. Maybe part of survival itself is being able to enjoy both the repetitive and the novel aspects of new experiences, in being able to compare, contrast, and create. For all these activities, it is necessary to retain memories of earlier experience, to retrieve these memories appropriately, and to apply them in a variety of ways.

Most adults—particularly those past middle age—worry about losing their memory. At least one member of every audience I have ever lectured to, or been part of, has asked about memory loss. So far, research results are as contradictory here as they are for perception and learning. Comparisons of the remembering done by older and younger people frequently—but not always— show age differences in favor of the young. Such age differences apply only to some kinds of memories, however, and are often attributable to differences in initial learning or to problems in retrieval.

Methods of Testing

Classical ways of testing memory are recognition, recall, and relearning. A common **recognition** method is to present material learned in an earlier session together with other similar material (digits or words, for example) and to ask subjects to pick out the items learned earlier. A common **recall** method is to ask subjects to report or reproduce as much of the earlier-learned material as they can. A common **relearning** test is to see how long it takes subjects to relearn material that was learned earlier (this test is most appropriate when a long period of time has elapsed between learning and remembering). Most adult developmental research has looked at the differences between recognition and recall. Different methods yield different findings at different ages. For instance, most research shows age deficits in recall, but few studies show any in recognition.

Primary and Secondary Memory

Before information theory began to displace earlier learning theories, memory was thought to be some kind of stamping in of stimulus traces, probably in some part of the nervous system. More recently, the emphasis has been on the processing of information, even while it is being stored.

Waugh and Norman (1965) propose a two-stage model of memory processing: **primary,** or short-term, memory and **secondary,** long-term storage. Primary-memory functioning would not deteriorate with age, but secondary-memory functioning would. This difference is partly due to the reorganization or higher-level processing required for long-term storage.

Many studies have failed to find significant age differences in digit span or word span, which are measures of primary memory. Even those studies that have found slight but reliable age decrements in memory span (for example, Botwinick & Storandt, 1974) have not found that the decrements are large enough to represent serious functional impairment. Older subjects do not do as well on backward digits—repeating numbers in reverse order—which requires processing and thus represents secondary memory. Younger subjects tend to receive the same scores on both forward- and backward-repeated digits (Botwinick & Storandt, 1974).

Secondary memory is considered timeless (Craik, 1977). There is no qualitative difference between what is remembered after 30 seconds and what is remembered after months or years. For secondary-memory material, however, the method of testing does make a difference. Older subjects do not show much forgetting in recognition tests but do in recall tests. Cross-sectional comparisons of memory for word lists show no age differences in recognition between 20-year-old subjects and any older groups, including those in their 60s (Schonfield & Robertson, 1966). Recall scores, however, are lower than recognition scores at all ages. Even 20-year-olds do not recall as well as they recognize, and people at each successive decade older show more discrepancy between the two methods. However, even 60-year-olds have not reached zero level.

Not only does method of measurement make a difference, but method

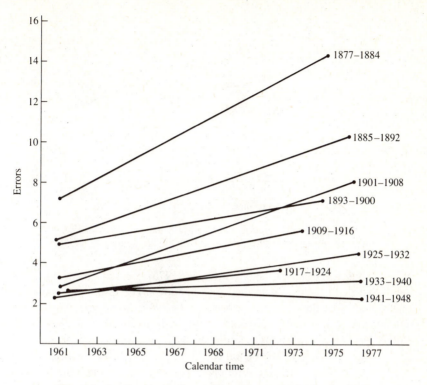

Figure 3 – 4.   Regression lines of Benton errors and calendar time for nine birth cohorts. (Source: Arenberg, 1982.)

of learning also affects memory. When information is heard or repeated aloud, it is remembered much better (and also learned much more easily) than when it is seen. Although visual/sensory memory has been found to last only about one-fourth of a second, auditory sensory memory may last as long as 2 seconds (Walsh, 1975).

Older people find it relatively harder to remember complex material, such as paragraphs, than to remember simple material, such as a list of color names. There is a decline with age in the ability to reproduce or recognize, but this decline does not seem to be noticeable until after 60 years of age. Figure 3 – 4 shows the number of errors in copying from memory a set of designs (Benton Visual Retention Test). These are cross-sequential data derived from the NIA Baltimore longitudinal study of men. The oldest group, born between 1877 and 1884, made more errors at the first time of testing in 1961 than did younger birth cohorts. They also got worse at each succeeding testing than did younger cohorts. In fact, the young adults, born in the 1930s and 1940s, stayed the same over 16 years (Arenberg, 1982).

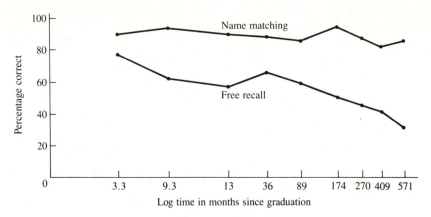

Figure 3–5. Recognition and recall of names and faces of high-school colleagues. (Source: Bahrick, Bahrick, and Wittlinger, 1975.)

Bahrick, Bahrick, and Wittlinger (1975) focused on memories of high-school colleagues, as verified by yearbooks. The results are shown in Figure 3–5. The deficits the researchers found seem to be for subjects over age 50, and that primarily in recall. Table 3–1 shows decrements in recall and recognition of news items according to age (40 and older) and time interval (6, 12, and 18 months) (Warrington & Silberstein, 1970). Again, recognition is better than recall, and age differences are more noticeable after 55 than before.

Deficits in memory, particularly secondary memory, are usually attributed to faulty learning or problems with retrieval. Another way of saying this is that the problem lies with ineffective attention or encoding of information to begin with or with difficulty in getting the information out of storage.

Retrieval

Problems with retrieval are a variant of the competence/performance issue. Older people's memories may be as good as ever, but they may not be able to get at the information. For some reason, it is harder for older people to "dredge up" large or complicated memories.

In one experiment (Craik & Masani, 1969), subjects were presented with word lists in an order alien to normal English usage; the words could not be combined to form a sentence. The investigators scored the number of "chunks" remembered, defining a chunk as a string of words recalled in the same order in which it had been presented. Older subjects recalled fewer chunks than did younger subjects, but they recalled as many words per chunk as younger subjects. Craik concluded that aging had a detrimental effect on

Table 3–1.   Percentage retention of public events after three time intervals

Age group	Recall			Recognition		
	Retention interval (months)					
	6	*12*	*18*	*6*	*12*	*18*
40	48%	37%	32%	77%	72%	69%
40–54	45	35	31	80	71	68
55+	36	29	26	75	69	68

Source: Warrington and Silberstein, 1970.

retrieval processes (fewer chunks retrieved) but that aging did not affect encoding ability (same number of words encoded into each chunk).

Many people, including many psychologists, assume that the major retrieval problem in later life is interference. But what exactly do we mean by interference? In earlier stimulus-response theory, interference meant response competition. It is harder to produce a stored memory when you need to because other competing memories are simultaneously evoked and you must go through a secondary selection process in order to sort out the particular memory you want.

In information-processing theory, a similar concept is used. Retrieval cues or categories become less effective if more items are included or evoked by them. It is as if older people are retrieving from larger categories. To counteract this overload and consequent blurring or suppression of memories, one could sharpen the cues or categories so that they differentiate more effectively among the confusion of relevant and irrelevant memories evoked. Furthermore, it is more important to "overlearn" as one gets older. On the comforting side is the persistent finding that meaningful material is remembered better than meaningless material, since most memories are of meaningful things. Also, using memory strategies helps, and most older people report that they use them (Perlmutter, 1978).

Higher-Level Thought

It seems incredible that there is so little research literature on the life-span development of higher-level thinking, considering that almost all the world's thinking is done by adults. Labouvie-Vief (1979) points out that while logical thinking is perfected in adolescence, it is not really put to use before adulthood. Only after individuals become committed and responsible do they use their logical abilities to help them choose the best course of action to solve life problems—to adapt.

Most data on development of higher mental processes are cross-sectional and thus can merely be suggestive. Let us first look at one of the few longitudinal studies so far. Arenberg (1974) used a display of ten lights to set up problems involving logical relations. He tested 300 well-educated, middle-class men between the ages of 24 and 87 at two times, six years apart. His cross-sectional results, comparing men of different ages tested at the same time, show unequivocally poorer performance by men over 60, with each younger age group progressively better. In the follow-up six years later, however, which included only 224 men who had succeeded the first time, age decrements were observable only for men over 70, who asked significantly more redundant questions than any younger age group.

Now let us look at other cross-sectional data. Wetherick (1964) found no significant age differences among 20-, 40-, and 60-year-olds in learning to work a switchboard. This finding supports Arenberg's conclusion that most cross-sectional age declines tend to be for ages older than 60. Collins (1964) also found no age differences on a complexity task, however, and his subjects ranged between 17 and 85.

Nehrke (1971), with a much larger sample (1151 people between 20 and 70 years old), reported that age, sex, education, and number of trials all produced significant differences in solving syllogisms. Better education was associated with better scores. However, subjects of each older decade of age scored lower, on the average. Older subjects also asked more questions, particularly more redundant questions.

Birren has long said that what we should be studying is the kind of cognitive strategies people of different ages use. Cognitive strategies include guessing and asking questions. They also include selecting different kinds of cognitive styles to approach different problems, as well as degree of impulsivity. For example, young people, knowing that they can function quickly, may be more likely to use relatively inefficient methods such as trial and error—to be more impulsive. Older people, finding that they are sometimes slower, may be more efficient. They may tend to think through a problem first—to be more reflective—so that when they go to work they can use fewer trials.

Such logic is at least partly supported by data that show no age differences in complex task solutions when unlimited time is available. Presumably, the extra time taken by older people is used for planning and deliberation. When Birren (1969) interviewed 100 successful older professional people, he found that most had not only long-range goals, but also tactical insight into how to achieve them. Some of their strategies were conservation of their resources and control of their emotions. In general, they were more focused on what they had decided was important than younger people tend to be. As he got older, B.F. Skinner, the noted behavioral psychologist, turned his attention to the strategies he was using to counteract the declines in functioning he saw in himself. His description of these strategies (Skinner, 1983) matches those of Birren's subjects.

Creativity

Problems of definition plague the studies of creativity. To begin with, are we talking about ability, or personality, or cognitive style? Is a person who produces many "creative" works more creative than one who produces fewer? Are we interested in productivity or capacity, in ability or performance? Is creativity different from general intelligence? Is qualitative change of cognitive structure, following Piaget's theory, an example of creativity? Can we thus consider anybody who reaches the *formal-operations* stage a creative person? Or is a creative act more specialized and limited—perhaps we should say more elite? Can we consider transformations of personality and lifestyle creative acts?

Flavell (1970) suggests that an act of creativity begins with the confronting of new information for which there is no existing category. If so, it would not necessarily be a decline in capacity for structural change that limits creativity after adolescence, but the adult's desire to maintain the stability achieved so laboriously at the end of the rapid changes of adolescence. Adults would try to ignore such new information. When events necessitate a restructuring of thinking, however, creativity can occur even among older adults. We could therefore say that there is a plateau in creative *capacity,* even though there is a decline in creative *performance.* The fact that most scientific and artistic productions occur in late adolescence or the early 20s may not be because that is the time of greatest potential but because that is the time of entering jobs and careers. Consequently, it is the time when fresh viewpoints are brought to the existing body of skills and knowledge. Should there be more career changes in later adulthood, we might see more creative output later in life.

The classic work on life-span creative achievements was done by Lehman (1953). He tabulated the output of notable people whose works were part of the public domain and announced that major creative achievements occur relatively early in people's productive careers, somewhere between their 20s and 40s, varying with their field. Furthermore, although their achievements may continue for many years after their peak, their later work is generally recognized (by other experts) to be less outstanding and significant than their early work. He assumed that people produce their best work when they are producing their most work.

Lehman's findings have been challenged. Dennis (1966), for example, reviewed the productivity of 738 scholars, scientists, and artists who had

Table 3–2. Percentage of total works between ages 20 and 80 that were done in each decade

	Men	Works	Age decade					
			20s	*30s*	*40s*	*50s*	*60s*	*70s*
Scholarship								
Historians	46	615	3	19	19	22	*24*	20
Philosophers	42	225	3	17	20	18	*22*	20
Scholars	43	326	6	17	*21*	*21*	16	19
Means			4	18	20	20	*21*	20
Sciences								
Biologists	32	3456	5	22	*24*	19	17	13
Botanists	49	1889	4	15	*22*	*22*	*22*	15
Chemists	24	2420	11	21	*24*	19	12	13
Geologists	40	2672	3	13	22	*28*	19	14
Inventors	44	646	2	10	17	18	*32*	21
Mathematicians	36	3104	8	*20*	*20*	18	19	15
Means			6	17	*22*	21	20	15
Arts								
Architects	44	1148	7	24	*29*	25	10	4
Chamber musicians	35	109	15	*21*	17	20	18	9
Dramatists	25	803	10	27	*29*	21	9	3
Librettists	38	164	8	21	*30*	22	15	4
Novelists	32	494	5	19	18	*28*	23	7
Opera composers	176	176	8	30	*31*	16	10	5
Poets	46	402	11	21	*26*	16	16	10
Means			9	23	*26*	21	14	6

Note: Maximum values are shown in italics. Adapted from Dennis, 1966.

all lived to at least the age of 79. His findings are summarized in Table 3–2. For most disciplines, the most productive (or almost the most productive) decade was the 40s; only in music was the 30s decade more productive than that of the 40s. Dennis also showed that scholarly productivity was maintained at a high level through the 60s, with only a slight decline in the 70s. Scientific productivity was also maintained through the 60s, but decline was more marked in the 70s. Artistic productivity declined gradually from the 40s through the 70s. Dennis interpreted the differences among the various fields in terms of individual effort versus assistance from others and the length of the training period. Artists today usually work alone, whereas laboratory scientists usually have teams of assistants and students.

When Taylor (1969) studied critics' reviews of noted pianists, he found the most-cited age changes to be (1) an inability to control complex materials, such as fugues, and (2) a lessening of "pounding" and fast tempos. (Age changes are not all bad, then!) Critics do not expect declines before the artists enter their 60s. Like Dennis, Taylor mentions overlearning, early learning, and frequent repetition of material as aids to maintaining repertoires; as well as such strategies as scheduling concerts less frequently and repeating old material. All these strategies have been discussed previously for more everyday types of performance.

An interesting longitudinal study of master chess players (Elo, 1965) found an inverted U-curve, peaking at about the age of 35. Performance levels at age 63 were comparable to those at age 20. These data replicate those of Lehman. When Charness (1981) varied both age (16–64) and skill of master chess players, he found that older players searched for problem solutions less extensively than did younger ones. However, older players were no different from younger players in rate of search or quality of the moves selected. Another interesting longitudinal study followed honors science students over four years (Cropley, 1969). Those who "bloomed" in the course of these few years were no different initially from their more everyday classmates in ability or achievement. But they did differ from them in style: they were more divergent thinkers.

Lehman's findings were also evaluated by Butler (1967), who cited the association between productivity and decline in time available for work. As people gain eminence, they are invited to enter administrative or honorary positions and thus effectively diminish their creative output. Scholars and scientists, for example, become department heads and deans. Artists become teachers.

Butler's second point is that when abilities are exercised, they do not decline. There are more within-age differences than between-age differences. One could cite such notable examples as Pablo Casals, who was still playing the cello brilliantly at 95; Pablo Picasso, who was painting in new ways at 90; and P.G. Wodehouse, who published one of his best books at 90. Women artists and writers between 26 and 74 years of age showed no negative correlation between age and creativity scores, in contrast to a group of noncreative women who did (Crosson & Robertson-Tchabo, 1983). Also, there are many instances of people who did not even begin their notable work until their later years.

Generational differences certainly exist in terms of opportunities and interests. If a culture emphasizes engineering at one point in history, for example, potential musicians—those who would be more creative as musicians than as engineers—are lost, becoming mediocre engineers. Such cultural emphases can shift quickly, too. Young people who turn creatively to physics when it is a challenging area in college may find opportunities closed ten years later, when there are more jobs in interpersonal fields—or vice versa.

IQ

Tests of general intelligence—sometimes referred to as "omnibus" tests—derive a single overall score, such as an IQ, by combining scores on diverse subtests and then dividing the obtained "mental age" by chronological age—up to adulthood.

Intelligence-test findings highlight the dangers of drawing age-change conclusions from age-difference data. In fact, it was his intelligence-test research that led Warner Schaie to see the problems with cross-sectional research (Schaie, Labouvie, & Buech, 1973) and to advocate cross-sequential and time-sequential designs. When people of the same age were tested at the same time, the highest overall scores were obtained by those between their late teens and late 20s. This can be seen in the upper curve in Figure 3–6. Progressively older subjects got progressively lower scores, particularly past the age of 60.

There is a correlation between number of years of school completed and general intelligence level. The more education people have, the higher their scores are to begin with and the higher they will continue to score throughout life, compared with others of their own age. Because most younger people over the last few decades have had more education than their parents and grandparents, they get higher IQ scores in the present. When they reach the ages that their parents and grandparents are now, they still will have higher IQs than their parents have at these ages now.

These age-cohort differences reflect a secular trend—a slow, persistent historical trend—toward higher ability (probably as a function of more education) similar to those trends found for increased height and weight, better health, and later onset of sexual maturity (see Chapter 2). It may be of interest to note that when the first edition of the Stanford-Binet intelligence test was developed in 1917, the ceiling age at which intellectual growth presumably stopped was 12. In successive revisions over the next 40 years or so, this ceiling rose to 16 and then to 21. Similarly, Jones and Conrad (1933) found the peak of test performance to be at about age 16 in the early 1930s, but more recent cross-sectional studies have reported peaks at 30 and, most recently, at 50 years of age (Botwinick, 1967).

The effects of cohort and period can be seen in Figure 3–6 which presents the results of testing three independent samples from the same general population of West Coast medical-plan members between 21 and 81 years of age (Schaie et al., 1973). The diagram in the upper part of the figure shows the cross-sectional gradients obtained by comparing the people of different ages who were tested at the same time. These age comparisons are not identical for the three times of testing (1956, 1963, and 1970). However, the differences among people the same age for different years of testing are not very noticeable for those younger than 53. As far as age differences are concerned, there is a plateau between 25 and 46 and then a gradual drop.

The lower part of Figure 3–6 shows the within-cohort gradients: the differences in scores between groups of people born at the same time but tested at different ages. Clearly, age cohort (see Chapter 1) influences intellectual performance. Those born most recently did not change much over the 14 years

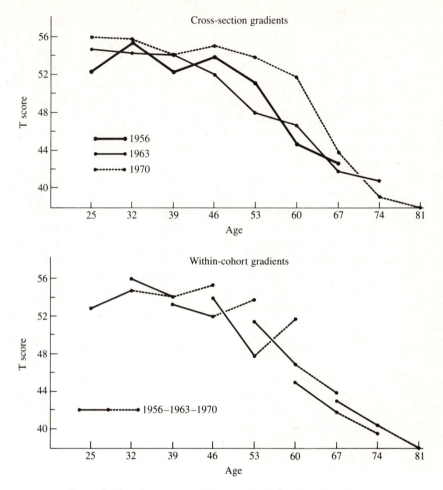

Figure 3–6. Age, cross-sectional, and within-cohort intellectual changes. (Source: Schaie, Labouvie, and Buech, 1973.)

between their first and last tests. But those born before the turn of the century—a period that may have been a watershed in American history—show dramatic drops from one test period to the next.

The kind of lives led by people born since 1900 has produced several generations whose intellectual performances have been more durable than those of their parents and grandparents. Perhaps intellectual performance is more central to our modern way of life. Perhaps, also, future generations who value education and intellectual pursuits less—as suggested by recent drops in national averages on academic-achievement tests—will show drops in intelligence-test scores compared to their parents and grandparents. If they do, cross-sectional curves of intelligence will look as if people became smarter as they aged.

Accumulated findings from longitudinal studies with intelligence tests—the same group of people retested one or more times over a period of years—almost all agree that there is some increase in scores at least through the 20s and no general decline throughout the years of adulthood, at least until about the age of 60. Most of these studies have been based upon superior samples, and the scores of better-educated people tend to increase more than those of people with less education. Health is also a factor: those in poorer health show greater declines.

Honzik and Macfarlane (1973) examined the personality characteristics of 7 men and 13 women who gained the most (8 or more IQ points) on the Wechsler Adult Intelligence Scale (WAIS) between the ages of 18 and 40. Compared with those whose IQs did not change, the gainers tended to have been children who were not gregarious, not highly sex-typed, and not liked or accepted. At age 30, they were less satisfied with their appearance and less likely to be asked for advice and reassurance. In general, therefore, they were more likely to be dissatisfied with their current lives and thus more likely to try harder and keep on trying harder.

Differential Abilities

So far we have been looking at omnibus tests, or combined measures of ability. Changes with age are a function of the kinds of abilities measured. Among the nine subtests of the WAIS, for example, those that require quick thinking—such as the Digit Symbol Test—show an age-change pattern similar to that for many perceptual abilities. They reach a peak in the 20s, plateau for a decade or two, and then decline steadily. Tests of stored information, such as vocabulary or general information, may continue to increase almost to the end of life. Certain types of reasoning tests, such as arithmetic reasoning, show an intermediate pattern: essentially, a plateau through the adult years. Most recent attention to adult intellectual development has focused primarily on these differential patterns, particularly on the model proposed by Cattell (1963) of a division between **fluid** and **crystallized** intelligence.

Fluid intelligence has been defined as an underlying or basic ability resulting from the interaction of physiological capacity and experiences. All active processing of information, whether coding during the acquisition phase or higher thought processes such as problem solving, involves fluid intelligence. The curve of growth and decline in this kind of ability would parallel that of various biological processes, perhaps declining steadily from the late teens.

Crystallized intelligence is the product of the action of fluid intelligence on life experiences. It can be defined as knowledge. Horn (1970) calls

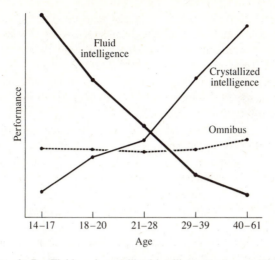

Figure 3–7. Fluid- and crystallized-intelligence patterns with age. (Source: Horn, 1970.)

it a "precipitate out of experience." This kind of ability continues to increase throughout adulthood.

Because IQ is a mixture of fluid and crystallized intelligence, it can remain stable through the adult years. As the proportion of fluid intelligence goes down, the proportion of crystallized intelligence goes up; the average remains constant (see Figure 3–7).

Sex Differences

Intellectual development during adulthood seems to be very different for men and women in North American society. All test findings agree in this respect. Girls are more advanced than boys in the preschool years, the sexes are the same during early and middle school years, and boys score higher starting in high school (Maccoby & Jacklin, 1974). Kangas and Bradway (1971) report retests spanning 38 years on the Stanford-Binet for 48 men and women between the ages of 12 and 50. Men who had higher IQs at 12 gained more in IQ by the mid-20s than did those who started with lower IQs, but women who had higher IQs at 12 gained less than those with lower IQs. Eichorn (1973) reported an increase in general IQ for men between 16 and 36 and a slight decline for women from 26 to 36 years. It is as if women use their intelligence to grow dumber, at least in the early years of adulthood. It could be adaptive for women to seem less competent than the men they seek to marry—and do marry—in a society that encourages men to "marry down." This subject will be discussed more fully in Chapter 5.

Follow-up testing with two Berkeley longitudinal samples—the Growth Study and the Oakland Guidance Study—also showed sex differences (Bayley, 1968; Honzik & Macfarlane, 1973). The largest gain on the WAIS between ages 18 and 40 was made by women on verbal IQ (more than 7 points) (Honzik & Macfarlane, 1973). This gain is really a return to the equality found in childhood, because the women at 18 scored much lower than the men. The same general effect holds for the full-scale IQ.

Schaie and his associates (1973) administered the Primary Mental Abilities Test to three independent samples of adults of all ages and found very stable and significant sex differences, at all ages and in all analyses. These differences varied in direction according to the particular mental ability tested. Women were superior in verbal meaning, reasoning, and word fluency; men were superior in space, number, and general intellectual ability (overall score).

Sex differences were particularly pronounced in the childhood personality antecedents of adult intelligence (Honzik & Macfarlane, 1973). For one thing, more of the girls' than the boys' early characteristics correlated with their intelligence at age 40. Honzik and Macfarlane suggest that the greater variety of men's occupational experiences produced more changes in their behavior. Women tended to change less. Those women who had the highest IQs at 40 had been productive, complex, self-doubting little girls and independent, interested 30-year-old women.

A Fels Institute longitudinal study (Sontag, Baker, & Nelson, 1958) of 72 women and 59 men found that those women who were highly social and dependent were more likely to have declining IQs than were those who were less characteristically sex-typed. From the standpoint of our new hard look at data on sex differences in achievement and performance, it seems more likely that we are dealing with the effects of sex-role socialization, which Matina Horner (1970) has dramatically called "fear of success," rather than with any basic sex differences. In other words, we are dealing with adaptation to the realities of adult sex-typed life rather than intrinsic sex differences. Similar factors probably apply to class, ethnic, and racial differences.

The Piagetian Approach

In the late 1970s and 1980s, investigations into cognitive functioning in adulthood have turned more and more frequently to Piagetian and dialectic models, moving away from mechanistic/quantitative approaches to more qualitative/structuralist ones. Previously, during the 1970s, Piagetian approaches were largely applied to children's cognitive development, mainly because the four stages of Piaget were presumed to have been completed by adulthood. These stages are:

1. Sensorimotor (birth to 2 years)
2. Preoperational or representational (2 to 7 or 8 years)
3. Concrete operational (7 or 8 to 11 or 12 years)
4. Formal operational (11 or 12 years to ?)

Note that the exact ages are flexible, depending upon the level of functioning attained.

Siegler (1980) notes that work in adult development has focused upon the last two stages: the development of number, length, width, volume, seriation, and classification of objects; and the development of abstract thought, involving reversibility, identity, and causality, as well as thinking about thought. In general, older adults have more difficulty with concrete and formal operations than do young adults, although differences are not important until after the decade of the 60s. Well-educated, verbal older adults, furthermore, have far less difficulty. Piagetian tasks, in other words, show the same pattern of findings as other complex cognitive tasks.

Piaget (1970) believed that most cognitive development in adulthood is quantitative rather than qualitative and more the result of experience than of biological change. He also wrote that although all normal adults have reached formal operations, they express it within the domain of their own specialization or aptitude. During their years of greatest cognitive power, in other words, adults function in highly specialized areas of life involvement. In line with this, Sinnot (1975) found less age deficit in adults' ability to solve formal-operational problems if these problems were within their own domain—and when they, the adults, were college-educated. Incidentally, a wide-range cross-sectional study of formal-operational performance (ages 10 to 50) did not support Piaget's belief that all adults had achieved formal operations (Kuhn, Langer, Kohlberg, & Haan, 1977). In fact, none of the subjects in this study did fully achieve it, although those between the ages of 21 and 30 did better than those either younger or older.

Summary

From the decade of the 20s to the end of the 60s, decreases in speed of cognitive and intellectual functioning and fluidity of processing new information are slow but incremental. These findings are often more the result of performance disadvantages than competence declines, however. When older adults are allowed to pace themselves in learning and memory tasks, age differences are often wiped out—particularly in recognition, less so in recall. Material that has been adequately coded and stored does not seem to "fade" over time. Differences between groups and individuals become greater over time, as does intraindividual variability. Problems of overarousal, susceptibility to distraction from competing stimuli, overcautiousness, and inefficient strategies account for many age changes. Paying closer attention, assigning meaning to novel information, and overlearning are all good ways to maintain optimal performance. Above all, maintenance of good physical fitness, particularly through appropriate exercise, seems to lead to minimal decline. While older adults may not be able to do very much about their "fluid" processing, they can enhance the growth of crystallized intelligence by maintaining intellectual pursuits during their adult years.

Chapter Four

Personality Development in the Adult Years

What will present-day 20-year-olds be like ten years from now—or 20 years from now? Will they become more sure of themselves? Will their interests change, or their ideas about what's right and wrong? Will other people like them better? All people operate by built-in life clocks that tell them at what age they should be doing particular things or how they should be acting at different ages. If they don't get married when they think they are supposed to, or don't "act their age," they feel they have failed in some way. They may want to stay 20, but they move along to 35 and 45 and 55; in some ways they are always the same person, but in other ways they are always changing. Sometimes that change is development.

In the preceding two chapters, it was concluded that there seem to be slow-moving, almost unnoticeable, but inexorable changes over the adult years in many areas of physical and intellectual functioning. It was noted that we have to be tentative about predicting or describing these changes because most information is cross-sectional. Furthermore, there is much more information about the transition from preadulthood to adulthood at one end and from middle age to old age at the other end than there is about the long years in between. The same problems exist in the area of personality.

In Chapter 3, it was pointed out that intelligence is a composite concept. Personality is even more of a grab-bag concept. It includes acts of behavior as well as feelings, attitudes as well as interactions with other people. However, many psychologists believe that personality is more than an agglomeration of aspects, parts, or traits. They see it as a kind of system—an integration of all behavioral elements into a "self" or "ego" or whole. Finally, personality refers not only to behavior as such but also to the appropriateness or efficacy of that behavior in the physical and social world.

Perspectives on Personality Development

Present theories about adult personality development assume one of three alternative perspectives. The first stresses stability. The self becomes "institutionalized" early in life, to use Neugarten's term, and in adulthood a lot of effort is spent in maintaining it. People strive for a consistent identity that can minimize the disturbing effects of changes all around. Changes that threaten to disrupt this self-system are likely to set off compensatory changes to minimize the disruptive effect. This can happen after physical alterations in the body, such as increases or decreases in strength, or after "significant life events" (Neugarten, 1977) such as marriage. Preserving maneuvers include distorting what is seen, what others are believed to be doing, or even what is felt. A person who feels unlovable, for example, counts the number of times he (or she) is ignored or not smiled at or not invited somewhere and forgets the many more numerous indications of love and admiration. It takes enormous efforts such as psychotherapy to produce any significant changes in habitual life outlooks. From this first perspective, then, personality development is not really a viable concept, for its theme is absence of development.

An opposite perspective views personality as the product of the situation. As life situations fluctuate, so do the people experiencing them. Like Heraclitus' river, the only thing that is constant is change; constancy is an illusion or a delusion. The same person can be a courageous leader in one situation and a dependent, unsure procrastinator in another. Furthermore, from this point of view, people can be made to behave in any particular way by arranging a situation so as to bring out that kind of behavior. Stability over many years would only reflect stability in life situations over those years. From this perspective, just as from the first perspective, personality development is impossible. Even though there may be many changes, they will not be related to each other in any intrinsic way.

It is only from the third perspective that patterned change or true development can be considered. The self-system, instead of minimizing changes by compensating to maintain stability, incorporates these changes and thus becomes transformed into a new and different whole.

Longitudinal data show that, in fact, there is more than one pattern of change. Some personality characteristics remain unaltered through adult life. Some characteristics change idiosyncratically or differentially for individuals or subgroups as a consequence of varying environmental experiences. And some characteristics show transformations of personality structure and therefore can be said to develop in the most exact sense of the term. Different kinds of stability and change are described in the following pages.

The Concept of Self

A half century ago, George Herbert Mead (1934) distinguished two parts of the **self:** the **I** and the **me.** The **I** is the core or center; it unifies diverse feelings and experiences as well as past, present, and future, and makes one feel the same person throughout the passage of time. The **me** is the part of the self that results from interaction with others in society; it is more likely to change over time.

As early as three or four months of age, the infant develops a sense of "existential" separateness from others, a sense of "I" as separate from "you" and "them" (Lewis & Brooks, 1975). There is a life-long effort "toward consistency in our perceptions of ourselves" (Clausen, 1972, p. 502). This feeling of being the same person all along is so stable and so pervasive that reunions with old friends or classmates can be profoundly shocking. When it is discovered that images of those people are not what those people are like now, the fact that we, too, have changed must be faced. However, it may soon be seen that changes are relatively superficial. After a few minutes of con- versation, we may go right back to where we left off, again seeing both our friends and ourselves as having remained the same people over time. At least, our relationship has stayed the same.

Maintaining a sense of continuity, of **I,** may become more crucial as people get older (Lowenthal, Thurnher, & Chiriboga, 1975). When multiple changes in body and in social position occur, it becomes particularly impor- tant—but more difficult—to keep one's identity.

The **me** consists of descriptive categories or classifications; it does not start to develop, according to Lewis and Brooks (1975), until about two years of age. It requires sufficient cognitive maturity to be able to classify: to compare oneself with others and to combine the characteristics that others attribute to one with those one attributes to oneself. Because these views of ourselves incorporate the views of others around us, the **me** is more likely to change with changing associations and experiences than the **I.** For instance, if one sees, in getting older, that most people now consider one powerful, or attractive, or irrelevant, or unattractive, one is likely to define oneself the same way, and to change one's behavior to fit this new self-definition: to act powerful, or attractive, or irrelevant, or unattractive, as the case may be.

In Erikson's theory, identity formation is—or at least is expected to be—completed early in adolescence. However, there are probably recurrent "identity crises" throughout the rest of life. Only a few people may really complete their identity formation by 15 or even 20 years of age. Erikson himself stresses that the process is ongoing. Identity formation may be the most important task faced by adolescents, but it may also be a task faced by older people, particularly by those whose life circumstances change. According to Erikson, this sense of being distinct individuals, and the distinct definitions of ourselves that we form, must agree with the definitions other people have of us. Some psychologists (such as Mischel, 1968) feel, however, that by early adulthood most people have long known who they are and what they are like. These images of themselves remain remarkably stable from then on, almost as stable as the sense of *I*-ness.

When a grandmother, her daughter, and her granddaughter were asked in what ways they had stayed the same over their life and in what ways they had changed, the 74-year-old grandmother said, "I think I was always good to the people I loved—especially my children and my husband. I've always tried to laugh—even now, when I can't get around so easily, I try to be happy. I think I've mellowed out over the years. Things that used to really bother me when I was younger don't seem to matter any more." Her 49-year-old daughter said, "I've always had a good sense of humor, been very dependable as far as my job is concerned, always been a good mother, always been a good wife—that will never change. I always used to be weak, but have found out that I'm stronger than I thought, more contented with my life than ever before." And the 16-year-old granddaughter said, "I've always taken things too seriously; I'm sensitive emotionally; I always think of consequences before I act. I've gotten rowdier and less cautious, living more for the fun of it." Thus, all three see essential sameness, even though they feel they have gotten better, too.

In order to maintain the integrity of self-definitions, people may go to great lengths to warp or mold experiences, selecting out evidence to confirm self-perceptions and discarding contradictory evidence. We surround ourselves with people who confirm our beliefs, and we put ourselves into situations that enable us to live up to—or down to—our self-definitions.

The **me** part of the *self* consists of self-definitions, self-images, or self-concepts. It includes a wide variety of individual characteristics, from temperament to need for achievement. These characteristics are used as labels in defining oneself and others. People are aware of, or conscious of, some of these traits, and unaware of others.

Mischel (1979) emphasizes the distinction between **stability** over time and **variability** from one situation to another. Figure 4-1 shows a diagram of this distinction. At Time 1—let us say, in early adulthood—the person shows three kinds of behaviors in Situation A (*l, m,* and *n*), one kind of behavior in Situation B (*m*), and two kinds of behavior in Situation C (*n* and *o*). This person is thus more variable in Situation A than in Situations B and C. At Time 2, perhaps 20 years later, and Time 3, perhaps another 20 years later, this same person shows the same behavior in Situation A as he or she did in youth: still *l, m,* and *n*. Measurements in Situation A would show exact

	Situations		
	A	*B*	*C*
Time 1	l, m, n	m	n, o
Time 2	l, m, n	m, p	p
Time 3	l, m, n	m, p	q

Figure 4-1. Stability and variability of behavior.

similarity of performance over the years and would justify a conclusion of stability of personality over time. But look what would happen if the measurements were in Situation B. The person would show personality change from youth to middle age, adding *p* to earlier *m* characteristics. But he or she would keep these characteristics into Time 3. If we drew conclusions about stability from Situation B, we would conclude that people change during early adulthood but then stay the same into old age. If the measurement were of Situation C behavior, there would be *no* apparent stability over time at all.

Now look at Figure 4-2. Even if measurement of a particular behavior is always in Situation A—the home, for example—the actual behavior— anger, for example—may be expressed differently at different times of life. At Time 1, anger may take the form of direct physical aggression; at Time 2, of sarcasm; at Time 3, of controlled facial rigidity. At Time 1, furthermore, the anger may not be very important to the individual's ongoing behavior—a momentary twinge, perhaps. At Time 2, it may color all other actions; at Time 3, it may again be of relatively low salience.

All these factors need to be kept in mind in interpreting longitudinal data—or, for that matter, any kind of data that are used to assess age change.

Longitudinal Studies

During the 1920s and 1930s, longitudinal studies of human development were begun in several locations across the United States. Most of the studies selected subjects in early childhood (even newborns and prenatals) and followed them—or, at any rate, the survivors—over time. More recently, a few studies started with measurements of adults.

	Expression of behavior 1	Importance of behavior 1
Time 1	l_1	low
Time 2	l_2	high
Time 3	l_3	low

Figure 4-2. Expression and importance of particular behavior.

Three long-term studies in California began with infants or children: Terman's study of gifted children; the Berkeley Growth Study; and the Oakland Guidance Study. Most subjects in these studies are now middle-aged. Follow-ups of these people have yielded interesting data on adult development.

So far as the constructs of "self" are concerned, most longitudinal data show more stability than change over the adult years. Sears and Sears (1978), who followed up the boys in Terman's group of gifted children when they were men in their 60s, found a high degree of consistency, as did Haan (1976) when she examined the follow-up data on the Berkeley subjects when they were in their 40s.

Byrne (1966) reported stability in self-descriptions over time, as did Kelly (1955) and Woodruff and Birren (1972). The subjects in Woodruff and Birren's study were originally administered the California Personality Test in 1944, when they were college students, and were given it again in 1969, 25 years later. Curiously enough, they described themselves very much the same way in 1969 as they had in 1944, even though they claimed they had changed a great deal. Their descriptions at age 45 of what they had been like as college students were very different from the way they had actually described themselves when they were students. Like the three women quoted above, they wanted to think they had improved over time.

Temperament

Basic differences in temperament or activity level mold most other individual differences in personality. Some babies move quickly, some are placid. Some adults rush through everything at a fast pace, and some are serene. Quickly moving adults were probably quickly moving babies (Honzik, 1964).

In follow-ups of adults in the Berkeley and Oakland longitudinal studies (Haan & Day, 1974), activity level proved to be one of the characteristics that stays most stable over the life span. The most active members of a birth cohort maintained their relative speediness, although their absolute tempo may not have stayed at the same high level. Active people slow down as they age, along with their peers, but they probably remain among the quickest of their peers to the end. The decline in general activity found for the Baltimore men in the National Institutes of Aging (NIA) longitudinal study, incidentally, did not begin before the age of 50 (Douglas & Arenberg, 1978).

Affect

Do feelings or emotions change over life? Are they stronger at some periods than others—stronger in adolescence than in late adulthood, for example?

Several psychologists suggest that facial expressions of affect may be more overt in children than in older people. Development during childhood and adolescence consists of the suppression of facial displays of emotion and the substitution of symbolic for motor activity (Izard, 1971). Haviland and Myers (1979) asked children, young adults, and older adults to construct faces (out of features drawn on paper, such as eyes, nose, and mouth) for children, young adults, and older adults. Most subjects constructed children's faces that were more open and expressive than those they constructed for adults. The ages of the subjects themselves did not seem to make much difference. These results suggest that people have age stereotypes of expressiveness.

When Rosen and Neugarten (1960) administered the Thematic Apperception Test (TAT) to people between 40 and 71 years of age, they found that older people tend less often to perceive emotion as important parts of life situations. Opposed to these cross-sectional findings are longitudinal data derived from the NIA sample of men (Douglas & Arenberg, 1978); scores on both restraint and emotional stability were stable over many years.

Innovative research by Csikszentmihalyi, Graef, and Larson (1979) asked men and women between 13 and 65 years of age to record their feelings whenever they were signaled by an electronic pager they carried with them. One finding was that older adults reported greater concentration, less distractibility, and less wish to be doing something else. Further, their feelings in one situation were less unique and more like their feelings in other situations than was true for younger subjects.

Life Satisfaction

Does getting older mean getting unhappier? Different approaches have been used to try to answer this. People have been asked how they feel, how satisfied they are with life, how much excitement or zest there is in their life, how good they feel about themselves, or how anxious or depressed they feel. There are tabulations of the frequency of depressive or pathological symptoms by age, of seeking psychotherapy or being committed to mental hospitals, and of suicide rates. Most of these studies are cross-sectional, a few are cohort-sequential, and some are longitudinal. Different approaches, not surprisingly, give somewhat different results. In general, longitudinal studies show stability over time, whereas cross-sectional studies show increases in unhappiness with age.

Let us look first at the longitudinal data. Kagan and Moss (1962) found that social anxiety in early adulthood could be predicted from the same kind of behavior in middle childhood. Block (1971) found that those senior high school students who showed personality changes by adulthood seemed to be in a state of "disequilibrium and tension both within themselves and in relation to established adult society and values, whereas nonchangers appear to be relaxed, effective individuals." Woodruff and Birren (1972) found "neuroticism" relatively stable from college to middle age, even though a new group of students tested in 1969 were more neurotic than those tested 20 years earlier. Maas and Kuypers (1974) found that anxious-asserting older women had been anxious, tense, and assertive in early adulthood. R. R. Sears (1977) found that optimism about life and feelings of self-worth persisted over three decades of adulthood. Costa and McCrae (1976) found remarkable stability of individual differences in such measures as anxiety and neuroticism among men over a ten-year period.

Now let's look at a cohort-sequential investigation. The University of Michigan's Survey Research Center conducted two parallel national studies of American mental health and happiness, one in 1957 and the second in 1976 (Veroff, Douvan, & Kulka, 1981). Tables 4-1 and 4-2 show some of their findings. First, as can be seen in Table 4-1, sex differences are more interesting than age differences. The percentage of men who said they were very happy in 1957 stayed the same in 1976. Remember, these are not the same men in both periods, just men from the same birth cohort—born at the same time. Thus, compare the percentage of men 21–34 who were "very happy" in 1957 (33%) with the percentage of men 35–54 who were "very happy" in 1976 (33%). The pattern is different for women, though. Both cross-sectionally and time-sequentially, younger women were happier than older women. In fact, more younger women than younger men said they were very happy. Table

Table 4-1.   Relation of age to happiness (by sex and year).

	Age					
	21–34		35–54		55+	
Happiness	*Men (%)*	*Women (%)*	*Men (%)*	*Women (%)*	*Men (%)*	*Women (%)*
1957						
Very happy	33	45	35	38	30	24
Pretty happy	64	48	54	51	55	57
Not too happy	3	7	11	11	15	19
	100%	100%	100%	100%	100%	100%
Total number	317	440	447	556	306	373
1976						
Very happy	29	35	33	31	30	28
Pretty happy	62	55	58	59	58	58
Not too happy	9	10	9	10	12	15
	100%	100%	100%	100%	100%	100%
Total number	340	467	306	383	294	433

Source: Veroff, Douvan, and Kulka, 1981, Table 2-22.

Table 4-2. Selected age comparisons of feelings of well-being (by year)

Measure of Well-Being	Age											
	21–29		30–39		40–49		50–59		60–64		65+	
	1957 (%)	1976 (%)	1957 (%)	1976 (%)	1957 (%)	1976 (%)	1957 (%)	1976 (%)	1957 (%)	1976 (%)	1957 (%)	1976 (%)
Present well-being												
Worries:												
Always, a lot	32	51	32	53	34	47	35	39	33	42	36	39
Zest:												
Highest third	—	37	—	43	—	41	—	39	—	31	—	23
Present happier than past:												
Yes	—	53	—	50	—	39	—	33	—	30	—	24
Past well-being												
Childhood unhappiness:												
Yes	38	52	31	34	22	26	18	20	11	20	12	13
Nervous Breakdown:												
Yes	17	24	21	25	21	23	20	18	16	23	14	14
Experience problems relevant for help:												
Yes	30	43	29	40	23	42	19	32	12	26	14	19
Overwhelmed by bad things:												
Yes	—	48	—	44	—	42	—	39	—	39	—	37
Future well-being												
Morale about future:												
Very happy	76	69	65	65	53	48	40	42	27	28	17	17

Source: Veroff, Douvan, and Kulka, 1981, Table 2-24.

4-2, which combines men and women, shows a steady drop in the percentage of respondents finding life zestful from the decade of the 30s to late adulthood. Other aspects of well-being, such as self-esteem, show parallel age patterns of decreasing positive feelings (Veroff, Douvan, & Kulka, 1981), particularly after 50.

A 1969 Gallup poll asked people "Is your life exciting?" (Alston & Dudley, 1973). The percentages of those who answered yes are shown in Table 4-3. Clearly, older adults felt less excitement in their lives than did younger ones. The only noticeable sex difference, incidentally, was in the youngest group: women in the child-rearing years found life duller than men of the same age. Three-quarters of men in their 20s felt that life was exciting. Fewer men *and* women over 50 thought life was exciting—only two-fifths. Again, before we conclude that life gets duller as one goes along, we should consider the effect of the self-actualization movement and its stress on excitement in life. In 1969, that movement was relatively new and thus would have had its greatest impact on youth. A 1982 poll asking the same question might find less age difference in this respect.

Although exciting lives may be more possible for youth than for their elders, an unexciting life is not necessarily unsatisfactory or unhappy. One can have high life satisfaction and high morale and be neither happy nor unhappy. Serenity is not exciting, but it is not depression. For example, the youngest San Francisco group studied by Lowenthal et al. (1975)—the high school seniors—were the least happy, the most lonely, the lowest in life satisfaction, and the highest in negative experiences reported—but they also reported the most happy experiences! We could call their lives both exciting and complex. When they weren't up, they were down. Their emotions were rarely calm.

The newlyweds in the same study were a little less complex. Overall, they seemed to be the happiest group. They were highest in life satisfaction and reported a majority of positive experiences. They were, however, the

Table 4-3. Percentage saying that life is exciting, by age and sex.

Age	Male % (N)	Female % (N)
20–29	75 (117)	65 (138)
30–39	56 (121)	55 (144)
40–49	48 (153)	49 (157)
50 and over[a]	40 (310)	36 (240)
Total	50 (701)	49 (679)

[a]Previous analyses indicated no statistically significant changes in proportions saying that life was exciting by ten-year intervals after the 50-year-old level.
Source: Alston and Dudley, 1973.

second highest in reported negative experiences, next to the adolescents, and they were lonelier than the middle-aged subjects. Their lives were not as exciting as those of the teenagers, but only slightly less so.

On the whole, the middle-aged parents of high school seniors were in the middle on most quality-of-life measures. The women's life-satisfaction scores, though, were the lowest of all age/sex groups. Overall, they were not as happy as the newlyweds, but were happier than the subjects who were their children's age.

The oldest group, in late middle age, was happier than those ten years younger. This group was as high in life satisfaction as the newlyweds (particularly the men), but had lower affect, either positive or negative, than did younger groups.

Self-Esteem

Lowenthal and her associates (1975) found that the high school seniors studied had the lowest self-esteem; the older subjects had progressively higher self-esteem with increasing age. Men and women did not show the same age pattern, however. The newlywed men and the oldest women liked themselves the best of the eight age/sex groups. Further, the age pattern of the men was more irregular than that of the women. The young-adult men had higher self-esteem than did the adolescent men and the middle-aged men. The women, however, showed progressively higher self-esteem with age. When these same subjects were reinterviewed five years later, there was no change in self-esteem for the middle-aged women. Noberini and Neugarten (1975) found similar stability for middle-aged women in their ten-year follow-up of Chicago subjects.

The San Francisco high school boys were painfully aware of their social inadequacies. One said, "Socially I have lots of room for progress. I'm the kind of person that most people don't think one way or the other about" (Lowenthal et al., 1975, p. 69). The high school girls were no different; they were "even more likely to question their ability to lead an independent life" (p. 72). It is interesting to compare these findings with those of a large national investigation ten years earlier. Young people who were asked about their past and future lives in a 1959 Gallup poll (Bortner & Hultsch, 1976) saw both the past and the future as better than the present. Thus, while they were currently "down in the dumps," they didn't expect to stay there forever. To the extent that we can compare San Francisco lower-middle-class youth in 1970 with a national sample drawn in a more stable and affluent era, the self-esteem of the San Francisco youth may have been low only in contrast to their high aspirations for the future. Their ideal selves were perhaps exaggerated, so their evaluation of their current state could only be low.

The newlywed young men felt great confidence in themselves, greater than did the newlywed women. This sex difference is consistent with findings generally reported, particularly among married adults. Women are more critical of themselves and devalue themselves much more than do men. Bortner and Hultsch (1976) found more of the pattern they called "great expectations"—exaggerated hopes for the future—among young adults than among the other age groups they studied, even the adolescents.

The San Francisco middle-aged men described themselves as dull, reserved, and lacking a sense of humor; they did not like themselves as much as the newlyweds liked themselves. The middle-aged women were not much more pleased with themselves than their male contemporaries. But the pre-retired men and women, who were ten years older (around 60), seemed much more comfortable with themselves. A woman at this time of life said, "I can say what I feel, I am not embarrassed by many things anymore, and my personality is better" (Lowenthal et al., 1975, p. 74). Bortner and Hultsch found, however, an "anticipating deprivation" pattern most common at this age. The feeling of ease and self-liking must thus be seen against a backdrop of doom to come. It is the *Götterdämmerung,* the "twilight of the gods."

Women tend, on the whole, to derive their feelings of self-worth from family circumstances; men, on the whole, derive their worth from job circumstances. Nowak (1976) found that middle-aged women, in addition, were sensitive to their appearance and didn't like themselves much when their skin began to sag and show other signs of aging. Others have suggested that men have similar sensitivity to their declining strength and power. It is interesting that in one study men's self-esteem was related not to the prestige or financial rewards of their job, but to their occupational achievement relative to others with similar education (Luck & Heiss, 1972).

Coping

Do people change over time in the way they cope with altered life circumstances? Longitudinal studies generally show increasingly effective ways of managing such stresses. When Haan (1976), for example, compared the coping of adolescents in the Berkeley longitudinal sample with their own coping when they were 30 and 45 years of age, she found that fantasy and "reaction formation" decreased while altruism and suppression increased. The proportions of "immature," "neurotic," and "mature" behavior of Harvard students over the years is shown in Figure 4-3 (Vaillant, 1977). Vaillant found, as did Haan, that there was a general progression toward more "mature" behavior—but not for all. A group he labeled "perpetual boys" became less mature as it got older. In the San Francisco study (Lowenthal et al., 1975), the older groups were more "instrumental"—less absent-minded, disorderly, lazy, and restless. They were also more skilled in interpersonal relations, less

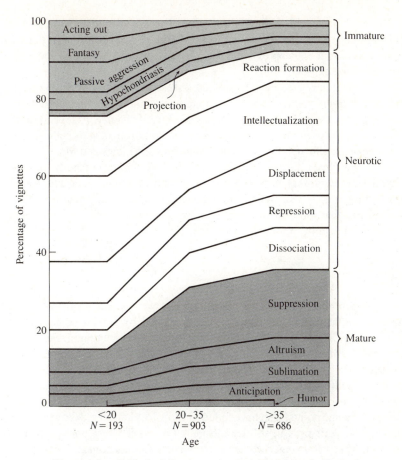

Figure 4-3. Shifts in defensive styles during adulthood. (Source: Vaillant, 1977.)

suspicious, and less embarrassed. Finally, men in the National Institutes of Aging longitudinal study reported progressively less daydreaming as they got older (Giambra, 1973).

Livson (1976) used other terms to describe age changes in coping styles of the Berkeley longitudinal subjects. Different ways of coping were adaptive at different ages, and for men versus women. In youth, mentally healthy men were ambitious and intellectual, and mentally healthy women were aggressively flirtatious. At the same age, less healthy young men were more likely to be rebellious, hostile, and impulsive; less healthy young women were more likely to be unassertive, gregarious, and conforming. In adulthood, healthy men were more rational and narrower in their interests than they had been in youth; healthy women were expressive, open, and nurturant. Less healthy adult men were productive but irritable; less healthy adult women were about the same as they had been in youth. In middle age, healthy men showed a rise in nurturant and expressive behaviors; both men and women were more dependent and expressive.

There have also been several cross-sectional studies of coping using objective measures rather than clinical judgments. Ilfield (1980) analyzed data from a large-scale study of mental health (Pearlin & Schooler, 1978) and found that older adults used more acceptance and less help from outside sources than younger adults, although the differences were small. Billings and Moos (1981), on the other hand, did not find any age effect in coping methods, nor did Folkman and Lazarus (1980). McCrae (1982) only questioned men and women who had reported a loss, threat, or challenge in the preceding year but found no evidence that more mature and effective coping strategies were used by middle-aged than by young respondents.

Stress and Transition

More than 20 years ago, psychologists were searching for universal life events that would inevitably be accompanied by stress and inevitably induce change. Then, empirical studies challenged this assumption. For example, Frenkel-Brunswik, whose work was completed by her colleagues after her death (Reichard, Livson, & Peterson, 1962), found that one such major life event, retirement, was often not stressful, at least at the time, and often did not lead to changes. The empty nest and the menopause, other presumably universal change points, also have failed to show inevitable breakdowns. Only widowhood, perhaps, can still be considered a classic stress point, although maybe more so for younger women and men than for older ones (Weiss, 1975; Noberini & Neugarten, 1975). Neugarten (1977) suggested that we see none of the expected signs of stress at times we expect to because people **anticipate** and rehearse for these major life events or turning points. We must therefore distinguish between normative, expected events and nonnormative, unexpected ones. There is anticipatory socialization for the normative, but not for the unexpected.

In their follow-up of the Midtown Manhattan Study, Srole and Fischer (1978) asked respondents to report their idea of what their major turning points in life were. The question was: "They say that life is the school of hard knocks that we all have to take. As you think back over *your* life, what heavy blows have hit you the *hardest* and upset you the *most* for some time afterwards? What happened and how old were you at that time?" (p. 16). Their subjects ranged in age from 40 to 79. The most frequent blows listed were family deaths and illnesses (more than half the illnesses were psychiatric), marital disruptions other than widowhood, events in job or career, and experiences in

World War II. Incidentally, only half perceived these blows as turning points in their life. Of these people, only half saw them as being turns "for the worse."

Parron (1978) asked golden-anniversary couples to describe their reactions to three presumed major life events: marriage, birth of first child, and departure of last child. Their responses indicated that these times were not as significant as others they themselves mentioned. At least in retrospect, personally important life events were not necessarily socially defined major life events. The respondents were more likely to attribute change in their lives to the Depression or to war than even to the birth of their first child.

Most adults are likely to experience at least one major turning point or crisis, it is true, and the wide range of chronological ages considered "midlife" suggests that those who speak of midlife crisis refer to this kind of more generalized experience, which can occur at almost any adult age depending upon life chances and circumstances. Since family and job loom large in everyday life, such crises are likely to be in these domains. It is customary, further, to look to biological changes for explanations of psychological changes, particularly in women's lives. A review of the ideas about women's midlife changes illustrates this point.

Women in Midlife

Once it was thought that women were supposed to fall apart at the time of the menopause. Chapter 2 presents evidence against this belief. Next, women were supposed to become depressed and mournful because of the empty nest. The evidence against this is presented later, in Chapter 5. Nonetheless, there remains a persistent underlying conviction that midlife is a period of unusual stress for women. If neither menopause nor empty nest is the reason, could there be another one—that is, if women are indeed more stressed at this point?

Two such reasons have occurred to me, and I have identified them by two Greek mythological characters: Cassandra and Tantalus.

Cassandra, the Trojan princess, worried a lot. Like her, the middle-class, middle-aged woman today is a worrier *par excellence*. From infancy, she has been socialized to be "tuned in" to the feelings and attitudes of others. Thus, she gives a lot of attention to the woes of her family. First, she worries whether her young adult children are turning out "right." Are they settling into a career, marrying, and having the appropriate number of children at the appropriate ages? If not, then she may feel that she has done something wrong in raising them—that she has not been a good mother.

The shift in the prevailing ideology toward "doing one's own thing" often means that middle-class young adults feel it is less important to take serious jobs and marry. This can be stressful on their parents, even though many of the parents eventually go through "reverse socialization," and accept their children's values (Troll & Bengtson, 1982).

The Cassandras of today also worry about their husbands, whose jobs may be in jeopardy or losing impetus; whose health may be precarious, raising the possibility that (like many middle-aged women they know) they may become prematurely widowed; or whose love may wane (like the husbands of many women they know who have left them for younger, less familiar women). As Lopata (1973) notes, it is not as bad being a deserted woman when you are 70 or older as it is when you are 30, 40, or 50.

These Cassandras are also worried about their parents, who perhaps show signs of aging and may actually need lots of care. Most studies show that when older parents need help, their daughters are their chief caregivers (Troll, Miller, & Atchley, 1979). Finally, Cassandras are worried about their own self-fulfillment, now that their children are supposed to be out of the nest (although many wonder whether their children will ever leave). This brings us to the second Greek myth.

Tantalus was forever "tantalized." Every time he reached for some of the good things that surrounded him, they withdrew just beyond his reach. The modern midlife middle-class woman has been led to believe that she should be actualizing herself. Some women find fulfillment outside family relationships by resuming old careers or pursuits. But many reach for something that they later find to be beyond them. They cannot make up for years spent as housewives, which for many women meant near—or total—isolation from public life, or they hit retirement when they are just getting into their stride.

Adaptation

Although life-span developmental psychologists may have gone down a blind alley in looking for the universal life-event turning points, they pointed to the essentially adult process of adaptation, the concern of a number of investigations. At Duke University, for example, longitudinal data were analyzed in terms of the effect of resources in moderating potentially cataclysmic events (Siegler, 1980). To begin with, it was found that of three kinds of resources considered—health, psychological (combining intelligence and adaptive capacity), and social (income, education, and density of social network)—only psychological resources predicted which people would experience stress. Older people with low psychological resources were more likely to experience a major medical event than those in poor health. The process of adaptation seemed to be homeostatic among these older people. That is, they changed just enough to return to where they were before the upsetting event.

Troll (1982) presented four possible ways to change following an upsetting event:

1. **Denial** of the change, which involves trying to continue as if it had never happened, usually a difficult and dangerous procedure;
2. **Homeostasis,** changing just enough to return to the pre-change condition, probably the most common response;
3. Over-welcoming of change, characteristic of some forms of therapy that believe it is necessary to destroy previous structures to achieve new and better ones, often leading to **fragmentation** of the self;
4. Creative and controlled **development,** or reconstruction of the self to adapt to new circumstances.

Siegler found that the Duke subjects, after an initial disorganization of behavior, tended to return to pre-event levels of functioning in both health and psychological behavior.

A somewhat similar investigation was undertaken by Fiske and her colleagues in San Francisco (Lowenthal et al., 1975). They considered not only psychological resources, but also psychological deficits. They describe four kinds of response, two for what they considered to be high-stress events and two for low-stress events. Some individuals were **challenged.** They had experienced what seemed to be a great amount of stress but did not seem overwhelmed by it. Others were **overwhelmed** after high stress. A third group was **self-defeating:** Their stress seemed low, but they were overwhelmed. And the fourth group was **lucky:** Their stress was low, and they adapted easily. The percentages of overwhelmed and challenged were about equal in two age groups, young and middle-aged, however. One-third of those in each age group were overwhelmed, and about 20% were challenged. For those experiencing light stress, about 20% were overwhelmed, and 30% were lucky. Although age differences were not significant, sex differences were; more women reported high stress.

When Livson (1976) looked at the lifetime records of the 24 women in the Oakland longitudinal study, she found that the adaptation patterns of those she had labeled "traditionalists" and "independents" differed. The traditionalists had maintained a high level of adjustment throughout, having, as Livson said, completed Erikson's tasks (see Chapter 1), but the independents had a rough time at the age of 40, repeating the difficult transition they had experienced in early adolescence. Even though they may be described as having gone through a midlife crisis, however, they had reorganized and restructured their lives by age 50 (as Jung would have predicted). It should be noted that these women were members of the cohort of the Depression of the 1930s (Elder, 1974), and that their personality changes need to be evaluated in terms of the times in which they grew up and lived. Options had been few when they were adolescents but became many when their child-rearing days were over, enabling them to reconsider their early-life decisions, which might have been difficult for women who were potentially independent.

Orientation to Life

One of the most prominent conclusions of the ground-breaking study of Kansas City residents undertaken by a team of scientists from the University of Chicago in the late 1950s and early 1960s was age differences in mastery styles (Neugarten & Gutmann, 1964). Sex differences were almost as clear as age differences.

Adult men—until about their 50s—seemed to show an **active-mastery** mode. If they wanted something, they were inclined to go out and try to get it. Their orientation was outward, toward the external environment, which they were intent on manipulating to the best of their abilities. During their 50s, perhaps as a result of diminishing success in using an active mode, men turned inward, becoming more interested in their feelings and ideas and using a **passive-mastery** mode. They seemed to be trying to get what they wanted by appealing to powers greater than themselves.

Younger women tended to use passive mastery. After all, women are trained from childhood to get what they want through the active efforts of others, especially men—fathers, husbands, or sons. In middle age, though, these efforts may no longer work—some say because of loss of sexual attractiveness or charm (for example, Kastenbaum & Symonds, 1977). At any rate, while men in their 50s apparently were turning to passive mastery, women of that age showed more active mastery. They turned outward while the men turned inward, and they became more comfortable with their assertiveness. Note that the era in which this research was done was also the period during which the influx of women—particularly middle-aged women—into the labor market was remarkable.

Livson (1976), reporting on the Berkeley longitudinal data, found that many nontraditional women—so far as "feminine" personality characteristics went—who had been leading traditional lives in their early adult years became more assertive or nontraditional in midlife. Monge (1975) found age differences in a number of self-concept components derived from analysis of semantic-differential responses. Figure 4-4 shows men, during their 50s, decrease somewhat in the achievement/leadership component of personality, increase sharply in congeniality/sociability, and decrease in masculinity. Women, at the same time, increase in achievement/leadership, more sharply than men decrease. They also increase slightly in masculinity.

Other research findings are less clearly supportive of mastery theory. Costa and McCrae (1976) factor-analyzed the responses of 969 men of different ages on Cattell's personality test. They found that young men appeared to have a dominant feeling function, and middle-aged men a dominant thinking function.

The most noticeable difference between the earlier and later life stages investigated by Lowenthal and her colleagues (1975) was in the expansiveness or constriction of their orientation to life. The two younger groups—high

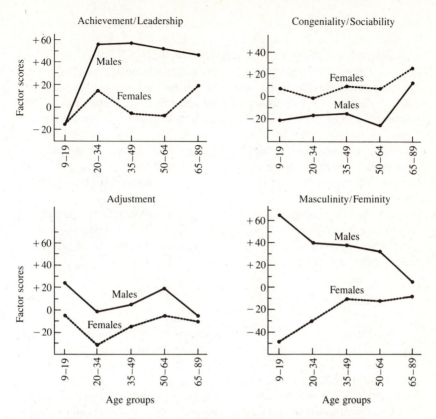

Figure 4-4. Sex and age differences in four components of the self-concept. (Source: Monge, 1975.)

school seniors and newlyweds—were more likely to refer to success and self-fulfillment. The two older groups were more likely to caution against setting goals too high. Remember here that these subjects were of the lower middle class.

High school boys and girls—and also newlywed men—placed the highest value on personal achievement and happiness. The men were likely to think in terms of occupational and personal success. A typical statement by a high school boy is quoted by the authors: "I figure that I'll be working for the most of my life, so I want to get a good job that I'll be able to enjoy. So then I'll be able to enjoy my life, because that will be my life. Of course, you can't really enjoy life unless you have a lot of money" (p. 178).

The high school girls focused on self-actualization and self-fulfillment. One of them said, "I think if people want something bad enough, they should go after it and prove themselves" (p. 178). Newlywed men responded not much differently from high school seniors, but newlywed women were more likely to stress giving oneself to others. One said she wanted "to bring good into the world. I find now that my main purpose is to please my husband, my family, to find happiness in life myself" (p. 179).

The middle-aged men and those facing retirement responded in a dry and conformist way about the dual tasks of earning a living and raising a family: "Well, I'd say probably earning a living. . . . I just think it's the responsibility that the husband should have to his family, to see that they're taken care of" (p. 179). Women of the same age, whose youngest children were high school seniors, tended to speak of "living a good life and bringing up your family well so they have a good life" (p. 180).

The men and women in the preretirement stages were more likely to mention humanitarian and moral purposes. The men also mentioned leaving a legacy, and the women mentioned some religious themes. As one man put it, "I think [a man] does well if he makes himself a decent and satisfactory part of society, with at least the sort of contribution that is recognized or recognizable" (p. 181).

Locus of Control

Rotter (1966) pointed out that some people, whom he calls **internals,** perceive that their own actions can have an effect on their lives. Others, called **externals,** feel that they are essentially powerless, controlled by powers outside themselves. That is, some feel that control is internal to themselves, others that it is external. If one believes that there is little one can do to change one's circumstances (external locus of control), one is likely to become passive and to depend on others to take care of one.

External locus of control has generally been found to be more common in women than in men, and in people over 65 than in those under 65. Longitudinal data at Duke University (Siegler, 1978), however, showed that for 70% of middle-aged and older people, locus of control remained stable over a six-year period. So far, studies of age differences in locus of control have produced conflicting results. Staats (1974) reported that older people were more internal than were younger people. Bradley and Webb (1976) found that people over age 60 were more external than were younger adults.

Sex-Role Characteristics

Differences between men and women are emphasized in almost every human culture. Men are encouraged from infancy on to behave in certain ways considered "manly," and women are encouraged to behave in "womanly" ways. What is labeled manly will differ from one society to another, as Margaret Mead illustrated vividly in her early books on cross-cultural differences.

In some parts of the world, a man is supposed to be nurturant and artistic. In other parts, he is supposed to be aggressive and independent.

Modern Western societies also emphasize sex differences, even though we have become aware that most of these characteristics and their prejudicial effects are not biologically inevitable. Before we were born, our parents were ready to find us vigorous, hardy, aggressive, and independent if we were born with penises; and fragile, delicate, sensitive, and dependent if we were born with vaginas. All through our lives, both our parents and the rest of the world in which we have moved have reaffirmed same-sex characteristics whenever they appear and have discouraged opposite-sex characteristics.

Longitudinal correlations from childhood to adulthood, over a 20-year period, are moderate and sometimes statistically significant for such traits as dependency and aggressiveness (Skolnick, 1966a, 1966b). Kagan and Moss (1962) found these traits most stable if they were congruent with prevailing sex-role stereotypes. Thus, dependency was more stable for girls and aggressiveness more stable for boys.

It is interesting that correlations about the same size as those found in these longitudinal studies have been found between two generations of related adults, particularly mothers and their daughters. Grotevant (1976) reports parent/child correlations ranging from .24 to .43 for being dominant, realistic, investigative, and artistic. But there were no significant correlations for being sociable or enterprising, which are not part of the sex-role definitions. Father/son correlations were not significant for being dominant, realistic, investigative, and artistic, but were significant (.31 and .34) for being sociable and enterprising.

Sexual Behavior and Attitudes

Almost all norms for sexual behavior have changed during the past few decades. Younger adults tend to be much less restrictive than youth of earlier times, than their parents, and than older people in general (Bengtson & Starr, 1975; Zelnick & Kantner, 1977). Many older people, of course, have also shifted with the times. They are more permissive now than they were 10 or 15 years ago (Bengtson & Troll, 1978). Some of this shift seems to be a **period effect**—showing the influence of historical changes in the society as a whole. Some is probably "reciprocal socialization"—youth influencing their parents. Middle-aged mothers of "avant-garde" youth admitted to an interviewer that their attitudes had changed as a result of trying to accept the "freer" sexual behavior of their children (Angres, 1975). The pull of family ties is strong. Rather than condemn their children or become estranged, parents reexamine their own attitudes in the light of their children's attitudes. Grandparents may also shift in order to accept grandchildren's behavior, though perhaps less than parents (Hagestad, 1983).

Achievement Motivation

There is an impressive amount of stability over time in orientation toward work and achievement. Longitudinal data on AT&T executives (Bray & Howard, 1983) suggest that, although the first job experiences may alter initial attitudes or values regarding work, orientations remain stable thereafter. The Berkeley longitudinal data (Haan, 1976; Elder, 1974) show even more consistency. Generational research, however, hints at a recent cohort shift toward valuing intrinsic aspects of jobs more than extrinsic aspects. If so, and if these new values are not modified by early job experiences, we may see a future emphasis on achievement and creativity instead of on money and status.

In *From Birth to Maturity,* Kagan and Moss (1962) reported that the motive to achieve is acquired early in childhood and tends to remain stable into the 20s. They found correlations (in age periods 6–10 and the mid-20s) of .68 for boys and .49 for girls between childhood achievement behavior and adult concern with intellectual competence. This finding sets the theme for most adult sex differences in this area. (Notice the sex difference.)

Comparison of college students' achievement needs with that of their parents (Troll, Neugarten, & Kraines, 1969) shows significant correlations among all four parent/child dyads (father/son, .45; father/daughter, 39; mother/daughter, .30; and mother/son, .27). The greater consistency in the male line can be attributed to historical shifts in women's achievement motivation. Otherwise, women en should be as much like their mothers as men are like their fathers, as may be the case for the next generations of mothers and daughters.

A study of Radcliffe graduates by R. Baruch (1966) points to the persistence of motive to achieve, as a trait, across an intervening period of submerged expression. This is what Kagan and Moss called the "sleeper effect." It reflects the competence/performance dilemma. Baruch found a significant relationship among the number of years a woman had been out of college, the level of her motive to achieve, and her return to work. As measured by responses to the TAT, the need to achieve was lowest for women 10 years out of college with very young children. But it was higher among women out for 15 years, even though this latter group had the most children under 8 years old. Women who had been out of college for 20 and 25 years showed high and stable needs for achievement. In fact, those with the highest scores had generally returned to work, particularly if their achievement stories were focused on female figures. Curiously, if their stories dealt with men who were achieving, the women were not likely to be working. Presumably, this latter group of women could have their achievement needs fulfilled through the efforts of the men in their lives—husbands or sons, for example.

Achievement, affiliation, and power motives may operate independently in shaping the kinds of lives men try to lead or the kinds and amounts of satisfaction they derive from their lifestyles. In women, these three motives may be interrelated in complex ways. Women may express their achievement needs either directly through their own actions, or indirectly, through the actions of others. If women express these needs directly, they may be operating more like men, with achievement motives independent of power and affiliation motives. But even if they are expressing achievement needs directly, their modes of expression may be quite different from those of men. Outside the job world, women may achieve by doing community work, gourmet cooking, decorating and gardening, or even superior packaging of their bodies for glamor. If they express their achievement needs indirectly, they may be just as satisfied by the successes of their husbands and children as by their own products. If they express such needs directly, it may appear superficially as if they were expressing affiliation motives (wanting to be close to their husbands and children) or power motives (wanting to influence husbands and children), when instead they are really expressing achievement motives (wanting to excel). Figure 4-5 presents a hypothetical framework for examining the various modes in which women might express achievement motives.

Switzer (1975) compared three generations of women—grandmothers, their daughters, and their granddaughters—on achievement-related variables. Interesting generational differences emerged along with intrafamily continuity. First, when the combined level of achievement motivation was considered, the correlation between the grandmother and her daughter was .26; between daughter and granddaughter, .42. The larger gap between the two older generations is partly attributable to the educational difference. Only a handful of the grandmothers had any college education. In fact, most did not complete elementary school. One-fourth of their daughters, however, had some college, as did one-half of the young-adult granddaughters. The level of achievement motivation went up progressively from the oldest to the youngest generation.

In a later analysis of these data (Troll & Schwartz, in press), cohort shifts in both arena (home versus job) and approach (direct versus indirect) appeared in both male and female lineages. Granddaughters were more job-oriented and direct than their mothers and grandmothers, while grandsons were also less traditional—less job-oriented and less direct. This "convergence toward the mean" may well be a maturational effect, as Arenberg calls it (Douglas & Arenberg, 1978). The men in his NIA longitudinal study showed progressively less "masculinity" as they got older.

There have been cohort shifts not only in education, in level of achievement motivation, and in arena and expression, but also in locus of control. The grandmothers and most of the mothers showed external locus of control—they felt that the power to control their lives resided in people or forces outside themselves. The granddaughters felt that it resided within themselves (internal locus of control).

Approach and arena	Achievement as task mastery	Achievement as recognition or status	Achievement as interpersonal influence	Achievement as creativity
Direct				
Home and community	Good housekeeper—clean, efficient, skilled	Best-dressed woman, Beauty queen	PTA president	House decorator, Gourmet cook
Traditional "feminine" job	Fast typist, Good classroom manager	Secretary of top executive, Principal	Social worker	Artist
Innovative "masculine" job	Skilled surgeon, Successful lawyer	Dean of college, Popular magazine writer	Executive in industry	College professor, Theoretical writer
Indirect	Husband good salesman or financially successful	Expensive home in exclusive suburb	Wife of powerful political person	Patron, "angel"

Achievement modes

Figure 4-5. Expression of achievement motivation in women.

Other Values and Interests

Lifestyle themes such as intellectualism, humanitarianism, or practicality tend to become increasingly more important from late adolescence to early adulthood and then tend either to remain stable or to increase a bit more through the adult years (Haan & Day, 1974). These adult themes show the same patterning over time from childhood through old age (Haan, 1976). Well-functioning, financially secure men and women remain dependable, straightforward, giving, warm, and sympathetic, and they continue to arouse liking. However, notes Haan (1976), the intimate, more tender interpersonal attributes of likability, givingness, warmth, sympathy, and straightforwardness have more important roles in older people's hierarchies than they did when these people were younger.

Generational studies (Troll & Bengtson, 1982) also suggest that such characteristics are often shared by members of the same family across generations. By their late 20s, for example, people settle into their basic value and interest patterns, and on the whole these patterns tend to be very much like those of their parents. Intellectual parents can look forward to having intellectual children, although the particular areas of study their children pursue may be very different from those that the parents pursued.

An examination of the values that appear to be least stable over generations suggests that these are the lifestyle traits used to highlight the unique status of an age or an age cohort. For example, college students in 1965 stressed self-realization, estheticism, and humanitarianism (Troll, Neugarten, & Kraines, 1969). Troll and Bengtson (1982) refer to these characteristics as "generation-keynote themes." Child-rearing values were those that changed most from the grandparent to the middle-aged parent generation in the Minneapolis families studied by Hill and his associates (Hill, Foote, Aldous, Carlson, & Macdonald, 1970). Permissive child rearing was a "keynote theme" of the forerunner youth of the 1940s.

Cross-sectional comparisons of middle-aged and young middle-class men on the Strong Vocational Interest Blank showed that the older men tended to like new activities less, to prefer cultural (rather than physical) activities, and to like solitary activities more than did the younger men (Strong, 1959). Older men expressed as many likes and dislikes as younger men, for both people and things. But the older men more intensely liked those people and things that they liked than did the younger men, and they more intensely disliked the people and things they disliked.

Havighurst (1957), about the same time, found that middle-aged men spend more time reading newspapers than reading books or magazines. They also read editorials rather than sports, crime, or disaster stories. They read more history and love stories than they used to, and fewer science and sports.

Table 4-4.   Birth cohorts and political tolerance, 1954 and 1973

Born in	Age in		Tolerance scale: percentage more tolerant			Listening in on conversations: percentage should not[a]		
	1954	1973	1954	1973	Change	1954	1973	Change
1925–1933	21–29	40–48	41	56	+15	32	49	+17
1915–1924	30–39	49–58	37	48	+11	31	45	+14
1905–1914	40–49	59–68	31	33	+ 2	29	35	+ 6

[a]Data pertain to attitudes about government investigators listening in on the conversations of communists.
Source: Reprinted with permission from Nunn, Crockett, and Williams (1978), p. 84.

When Moss and Susman (1980) reviewed existing longitudinal studies of personality, they concluded that consistency over the years is most obvious for personality characteristics that are emphasized as good by the culture in which people live. In our society, achievement and appropriate sex-role behavior are valued, and these characteristics are among the most stable from middle childhood through adulthood. Attitudes, which are susceptible to changing cultural values, are among the least stable.

Three related questions concern not only developmental psychologists but also sociologists and political scientists: (1) Do people get more conservative as they get older? (2) Do they get more religious as they get older? (3) Are they less likely to change as they get older? An example of the type of research findings that are relevant can be seen in Table 4-4. Older cohorts show less political tolerance, and they change less over time. Glenn (1980) cautions us, however, about assuming that aging brings conservatism. For example, he found in one study (Glenn & Hefner, 1972) that influences that produced change in younger cohorts produced the same kind of change in older cohorts about four years later. This is reminiscent of the reciprocal socialization seen in generational findings (Troll & Bengtson, 1979). Further, the 1980s swing to conservatism in both politics and religion started with the youngest adults. It may be that late adolescents or young adults have less resistance to changing with the times.

Mental Health

In 1954, a cross-sectional study of the health, both mental and physical, of 1660 Manhattan residents between the ages of 20 and 59 found that mental health declined as age increased (Srole & Fischer, 1978). Twenty years later, 695 of those located from the original sample were reinterviewed. They were now between the ages of 40 and 79 and had scattered across the world.

Table 4-5.   Midtown Manhattan mental-impairment rates, follow-up panel ($N = 695$)

		Cohorts (decade of birth)		
		A *b. 1900* *(N = 134)*	*B* *b. 1910* *(N = 199)*	*C* *b. 1920* *(N = 195)*	*D* *b. 1930* *(N = 167)*
1954	Age	(50–59)	(40–49)	(30–39)	(20–29)
	Rate	22%	16%	14%	7%
1974	Age	(70–79)	(60–69)	(50–59)	(40–49)
	Rate	18%	12%	10%	8%
	Difference	−4%	−4%	+1%	−4%
	Significance of difference	NS	NS	NS	NS

Note: NS = not statistically significant.
Source: Srole and Fischer, 1978.

These follow-up data did not replicate the original findings: there was no sign of intraindividual decrease in mental health. Men stayed pretty much at the levels they had been at earlier, and women even improved. Cross-sequential comparisons are presented in Table 4-5, without regard to sex. Group A (born about 1900 and in its 50s in 1954 and its 70s in 1974) changed from 22% rated mentally impaired at the first round of study to 18% at the second round, a nonsignificant difference. Comparing Group A (in its 50s at the first round) with Group C (in its 50s at the second round), we see improvement, from 22% to 10%.

When men and women are considered separately (Table 4-6), we see a marked drop in mental impairment for female 50-year-olds from the first to the second round of the study—from 26% in 1954 to 11% in 1974. The same

Table 4-6.   Midtown Manhattan mental-impairment rates, follow-up panel ($N = 695$), by generation-separated pairs of like-age cohorts and gender subgroups

Cohort	Men	Women
A (aged 50–59 in 1954)	15%	26%
C (aged 50–59 in 1974)	9%	11%
Difference	−6%	−15%
Significance of difference	NS	<.01
B (aged 40–49 in 1954)	9%	21%
D (aged 40–49 in 1974)	9%	8%
Difference	0%	−13%
Significance of difference	NS	<.02

Note: NS = not statistically significant.
Source: Srole and Fischer, 1978.

Table 4-7.   Diagnostic classification of men and women (1954) by economic deprivation and class origin, in percentages

	Middle class		Working class	
Health groups	Nondeprived	Deprived	Nondeprived	Deprived
Relatively symptom-free	11	38	18	13
Anxiety and tension states	11	7	27	21
Psychosomatic illness	29	21	36	17
Behavior disorders	26	7	9	25
Somatic illness (serious)	20	19	9	17
Psychotic reaction	3	7	0	8
	100	99	99	101
Total number of cases	35	42	11	24

Source: Elder, 1974.

is true for 40-year-old women, but not for men. As a result, women, who had had much higher rates of mental illness than men before, moved to rates that were comparable to those for men.

Elder's (1974) longitudinal comparisons of mental or physical problems of children of the Depression show complex interaction effects between social class and deprivation. Table 4-7 shows that deprived middle-class children and nondeprived working-class children were in the best health 20 years later. The most striking effects are seen for psychosomatic illness and behavior disorders. The nondeprived working-class subjects were most likely to develop psychosomatic illnesses. The nondeprived middle-class subjects and deprived working-class subjects were most likely to develop behavior disorders such as alcoholism. Finally, those subjects who had experienced deprivation in adolescence were more likely to change in anxiety or emotionality scores during adulthood than were those who had experienced no deprivation. The latter group showed stability over time: those who had been anxious adolescents were anxious adults; those who had not been anxious also did not change. Elder's subjects, incidentally, were the same as Block's, who found the same effect using other measures (J. Block, 1971).

Could it be that the women who improved so much in the Mid-Manhattan study were exhibiting the same kind of deprivation effect? Opportunities opened up for women during the 1960s and 1970s; women had a chance to adapt and improve. Because those opportunities had already existed for men, no change occurred for them.

Similar findings are reported by Livson (1977). Middle-aged women in the 1970s who became more androgynous—more balanced in sex-role characteristics and thus more flexible and adaptive to opening opportunities— were judged in good mental health. In fact, their mental health was better than it had been earlier in their adult years. All the men had moved toward androgyny, incidentally, and all were judged in good mental health. However, the women who clung to their femininity and who did not change in middle age were judged in more precarious mental health. A review of their earlier records showed that they tended to have been the more fragile girls.

Summary

Several stage theories were described in Chapter 1. These models of adult development assume that there are noticeable changes and that these occur in a progression. What can we say from the data presented in this chapter about the validity of these theories? First, the "self" can be said to go through a sequence of orderly changes only in retrospection. People who believe in stages may look back and reconstruct such changes, but the weight of the evidence from longitudinal studies so far favors stability rather than change, or certainly any pattern of change. What evidence there is for change is for slow processes that are hardly noticeable before late middle age. Happiness and a feeling of excitement in life show such decreases, although some data show greater unhappiness in middle age than at earlier or later ages. But other studies show that those who are unhappy or "neurotic" in middle age were unhappy or "neurotic" earlier in life, or at least in earlier life transitions such as early adolescence. The evidence for universal turning points, such as middle age, is confusing at best, particularly if these turning points are indexed by distress. In part, "anticipatory socialization" for expected life events prevents such distress. When major crises are met, however, most people change just enough to return to their previous level of functioning. Personality changes need to be evaluated in terms of lifelong patterns of adaptation and living style and of the sociocultural circumstances in which they occur. Sex differences are profound in most aspects of adult personality development, although there is some suggestion that they are diminishing with historical/cohort changes, at least so far as achievement and mental health are concerned.

Chapter Five

Family Development

The decade of the 1970s saw repeated evidence that people live in families, even though not necessarily in the same households. In a recent national survey conducted by the University of Michigan Survey Research Institute (Veroff, Douvan, & Kulka, 1981), for example, respondents of all ages and of both sexes said that their family roles were most important. In fact, the percentage saying so in 1976 was even greater than in an earlier, matching study in 1957. In spite of alarming increases in divorce, ideological norm shifts toward individual self-fulfillment, and geographic mobility, therefore, we can conclude that the family lives.

Much of the meaning and drama of adult life takes place within the family. Although it has many forms, and these forms change to adapt to changing historical conditions, the family is the most basic primary social group. "Families differ from other groups in having powerful bondings, special rules, homeostatic mechanisms, telegraphic styles of communication, private meanings, myths, regressive features, alliances, loyalties, and dynamic influence from previous generations" (Framo, 1979, p. 4). Relationships with kin are models for most other intimate relationships. In fact, many close relationships are given a kin name: "Aunt Jane" is not necessarily a parent's sister but may be a parent's close friend.

The family is often thought of as the woman's domain—just as the job is considered the man's domain; yet this distinction is not completely true. Being married is also not a requirement for membership in a family. Single, widowed, and divorced men and women have relatives. In fact, when an important family relation is lost—as by death, divorce, or moving away—another may be substituted out of a reservoir of more distant relatives.

For more than half of this century, census figures showed that overwhelming proportions of Americans were marrying, more than at most other times in history and more than in other countries. Until 1956, there was a trend toward earlier age of first marriage, as well as a trend toward more divorces. These factors, incidentally, tend to be related: the younger people are when they first marry, the more likely they are to divorce.

The 1980 census showed that the median age for first marriage has gone up over the past two decades and now approaches that of the beginning of the 20th century. Women are marrying for the first time at an average age of 22.3. In 1979, P. C. Glick reported that the average age was 21.0 years; it was 19.9 years in 1967. Furthermore, many women in their 20s were postponing marriage and living with a man without legal marriage—"cohabiting." Most such women, however, said they planned to marry, even if not the man they were currently living with.

Even though they often plan to marry eventually, however, many more women do not and will not marry than in previous cohorts; like age at first marriage, the number of never-married women is approaching the percentage of 1900. If you look back at Table 1-5, you can see that part of this change is connected with changes in sex ratio. Guttentag and Secord (1983), in a provocative book entitled *Too Many Women?,* argue that the shift in sex ratios following World War II—from more men than women to more women than men—resulted, among other things, in a "marriage squeeze" for baby-boom women. When they reached maturity, the men two or three years older, whom they would "normally" marry, were in shorter supply because they were from the pre-baby-boom birth cohort.

As for divorce, Glick (1979) says, "The longtime upward trend in divorce became an upsurge between 1965 and 1975, when the U.S. divorce rate per 1,000 married women nearly doubled, from 10.6 per 1,000 in 1965 to 20.3 in 1975" (p. 3). Since 1975, though, the divorce rate has been rising much more slowly. Divorce will be discussed later in this chapter.

Demographic shifts such as these can be responses to historical events, such as economic affluence or depression and wars, or to ideological movements. More people marry, and marry at relatively earlier ages, in times of economic prosperity, for example, or when social norms do not require preparatory economic "nest building." A couple can catch up on furnishing a home during the early years of marriage if both husband and wife earn money and do not have children. Sigmund Freud repeatedly soothed his impatient fiancée by reminding her that they still did not have enough linen ready. In those days, it was taken for granted that household goods had to be acquired before marriage, because the couple was expected to start child rearing, housekeeping, and entertaining right after the wedding (E. Jones, 1953). The couples who married in the 1950s also may have had added motivation to marry early because of their own deprivation as children in the Depression of the 1930s (Elder, 1974).

Development of the Marital Dyad

In traditional couple formation, there is often a sequence from casual dating to steady dating, going steady, engaged to be engaged, and engaged. This sequence has a number of filter or choice points along the way. Initial idealization of the partner tends gradually to give way to a more realistic appraisal. Partners who start dating at an early age and who see each other often are more likely to go through the dating progression quickly and to marry young.

More than 20 years ago, Kerckhoff and Davis (1962) observed "seriously attached" college-student couples over a period of six months. Using their findings, Adams (1979) constructed the following sequence:

1. Attraction to marriage itself—a conscious, expressed desire to marry
2. Propinquity
3. Early attraction, based on such surface behaviors of the partner as
   a. Gregariousness
   b. Poise
   c. Similar interests and abilities
   d. Physical appearance and attractiveness, particularly in girls
   e. Similarity to one's ideal image
4. Perpetuation of attraction, aided by
   a. Reactions of others, including being labeled as a couple
   b. Disclosure, opening up to each other
   c. Pair rapport, feeling comfortable in each other's presence
5. Commitment and intimacy, establishing a bond
6. Deeper attraction, enhanced by
   a. Value consensus or co-orientation, providing validation of each other's viewpoints
   b. Feelings of competence reinforced
   c. Perception of other similarities in the partner, such as
      Attractiveness
      Levels of emotional maturity
      Affective expressiveness
      Self-esteem
      Race, ethnic group, or religion, if important to members
7. Deciding this is "right for me" or "the best I can get"
8. Marriage

Once "dyad crystallization" occurs, there are still the reactions of others to consider. And there are barriers to breaking up, such as the effort involved in forming a new relationship and the problem of hurting one's partner. These barriers help to move the sequence to the final step.

The recent increase in cohabitation—living together without marriage—has led some theorists to view it as a new stage of the getting-together process rather than as an alternative to marriage, at least among college students. One study (Macklin, 1978) found that one-fourth of students admitted to cohabiting; a few years later, the figure might have been higher. Broader surveys showed, however, that only about 2% of all couples were cohabiting in 1978 (Glick & Spanier, 1980). Almost all Macklin's respondents, incidentally, said they eventually planned to marry someone, though not necessarily their current partner.

The vast majority of cohabiting couples have no children. Further, they tend to live together no longer than two years, on the average, before they either marry or separate (Glick & Norton, 1977). One-half of the cohabiting men—of all ages—and three-fifths of the cohabiting women had been married before. Most of these were urban dwellers, relatively poor, and unemployed. In this larger picture, the college couples interviewed by Macklin (1978) may be a special segment of general cohabiting pairs. On the other hand, Glick and Spanier point out that many more people might have participated in a cohabiting union at some time in their life.

Government interest in the consequences of teenage parentage has led to a large number of recent studies on age of marriage and parenting. The association between early ages and poor socioeconomic conditions makes it hard to see the effect of age itself. Certainly many societies, including ours in the not-so-distant past, expect women to marry and bear children at an age now considered too young. Women in such societies would not be expected to need much education, nor would they be expected to support their children on their own. In other words, it may be the fact that early marriage is now considered deviant that makes it harmful, not the age itself. Age at first marriage is, not surprisingly, highly correlated with age at first birth for both sexes (.81) (Marini, 1981). Not only is marrying young associated with having a first child young, it is also associated with having more children.

The impressive National Longitudinal Survey (McLaughlin & Micklin, 1983) found that early first birth—before the mother was 19 years old—was highly related to poor personal efficacy: those who felt they had little control over their lives were more likely to have a birth at a "too-early" age—and to continue to feel that they had no control over their lives. Studies such as those of Furstenberg and Crawford (1978) in East Baltimore and Kellam, Adams, Brown, and Ensminger (1982) in the Woodlawn area of Chicago show that in poor, Black, urban neighborhoods very young mothers tend to lack educational and marital resources for raising children effectively. Most who marry end up alone in a few years or even sooner. Those who do not marry before they have a child are not likely to marry later. White early mothers suffer even more than Black (Howell & Frese, 1982), since their parents tend to lower their educational expectations—and help—for early-marrying daughters, though not for early-marrying sons.

An interesting sidelight on age and marriage was reported recently by an English researcher (Bytheway, 1981), who found that the well-known generalization that men marry younger women seems to be reversed around the age of 50.

In a longitudinal study of couples, Paris and Luckey (1966) found that those who continued their relationship over two years were more likely to have scored higher on role fit at the beginning of the study. In a sense, they had started off "ahead of the game."

Identity as a couple is analogous to Erikson's (1950) concept of individual identity. It assumes recognition of "couplehood" both by the partners themselves and by other people in their social world, especially family and friends. Lewis (1973) found that couples were more likely to stay together longer than 10 weeks and to develop their relationship if they were recognized as a couple by others.

An examination of long-term relationships—parent/child, sibling, old-friend, and long-married couple relationships—suggests that there may be an inverse relationship between attraction and attachment. In the beginning of a relationship, attraction is high, because part of its impetus is novelty and discovery. But attachment is low, because bonds are not yet cemented. A breakup of the relationship at this stage would cause only temporary distress, and substitutions for loved ones would be relatively easy—there are many more fish in the sea! In the course of repeated interaction, however, novelty is gone and attraction is reduced—but attachment may have become very strong. The two members of the dyad have become part of each other; they have achieved a joint identity. A breakup at this time may never be completely overcome. No substitution of loved object may be possible, and a "phantom-limb" pain may persist.

An interesting small-scale study of types of marriages among successful Americans describes five ways of expressing love, if not attachment (Cuber & Harroff, 1963):

1. **Conflict-habituated:** conflict and tension become part of an ongoing pattern. This can (and does, for some) last a lifetime.
2. **Devitalized:** no serious tension, but no zest either. There may be aspects of marriage that are satisfying, such as children, property, or family tradition, and occasional feelings of sharing something, if only memory.
3. **Passive/congenial:** passively content, not disillusioned with what is there.

4. **Vital:** vibrant and exciting sharing of some important life experience, such as sex, work, child rearing, creative endeavor, or even a hobby.
5. **Total:** like vital, but multifaceted. All important aspects of life are shared. This type of relationship is rare.

Reedy and Birren (1978) studied 102 happily married couples of all ages. They concluded that there are two main types of loving: a **companionship** type, based on expression of love, communication, and respect, and a **traditional** type, based on mutual material and emotional investments. The companionship type is most common among young adults and the traditional type among older adults. In part, this is probably a cohort difference. However, it is probably also in part a developmental change. Intense communication and self-disclosure may be more important to affectionate bonding early in a relationship. Loyalty, investment, and commitment to the relationship—the traditional way of loving—may develop over time.

Choices have multiplied in love, sex, and marriage behaviors (Fox, 1975). With more options available, there are more decision points along the way. The result is greater complexity in the conduct of life and more conscious control over decisions—and, thus, probably more agonizing over decisions. At the same time, a consequence of having many choices is their reversibility—it is now easier to change one's mind. This reversibility can blur choices. No one choice or decision is irrevocable, and thus no one choice is very important. In a way, marriage itself is of less strategic importance than it once was; the distinction between marriage and singlehood is less acute.

Although the time allowed for getting married has lengthened somewhat, there is still a definite time limit for women during which the mate-selection process must occur, particularly if children are desired. This limitation adds to the stresses of decision making.

More than half of all college women in the United States in the late 1970s no longer saw virginity as a valuable asset in acquiring a husband (Zelnick & Kantner, 1977). The average American woman today is sexually knowledgeable—or at least has had some sexual experience—by the time she marries. A national survey by Zelnick and Kantner (1977) showed that 55% of never-married young women had engaged in sexual intercourse before they were 19 years old. In 1953, Kinsey found that only 20% had been sexually active before the age of 20. Thus there was an impressive increase in 25 years. Similarly, men no longer must demonstrate economic capability before marrying.

Getting married is considered an important event that changes the lives of both partners. Even during the height of the youth movement, about 80% had a religious ceremony (Lopata, 1971). Separation of the sexual rite of passage from the social rite of passage may be one of the more permanent legacies of the sexual revolution.

Sex Differences

Sex differences tend to pervade all courtship. They showed up in an intriguing study by Coombs and Kenkel (1966) of computer dating among first-year college students. The women had more rigid standards than the men had for selecting and judging their dates and also had higher expectations of them. They wanted their dates to have socially desirable characteristics such as seriousness, intelligence, occupational potential, and general capability. They were much more cautious than the men in deciding whom to date and in stating whether they would like to date their partners again. The men limited their specifications to physical attractiveness. They were more easily satisfied with their dates and more ready to date them again. For most women, getting married and having children is still a very serious decision. Because the man a woman marries defines much of her future life, she is more emotionally involved and goal oriented in dating. As a result, she is more vulnerable and has less control over the whole marital process.

Within the last year, students in my family psychology classes have interviewed both members of two couples differing in how long they had lived together; they did not necessarily have to be married legally. One of the questions dealt with the reactions of their respective families when they were first introduced. That attitudes have changed hardly at all is evident from the responses. Parents of women were all very critical of the young man's economic potential, but parents of men were satisfied with their choice if their sons were.

Historically, men have usually had more control over marital choice than women. The cost of abstaining from marriage is still greater for women than for men, even though, as Bernard (1973) eloquently points out, the negative consequences of marriage are also greater for women. Some reasons for men's greater power in this sphere are as follows. First, women "marry up" because their marriages are seen as conferring social status. Second, marrying up or down applies to age as well as to social class, intelligence, and education. Third, women have a shorter age range of marriageability and a longer life span, factors that put them in a position of greater supply and lesser demand.

The man usually takes the most active role in asking for a date, makes most of the decisions about what to do on a date, and makes the final decision about getting married. Once a woman accepts a man as a legitimate suitor, he is expected to shoulder most subsequent responsibilities. It is not surprising, therefore, that women are much more sensitive to the characteristics and wishes of men than men are to the characteristics and wishes of women. In fact, the progress of courtship can be predicted from the woman's ability to sense her partner's perception of himself (Murstein, 1972). Because the man has more options all along the way, he does not risk as much at each choice point. He can always withdraw.

Development of the Couple

In 1890, a marriage was expected to last less than 25 years before one of the partners died. During this time, children were almost always in the home. Death of one spouse terminated the marriage about two years before the marriage of the last child. By 1970, the average life expectancy from the time of marriage had risen so that couples married in their early 20s could expect to stay together—if they didn't separate—for 45 years. Furthermore, there would be no children in the home for the last 20 years or more.

Most young men and women enter marriage with a formal commitment to an enduring relationship. They look forward with excitement and pleasure to shared activity and interest and to total involvement. Partners expect to be each other's main companion, concerned with all aspects of each other's lives and feelings.

Newlywed and childless couples enjoy a relatively high standard of living; both husbands and wives are likely to be working. Lacking other major responsibilities, they buy more cars, furniture, appliances, clothes, meals out, and recreation than at any other time of life. This buying spree, Aldous (1978) wryly notes, ends with the arrival of the first child. Then comes a time of buying homes, washers and dryers, food and medicine, and toys and children's equipment.

Both cross-sectional and longitudinal data show tnat over the years of marriage, husbands seem to participate less and less in household activities (Pineo, 1961). They also show decreasing interest in their families and engage in less sexual activity with their wives as their preoccupation with jobs and outside activities increases. What they value in marriage, if they are generally successful in their occupational careers, is companionship and mutual understanding. Those who are less successful are, curiously, as interested in children as they are in companionship (Elder, 1974). At the beginning of marriage, the companion role is usually at its peak, partly as a carryover from the courtship relationship. Young wives turn to their husbands both for sympathy and in anger. But as time passes—and particularly if children intervene—intimacy wanes, anger is held in, and wives turn to God, other people, housework, and for some, their own "careers."

A nonemployed wife who has young children at home is markedly restricted. If she does not live near her mother or sisters, she depends on her husband for help, companionship, and news of the outside world. A woman in one of my classes said that she felt our discussions of friendship among housewives were meaningless, because she never met anybody outside her family—and she was even taking courses at the university. As children get older, many women tend to reach out more, partly through activities around their children's broadening world (for example, PTA and Scouts). They are more likely then to help their husbands "get ahead" by earning some money, by giving husbands emotional support and encouragement, or by entertaining their husbands' friends and business associates. These activities vary by social class, but not in a simple fashion, because personality, family background, and other factors are also important influences. Entertaining in order to help a husband's career, for example, is a high-status role. Lopata (1971) found such entertaining more common among suburban women than among inner-city housewives.

Some—but not all—investigations find an upswing in marital satisfaction after the children are grown. One contributing factor here is probably fewer obligatory expenditures on children as well as an absolute increase in economic resources, at least for middle-class couples who are at the peak of their earning power. But, as Aldous points out, this period can be truncated by a new set of financial responsibilities for ill and aging parents, or even for ill or aging husbands or wives. Some couples survive to old age with sufficient funds or securities to continue to live comfortably, particularly if they reduce their wants and particularly with our present policies for Social Security, Medicare, and Medicaid, meager as they are.

Pineo (1961), reporting on the Burgess/Wallin longitudinal study of couples, found decreased companionship, affectional demonstrations, and sexual activity in these 20-year married couples, and called the change **disenchantment.** He believed that this was the result of a progressive lack of fit between partners who had originally chosen each other because they were the best match they could find.

Figure 5-1 shows the conditions under which a good fit could—or could not—be maintained, using the example of change in complexity. Either partner could become more complex, less complex, or stay the same. According to this model, if both husband and wife remain stable in personality over the years of their marriage, their match can remain good. This positive match may not be apparent while their children are present: the fit was just between the two of them. After the children leave (or at least become somewhat less intrusive), however, the original good match can shine through. Incidentally, in other kinds of societies, where marriages are arranged by extended families for the benefit of a larger unit, the couple relationship may even be enhanced by the arrival and presence of children.

If both husband and wife develop toward greater complexity over time, their fit can remain good—or perhaps even improve—only if they both develop "on the same wavelength." However, husband and wife may grow apart instead of together. In fact, those who are able to grow in unison may be rare exceptions. The same conclusions may be drawn for couples who decrease in complexity, or deteriorate over time. If they deteriorate in the same way (for example, if both "cool off"), they may remain well matched. Finally, if one partner increases or decreases in complexity while the other does not, the match will no longer be good. The same process of decreasing fit could come about through any kind of individual-change process in husband and wife.

Development of husband	Development of wife		
	None (stable)	*Becomes more complex*	*Becomes less complex*
None (stable)	Match should remain good. Perhaps dormant while children intervene, but when they leave, may get a "second honeymoon."	Match deteriorates. Wife's needs no longer met.	Match deteriorates. Husband's needs no longer met.
Becomes more complex	Match deteriorates. Husband's needs no longer met.	Relationship has chance to develop if individuals' changes are on same path. But they could each develop in different directions and would no longer match.	Match deteriorates. Husband's needs no longer met.
Becomes less complex	Match deteriorates. Wife's needs no longer met.	Match deteriorates. Wife's needs no longer met.	Relationship has chance of staying matched if negative developments of both are synchronous; could be like "cooling off." But if not, synchronization will disappear.

Figure 5-1. Possibilities for husband/wife matching over years of marriage as a function of personality development in either or both.

Couples who never have children also seem to experience a cooling-off process, although perhaps not to the same extent as do parents. Couples who marry when they are older (Blood & Wolfe, 1960) seem to show the same pattern of initial euphoria and high emotional interaction followed by gradual cooling, although the time sequence may be different. Couples married in high school follow this trajectory at a markedly accelerated pace (De Lissovoy, 1973; Kellam et al., 1982). They reach "disenchantment" after only 18 months of marriage instead of after 20 years. Furthermore, Kelly (1955) found that partners who are not close to each other when they are engaged are not likely to be brought closer together after 18 years of marriage.

The interaction patterns of newlywed couples are markedly consistent across studies. Feldman (1964) reports that partners talk to each other about subjects close to their hearts: their homes, their children, and their parents. They often get very excited when they talk, and they can easily get into fights. Whether or not they fight, their interactions usually make them feel warm and close to each other. The younger couples also go out more together and have more fun, particularly if they are middle-class.

Disagreements between younger partners are mostly over in-laws. Later on, when the wives quit their jobs to have babies, the partners fight more over money. Later still, they fight over the absence of joint recreation. They don't report fighting over their children until the children are old enough to get into deliberate trouble—in adolescence, usually.

The interactions of couples married about 20 years are markedly different from those of younger couples. The partners talk about subjects outside themselves: home repairs, religion, news, culture, and sports (Feldman, 1964). Their conversations are much calmer. They neither criticize each other nor run out slamming the door. They don't go out much with each other but are more sober and sedentary. This may be partly a cohort difference, of course, because these findings are based on cross-sectional research. Couples now older may not have been as recreation oriented even at the beginning of their marriages.

Sex-Role Differentiation

One way of looking at marital interaction is along a role-differentiation dimension. At one end is the traditional marriage, in which the husband is expected to earn a living and protect his family from the outer world, while the wife is expected to raise children and maintain a smoothly running, comfortable home. Little is expected in the way of love, warmth, emotional support, or shared thoughts and interests. The husband finds his friends among his work associates or neighborhood bar cronies; the wife finds hers among sisters and neighbors. At the opposite end is the expressive, shared relationship, in which love, warmth, and companionship are primary expectations. In such marriages, role differentiation is often at a minimum, with husband and wife expected to share and interchange roles.

Ethnic, social-class, and generational differences exist among couples with respect to sex-role differentiation. The more traditional social groups—lower classes, less educated people, and older generations—tend to expect a high degree of role differentiation. The more modern groups—urbanized middle and upper classes, more educated people, and younger generations—expect little role differentiation. Recent data, in fact, suggest that it is primarily education that makes the difference in marital patterns (Locksley, 1982).

All studies agree that wives are responsible for and actually perform almost all janitorial services, child-care tasks, and meal preparation. Husbands are responsible for and generally perform a very few "masculine" tasks that, in any case, occur less frequently: minor repairs, shoveling snow, and mowing the grass. Emptying the garbage is a "masculine" task that is performed more frequently, but is hardly time-consuming. Most studies do not even consider kin-keeping functions performed by wives such as visiting, keeping contact with, and writing to all geographically distant relatives (and friends).

Over the life course, there is somewhat more sharing of household work before the first child is born (Hoffman & Manis, 1978). The relative amount of housework done by wives as compared with husbands in Blood and Wolfe's large cross-sectional Detroit sample (1960) remained relatively constant after the children were of school age. There are few signs that couples return to egalitarian family orientations once the pattern has shifted after the birth of the first child. The wife takes on almost all the family responsibilities. In addition, she emotionally—and often practically, as by entertaining—supports her husband in his work role.

A later study, by Campbell, Converse, and Rodgers (1976) found, further, that the more children a woman had, the more housework she did. Only after the birth of the fourth child did husbands increase their work around the home. Husbands do not increase their family work when their wives are employed, either (Pleck, 1977). Although it is true that occupational and family work are inversely related to each other for both sexes, employed men still do only a fraction of the family work (one-third) that fully employed women do. Further, men's family roles do not intrude into their work lives, but women's family roles *do* intrude into *their* work lives. Many husbands take work home; not many wives do.

A time/motion study of Syracuse, New York, families (K. Walker, 1970) and a multinational time-use study (Szalai, 1973) both found that husbands spent an average of about an hour and a half per day altogether in family work. Their wives' employment made a difference in men's housework only if they had babies under 1 year old.

Although being a housewife today is not personally rewarding to many women, some do find this role fulfilling. Those with strong achievement motivation can express these strivings through fostering their husbands' careers and participating in their successes, if the husbands are successful—an indirect approach to achievement. The traditional marital role also seems to satisfy grade school-educated women with high power needs. If other arenas of displaying power are limited, running a house and directing young children can be gratifying. Remember the discussion of achievement motivation in the previous chapter.

Many of the women in the Oakland longitudinal study (Elder, 1974) who were adolescents during the 1930s Depression, did enjoy housework and being housewives. They preferred their family role over all others—even if they were active in other roles, and even if they were not happy with their marriages. More than half of them thoroughly enjoyed taking care of their homes and rejected the statement that cooking, sewing, and cleaning are just jobs that have to be done. Only 10% clearly disliked the duties of homemaking. Women from deprived backgrounds liked housekeeping even more than did those from nondeprived backgrounds. Some of them continued in this vein even in their post-child-rearing years (Livson, 1977).

A high level of role differentiation has been associated with the existence of the extended family, because the woman who gets companionship and daily help from her mother and sisters is not as dependent on her husband for household services. Conversely, if her husband shares her work, she need not turn to her mother and sisters for help.

Starting in the late 1960s, and perhaps precipitated by such feminist books as Simone de Beauvoir's *The Second Sex* (1953) and Betty Friedan's *The Feminine Mystique* (1963), the women's movement became a major influence on the American scene. A burgeoning literature suggested alternatives ranging all the way from rejection of childbearing and heterosexual relationships altogether, to equal husband/wife sharing of child rearing, housekeeping, and providing income. Some plans for sharing involved the interchangeability—either simultaneously or sequentially—of home and job roles between both sexes. Others stressed the need for community provision of child-care facilities and centers that would free parents of young children from confinement to the home, for at least part of the day or week.

Present-day husbands and wives are probably not as differentiated either in function or in behavior as some family theorists believe, nor as interchangeable as other theorists assert. Furthermore, *perceptions* of role changes may be greater than the actual changes. For example, the youngest couples in Hill's sample (Hill et al., 1970) described their marriages as markedly egalitarian and as being different in this way from their parents' and grandparents' marriages. But their behavior, as described by the interviewers, did not seem very different from that of their parents and grandparents. More change has probably taken place in ideology than in behavior. Of course, ideology can be the forerunner of new behavior.

Recent surveys (for example, Condran & Bode, 1982) have shown that, in spite of ideological pressure for more egalitarian husband/wife behavior, husbands and wives remain traditional. What is more, most husbands and wives like it that way (Pleck, 1975).

More than 20 years ago, Detroit-area women reported that their husbands participated very little in washing the evening dishes, straightening up the house, or preparing their own breakfasts (Blood & Wolfe, 1960). They participated more in grocery shopping and in keeping track of financial assets and bills. Fifteen years later, after the impact of the women's movement, another study in Detroit (Duncan, Schuman, & Duncan, 1973) found remarkably little change. In 1976, three-fourths of the female physicians in Detroit were doing all the cooking, shopping, child care, and money management for their families, and one-third did all the laundry and heavy cleaning (Heins, Smock, & Stein, 1976).

Many adults in our society dislike housework, especially men and college-educated women, and this trend may be increasing. Therefore, we may find that less housework will actually get done, that standards of cleanliness will decline, or that new lifestyles will be found that minimize the need for housework.

The Effect of Parenting

What is there about being parents that makes marriage so different after the birth of the first child? Not all adults in the United States are parents, but a vast majority are. For those who are, becoming parents is one of the important events of their lives. Parents generally have different developmental trajectories from nonparents, at least in the older cohorts of adults alive in the 1980s.

An ongoing study on family/career transitions in women's lives (Weingarten & Daniels, 1978) finds a dramatic difference in the effect of parenthood on women's and men's work histories. Regardless of generation, educational level, or family timing pattern, parenting alters women's lives much more than it does their husbands'. The first child almost always draws the mother back into the home. No man in Weingarten and Daniels's study dropped out of school or left a good job on account of becoming a father. In fact, the men reported that becoming fathers gave them an impetus to "make it" on their jobs and intensified their sense of financial responsibility. Thus, the baby drew its mother into the home and pushed its father out.

Women accommodate their work lives to meet the needs of their families. Some adopt a sequential pattern: either having children early and starting a career later, or first pursuing a career and then having children. Others adopt a simultaneous pattern, making daily transitions from one sphere to the other.

The sequential pattern provides a more radical transition. It is interesting to note that most of the simultaneous-pattern women were college-educated *late* first-time mothers. Those mothers who were able to choose the timing of their entry or reentry into the work world did so in relation to their children. Those who stayed home during the early years of parenting used the time to forge new identities, including occupational identities. In contrast to the mothers and grandmothers of today's younger women, who saw their first children as the end of their job careers and the beginning of home careers that would last the rest of their lives, the newer generation of women have a broader life-span view.

Some couples find that trouble begins during pregnancy (Masters & Johnson, 1966; Meyerowitz & Feldman, 1967). Restrictions on sexual activity and feelings about loss of attractiveness are major contributors. Newly married couples chose sex as one of the important aspects of marriage—men chose it as the most important. After the birth of the first child, sex dropped to the least important aspect for the women and to second place for their husbands (Reedy, 1977). Many husbands, however, show increasing solicitude toward their wives during pregnancy and take over more household tasks than at any other time of marriage. In fact, they would be willing to do more than their wives let them (H. Feldman, 1971).

A number of explanations have been offered for the crisis nature of the first birth. One is the shift from dyad to triad. Small-group psychologists have demonstrated that the triad in human groups tends to be unstable, with the weakest member forming a coalition with one of the two stronger members. In the case of the mother/father/newborn triad, this usually results in the baby and mother becoming the strongly knit element, leaving the father out (Freilich, 1964).

New mothers whom Russell (1974) studied worried about their appearance and their physical condition. They complained of fatigue, exhaustion, loss of sleep, and inability to keep up with housework. They worried about being competent mothers and at the same time resented being tied down. Their husbands also lost sleep and had to adjust to new routines and responsibilities. And then there was money—the burst of new expenditures that sends young fathers out to increase their income.

Aldous (1978) says that most couples "negotiate the transition period with no great sense of crisis" (p. 162), however. Couples that found time to be alone together in the evening and in which the husband got up at night with the baby reported fewer problems.

The Child-Rearing Period

During the ensuing child-rearing years, the theme is one of separation of interests and activities between husbands and wives. Husbands, particularly if they are successful, grow increasingly immersed in their jobs and personal

interests. Wives immerse themselves primarily in home and family and sec-
ondarily in jobs.

The presence of children is critical. On the one hand, children are
associated with lower communication and satisfaction; on the other hand, they
are associated with valuing a marriage, being needed, and being in love.
Couples with no children are more concerned with getting ahead, cultivating
intellectual capacities, and developing personal interests. They are able to
express both conflict and affection more freely and openly than couples surrounded by children. Of course, child-free couples that stay married are more
likely to be harmonious; less harmonious couples would probably have divorced.

An ingenious study by H. Feldman (1981) compared couples who
were intentionally parents with those who were intentionally not parents. Both
husband and wife were interviewed. Aside from the parenting issue, the two
groups were well matched as to education, age, and occupation, although the
mothers had less schooling than the child-free wives. The two groups turned
out to be similar in self-esteem and also in marital satisfaction. Where they
differed significantly, though, was on "positive marital interactions." That is,
couples without children had more fun away from home, more stimulating
exchanges of ideas, more joint projects, and more sexual relations. While the
childless discussed their work, culture, their feelings, and sex, the parents,
not surprisingly, talked about their children. It is possible to interpret these
differences as evidence of the negative effects on marriage of having children—Glenn and McLanahan (1982), for instance, conclude that there is a
generally negative effect—but turning attention from exclusive focus on each
other to a wider range can also be seen as positive growth.

The parents of high school students in the San Francisco study (Lowenthal et al., 1975) believed in being married and having children, and they
also appreciated their children. But the disruptive effect of their children on
their marriages and their lives was a recurrent theme in their interviews.
Childless couples who had been married about the same length of time—and
were still married—were more like newlyweds in their interactions (H. Feldman, 1964). Moreover, women most heavily involved with parenting who did
not turn to other, more personal interests about this time tended to be more
troubled (Spence & Lonner, 1972; Bart, 1970).

The Empty Nest

As noted earlier, the number of years that partners are likely to have
alone together again after the children are supposed to leave home has increased
greatly over the last century. Today, the empty-nest transition occurs in middle
age rather than in old age. Furthermore, many nests never truly empty, or
empty in a nominal rather than an actual way. One woman in the San Francisco

sample suggested that the empty nest is surrounded by telephone wires. Others remarked "What empty nest?" Their children continue to hang around in fact, even though they have moved out in theory. A study of newlyweds by Ryder (1968) found that although some newlyweds do have little contact with their parents, others visit and telephone often and still use their parents' closet space, checking and charge accounts, cars, and so on. As economic conditions deteriorate, children who have moved out may return—often with spouse and children.

Feldman (1964) finds that partners in the "launching stage," when one or more children are still at home tend to be calm and objective rather than emotional—as in Cuber and Harroff's (1963) **passive/congenial** relationship. Their focus is still on their children. They spend a lot of time talking about their children, and much of their interaction involves them. They still fight, but while their early fights tended to end with lovemaking and increased happiness, they now tend to look back without much pleasure on the course of the marriage. Women at this time are more likely than men to express concern about the coming transition (Lowenthal et al., 1975). They are also more likely to look forward to increased freedom and to see their children as new social resources (Hagestad, 1982).

The lengthening of the period when the couple is "alone again" has been accompanied by a number of new relationships between husbands and wives, most of them still unstudied. Many contradictory statements appear in the family literature. For example, there are popular reports that marriages are more likely to break up when the children leave home, with a second peak in divorce rates comparable to that for beginning marriages (so far unsupported by any demographic data). These reports are counterbalanced by other reports of second honeymoons. There are statements that women are more affected or more changed in their feelings and behavior by the emptying of the nest than their husbands, but there has been little systematic research on how husbands are affected.

There are reports that sexuality terminates for most couples at this time, counterbalanced by reports of revitalized sexuality. There are reports of heightened marital satisfaction—but these are often tied to reports of cooling interpersonal interactions. Unfortunately, most of our research information is still so tenuous for these later years that we must proceed cautiously in drawing anything but tentative conclusions. It would not be too farfetched to presume that diversity of marital style in later years is even greater than in earlier years. After all, variation increases on almost every other measure with each succeeding decade of life. It is possible that many of the preceding reports are true—each for a different segment of the population.

Not only is diversity probably greater as marriages last longer, but different components of marital quality probably show different time patterns. Gilford and Bengtson (1979) showed that negative feelings went down steadily with age—among surviving couples, cross-sectionally—but that positive interactions showed a U-shaped curve. Such differentiation in feelings and behaviors is shown in Figure 5-2, the findings of a careful area probability study by Anderson, Russell, and Schumm (1983). Notice that marital satisfaction reaches its lowest point when children are school age and then goes up again. Couple communication—discussion and self-disclosure—goes down less than satisfaction from the high point at the beginning to the low at school age, but then goes up for a while to the launching stage, to drop once more. Remember that a rising number of studies consistently show that children put a damper on couple communication. An ingenious study that observed men and women's behavior toward each other in public places found that if they were accompanied by children they touched each other less, talked to each other less, and smiled at each other less (Rosenblatt, 1974).

The Couple as a System

There is more than one way to view a family over its lifetime. We can focus on the individual members, in this case the husband or wife. We can also shift our focus to the couple as an interactional, bounded system. As noted earlier, a system can react to change in one of four ways: it can deny change; it can alter just enough to return to equilibrium, or homeostasis; it can fragment and fall apart; or it can "develop."

Denial could operate thus: in spite of changes in a husband or wife, or in any strategic part of the situation in which they interact, the marriage could continue as if there had been no changes. For example, partners whose children were adults and living in their own homes could continue to focus

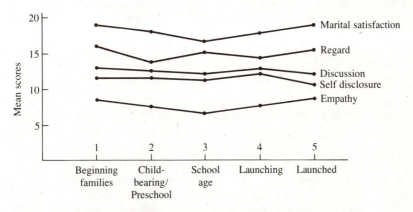

Figure 5-2. Equally weighted means for each criterion variable for each category of family life cycle. (Source: Anderson, Russell, and Schumm, 1983.)

their relationship on their children as much as when the children were still in need of a great deal of parental care. Or, to return to equilibrium, the marriage could change just a little. For example, a husband and wife could act toward each other as if the other were the children who had left, and thus could treat each other with extra nurturance and protectiveness. Or the marriage could fragment and end in divorce or alienation between spouses. Marriages do exist in which one partner has not talked to the other for years. Finally, the marriage could develop in any of a number of ways, leading to a "second honeymoon" or a richer relationship.

Winter, Ferreira, and Bowers (1973) found that married couples showed greater "spontaneous agreement" without consulting each other than did "synthetic" couples (men and women paired randomly). The married couples also required less explicit informational exchange and reached joint decisions in a shorter time. The better the spontaneous agreement, furthermore, the longer the duration of the marriage and the higher the satisfaction with the marriage.

Raush, Barry, Hertel, and Swain (1974) provide us with some valuable longitudinal data. They followed 46 young couples from their fourth month of marriage for about two years. First, they noticed that these couples had established stable and characteristic communication patterns by the fourth month. Second, these patterns were maintained over the next two years. In fact, these couple patterns were more stable over time than were the individual patterns of either husband or wife.

Comparisons of communication between men and women married to each other and those paired randomly show that husbands are more likely to lead the conversation with their wives but not with strange women and that wives laugh more and disapprove more with their husbands than with strange men (Ryder, 1968). An examination of the affect of communication—positive or negative—found that couples more satisfied with their marriage had more positive affect in their messages (Gottman, 1979), and longitudinal data showed that engaged couples expressing more positive affect had more satisfactory marriages five years later (Markman, 1981).

Marital Satisfaction

Marriages are usually assessed according to two separate criteria: happiness and stability. People who have happy marriages can get divorced, and people with very unhappy marriages may stay together for 50 years. Although stability of a marriage is no indication of its being satisfying to either partner, stability does have value in our culture, which stresses success. A stable marriage—one that lasts—is seen by many as a successful marriage.

Paris and Luckey (1966) followed 31 satisfied couples and 31 dissatisfied couples from 1957 to 1963. The satisfied couples tended to decrease in satisfaction, and the dissatisfied increased somewhat in satisfaction, suggesting a "regression to the mean." Nevertheless, there was an overall trend toward decreased satisfaction over time.

Happiness in marriage depends as much on the partners' expectations as on their actual relationship. Highly educated men and women who stress self-actualization and romantic love may not tolerate a relationship that would seem good to a working-class wife who is satisfied with an occasional paycheck and not being beaten. In general, couples with traditional expectations for marriage say they are happier than do those with more expressive expectations. Perhaps the rules are clearer in traditional marriages, and other options more limited.

Sex Differences in Satisfaction

In general, husbands tend to find marriage more satisfactory than do wives. When Veroff and Feld (1970) asked respondents to list things about their marriages that they did not like, 45% of the married men said "nothing," as compared with only 25% of the women. Husbands' satisfaction did not decrease over time, as their wives' did (Luckey, 1961). When men do say that they are dissatisfied with their marriages, they are more often reflecting discontentment with their life situations—with their children or their jobs—than with their relationships with their wives. More educated men are happier with their marriages because their lives are likely to be more comfortable all around. Younger men, particularly those with children, are less happy about their marriages than older men; younger men are also more likely to be financially disadvantaged. Finally, when a husband is unhappy, the couple is unhappy; but a wife's unhappiness does not seem to transfer to her husband in the same way.

One paradoxical finding is that wives report more marital stress than their husbands do, but they also report more overall satisfaction. Bernard (1973) believes that wives have to pay more for companionship and sociability. Love seems to be so important to women that they are willing to pay an exorbitant price for it. Veroff and Feld (1970) found that just getting married and being married are themselves important sources of gratification of affiliative needs for many women.

Sexual Behavior

We have witnessed a "sexual revolution" over the past decades. Diversity of sexual values and practices is accepted more now. However, a new mandate for sexual skillfulness may be superseding the old one for sexual naiveté—at least for women.

The traditional view of sex is that it must have a purpose, either for procreation or to express affection. Thus, the greatest change has been a shift from extrinsic to intrinsic value. Sex has become a pleasure instead of a duty—unless what has happened is that it is now a duty to get pleasure. Twenty years ago, Komarovsky (1964) noted that blue-collar women learned to negotiate what they wanted from their husbands before sexual intercourse. Although there are no recent data on this point, there is also no reason to believe that the bargaining power of sex has decreased.

The effect of pregnancy and childbirth on sexuality is pronounced (Masters & Johnson, 1966). A total of 79 middle-class wives were interviewed three times during pregnancy, and both they and their husbands were seen again after delivery. Of the 43 women who were pregnant for the first time, 33 said they had lost interest in sex and were less effective in sexual performance during the first three months of pregnancy. However, they felt heightened eroticism and activity during the next three months. This increased sexuality during the middle trimester of pregnancy was also reported by women having second or later children. During the last three months, a combination of physical symptoms and doctors' advice led to decreased sexual activity and, for some partners, cessation. Physical discomfort at all stages of pregnancy was more common among women who already had children, because of increased fatigue—they had their other children to take care of.

Even after the birth, one-half the women reported less interest and activity in sex for at least three months more. However, some women, either because of their own heightened interest or because they wanted to satisfy their husbands, resumed intercourse as early as three weeks after birth. The husbands' reports were consistent with those of their wives. Most mentioned a decrease in sexual activity, and most who did said they decreased activity because of concern for the coming baby.

A few men did say that they were not attracted to their wives during this time, and some of these men turned to extramarital sexual activity during the later prenatal and early postnatal months. Not surprisingly, their wives were not happy about this situation, and this factor alone accounted for much stress both before and after the birth.

In a study of 102 happily married couples of a wide age range, Reedy and Birren (1978) asked both members of each couple to rank the importance of six kinds of love: sex, loyalty, emotional security, companionship, respect, and communication. The newlywed couples ranked sex at the top, but in those couples who had a baby, the wife ranked it last and the husband second. By the time the children had left home, it was in last place for both members of the couple, and it stayed there. What replaced it at the top of the list was emotional security and loyalty. A retrospective rating with the same scale by golden-anniversary couples (Parron, 1978) duplicated these findings.

As far as sex in marriage is concerned, Clark and Wallin (1965) concluded, on the basis of longitudinal data, that women who have mutual love and respect in their relationships with their husbands are relatively high in sexual responsiveness and become more responsive with increased coital experience. Women whose marriages have had a persistently negative quality tend to remain relatively low in responsiveness. Shope and Broderick (1967) found that sexual experience before marriage was not necessarily conducive to good sexual adjustment in marriage.

Much has been said about the sexual boredom that goes along with long-lasting marriages—at least in this culture, where sexuality has been given much attention in recent years. Masters and Johnson (1966) prescribe variety in positions and foreplay. Some authors recommend open marriage and extra-marital explorations. Others recommend serial marriages with reappraisal and easy divorce built into the marital contract.

Masters and Johnson (1974) suggest that the often-reported second honeymoon of middle age may be partly due to the unleashing of sexual desires in previously inhibited women who no longer fear getting pregnant. The women's upsurge of sexual interest may then induce renewed sexual interest in their husbands. Another possibility is that there may be a baseline of pleasure and stability in the sexual component of marriage to which many couples can return after the interfering preoccupations of child rearing are removed.

Again, the phenomenon of renewed sexuality in middle age may show a cohort effect, because a generation that started sex life and marriage with "the pill" would not be as hampered by pregnancy risks as earlier generations were. A different reason for a woman's greater satisfaction with her sex life in middle age may be her husband's decreased sexual activity. If her husband's earlier sexual appetite was greater than hers, his decrease with age may match them more comfortably, so that they can now be more pleased with each other and thus also with themselves.

Divorce

The rate of divorce has been rising steadily over the past 60 years. Its timing in the marriage has stayed about the same, however. Divorce—or at least separation—is most common just after marriage; its frequency drops markedly during the first seven years, and at a slower rate thereafter. P. C. Glick (1979) calculated that one-half of all divorces following a first marriage occur within seven years after the marriage. It looks as if there may be a slowing of this rate in the last few years, attributed by some to the increase in cohabiting couples, whose separations are not counted.

Age at marriage is related to duration of marriage. Men who marry before age 21 and women who marry before 19 are least likely to stay married. Men who marry when they are over 30 tend to stay married, even though they may say they are unhappy. Partners whose income is low or who have children soon after marriage are more likely to divorce (Norton & Glick, 1976). Finally, divorce can be said to run in families. Children of divorced parents tend to marry children of divorced parents, and their marriages, too, are likely to end in divorce.

The relation between marital patterns of parents and those of their children may be explained in part by personality and couple-interaction factors. Children of divorced parents tend to date at an earlier age, for example, and thus to marry earlier, making less mature decisions and choices. Some divorces are attributable to difficulties in ability to form attachments to others (Kitson & Sussman, 1982). How husbands and wives handle conflict has also been found to be important (Raush et al., 1974).

In their longitudinal study of 48 White, middle-class couples, starting during the newlywed period, Raush et al. found remarkable consistency in interaction patterns. Both partners tended to use the same mode of resolving conflict, and these modes tended to stay the same over time. If one spouse, for example, reacted to induced conflict emotionally or coercively, so did the other, and the situation thus got worse. Such couples were likely to engage in power struggles in which neither listened to the other and both resorted to personal attacks, while the happily married were more likely to provide information about the issue in question and to suggest a solution. This was even more noticeable among the happily married husbands than among their wives. The happily married husbands initiated peace-making statements that encouraged diminution of conflict.

In a less powerful study of marital communication—because it looked at self-reports, mostly of university students—Honeycutt, Wilson, and Parker (1982) focused on how marital communications differed from communications with others. Happily married men reported a more relaxed style of communicating with their wives than with others. Happily married women were not only more relaxed, but also more friendly, open, dramatic, expressive, and attentive with their husbands. Men and women who reported less happiness in their marriage reported no difference between their marital communication styles and their general communication styles.

Of course, we must remember that happiness in marriage is not equivalent to less likelihood of divorcing. The importance of maintaining the marriage is an intervening factor. Couples that believe it is most important to "make a go of it" will live with very unhappy marriages, perhaps awaiting the "death do us part."

What happens after divorce? Hetherington, Cox, and Cox (1976) compared 48 divorced couples with 48 still-married couples over a period of two years. The greatest amount of readjustment and unhappiness occurred in the first few months after the divorce was granted. Men who had depended on their wives' care now had to learn to take care of themselves. Their wives were also learning to assume the tasks their husbands had performed. Relations with their ex-spouses occupied most of the time and energy of both ex-husbands and ex-wives. Two-thirds of these encounters followed the interaction patterns of earlier times. Conflicts were particularly bitter over finances, which now had to be spread over two households instead of one. Husbands tried to work harder to get more income but found it difficult to work at all because they were so upset. Their wives may also have had trouble working, either at home or on the job.

Curiously, not all the interactions were negative. Old affection patterns also persisted. In fact, 6 of the 48 divorced couples had sexual intercourse during the first two months. And most of the men and women said they would turn first to their ex-spouses if they needed help in a crisis. Remember, the hypothesis of attachment versus attraction? Although divorce may result from loss of attraction—or shifts in attraction—or from unhappiness and conflict, attachment is not so easily dissipated.

The dissolution of a marriage is almost always accompanied by enormous stress for both partners. It involves changes in role and status and reexaminations of identity. These strains can be particularly acute for women who have primarily defined themselves as being their husbands' wives and who must now figure out who they are on their own. Also, such women must do so at a time when they have lost most of their social ties, who were "family friends" connected to their husbands' occupations. These difficulties are further compounded by feelings of failure and by financial crisis.

A woman traditionally measures her success and derives her feelings of worth from first capturing a man and then holding onto him. In spite of demographic changes, most divorced women are still subject to derision as failures and are vulnerable to self-accusations by the same standards. In Douvan's (1979) Michigan study, the two groups in the American population showing notable symptoms of stress were divorced women and single men. This was as true in 1976 as it was in 1957.

Consistent with Hetherington's findings, in a carefully chosen sample of divorced men and women who lived in suburbs of Cleveland, Kitson and Sussman (1982) found that six months to a year following the divorce, more than 80% were still attached to their ex-spouses: they spent a lot of time thinking about them and wondering what they were doing. This was as true of men as of women, and of those married only two years as of those married longer. While the amount of attachment was related to the amount of distress experienced, distress yielded to comfort of friends and relatives, but attachment did not seem affected by this kind of support. Highly attached people said that their most difficult adjustments were living alone and feeling lonely, being independent, and being a single parent. Low-attachment people, on the other hand, mentioned role changes such as household chores and shifts in living arrangements and employment. Predictably, cohabiting or remarrying was associated with lower attachment. Curiously, while women had higher distress scores, men had higher attachment scores—the only sex difference, and a subtle one.

Only one-third of divorces during the 1970s represented marriages that had lasted more than ten years (U.S. Department of Health, Education, and Welfare, National Center for Health Statistics, 1975), and only 1% represented people over 65 (Hagestad, 1982). Older people who do divorce, however, are much less likely to remarry, particularly if they are women.

The effects of divorce are experienced at all ages, however. Hagestad (1982) calls these "family ripple effects." Parents, siblings, and children of a divorced couple all participate in some way. Many young women with children to support and little or no money from their ex-spouse turn to their parents for financial as well as emotional help, "coming home" with their children for a shorter or longer period of succorance. Recent research on children (for example, Kellam et al., 1982) shows that mothers and children who have this kind of resource fare much better than those who don't. The unexpected refilling of the "empty nest," though, may disrupt the plans and relationships of middle-aged parents and grandparents.

According to Douvan (1979), the divorced woman, particularly if she is raising children alone, faces poverty and role overload that are so oppressive that the social stigma of divorce pales by comparison. Only 14% of American women are awarded alimony, and less than half of them get it regularly. Only 44% are awarded child support, and less than half of these get it regularly (Lake, 1976). Furthermore, older women who have been brought up to believe that getting married means economic security, and who have few employable skills or experience, find themselves on a steep downward curve socioeconomically. Chiriboga (1979) found that, while both women and men experienced much stress during the divorcing process, the men seemed even worse off than the women. These findings are consistent with those of Kitson. Older people of both sexes were more disrupted socially than were younger people. The ages of the 50s and 60s are times when some couples enjoy being together again after their children are less intrusive, and a separation at this time can be particularly distressing. Starting to date again can be awkward, and it is often complicated by disapproval on the part of children.

Older couples are not immune to the tenor of the times, however, which makes divorce almost imperative for unhappy marriages. In fact, we may have reached a "tipping point," a reversal in general attitudes, a general belief that marriages that are not happy should be terminated. Once, partners felt obligated to stay together even if they were highly incompatible and unhappy, and they were ashamed if they did divorce. Now such couples feel apologetic if they *don't* divorce.

Widowhood

In the United States, there are at least 90,000 men and women under the age of 60 who are widowed, and half of these are under 45. These numbers do not include those who have remarried. Thus, widowhood is not necessarily an old-age phenomenon.

A younger widow is apt to be lonelier than an older widow, who is more likely to have many friends in the same position. Furthermore, older people might be better prepared psychologically for widowhood because they have had occasions—the deaths of friends and relatives—to "rehearse" for the deaths of spouses.

"Anticipatory socialization" had not occurred for the 40 Kansas widows studied by Gibbs (1979), however. They had little preparation for widowhood, even though all were over 50 years of age. Intensive interviews with widows of three age groups (30–40, 41–59, and 60 and older) revealed some common problems as well as some problems that differed by age (Wyly & Hulicka, 1975). All complained of loneliness and of difficulties in maintaining homes and cars. The two younger age groups also mentioned problems with decision making, child rearing, sex, and money. The oldest widows cited difficulties in learning how to manage money, problems of transportation, and fear of crime. Although some younger widows acknowledged that they felt more independent and free than they had while married, the oldest widows saw no advantages to their condition.

Because widowers who have not remarried are not very common in the community until after age 75, they are not as likely to join each other in groups. Men generally join support groups less readily than women. Like widows, they are expected to preserve the memories of their wives and are expected not to show interest in other women. Remarriage rates suggest that the former expectation is stronger than the latter.

Because men's identities only partly come from being husbands, widowers are probably not as apt as widows to face acute identity crises when they lose their wives. Yet, because they are likely to have seen their wives as important parts of themselves (Glick, Weiss, & Parkes, 1974), they may feel more lost. Their wives were probably their only close friends, their main confidantes, and their links to family and friends.

That bereavement is a source of stress for both men and women is attested to by Parkes's (1964) data, which show that the life expectancy of a surviving spouse is shortened for about five years following his or her partner's death. By simply following the vital-statistics records of surviving spouses, Parkes found that the survivors' death rates were higher than would be predicted for their ages. Eventually, however, death rates for those who survived returned to the average for people their age.

A different way of assessing the process of bereavement is by looking at mental health. A 13-month longitudinal study (Bornstein, Clayton, Halikas, Maurice, & Robbins, 1973) found that 35% of widows (men and women) were diagnosed as depressed one month after the death of their spouses, but only 17% were so diagnosed after one year.

A follow-up study was made of 56 women out of an original group of 100 who had been studied ten years earlier (Noberini & Neugarten, 1975). Those women, now aged between 55 and 67, who were widowed in the interim did not show any significant difference from the others in mood tone, sense of self-worth, sense of accomplishing their goals, or sense of integrity.

Clearly, women vary in the extent to which the role of wife is central to their identities. For many, motherhood supersedes wifehood. Others never develop close, intimate relationships with their husbands. Thus, it is not surprising that widows vary widely in their adaptations.

Remarriage

Paul Glick, a leading demographer, has estimated that about three-fourths of the women and five-sixths of the men who divorce eventually remarry within an average of three years after their divorce, and that more than half of these remarriages then last the rest of their joint lifetimes (Glick, 1977). The younger people are when they divorce, the more likely they are to remarry. Remember that most divorces occur soon after marriage, so that the relatively high figures in Glick's estimate reflect the preponderance of young divorces and remarriages. Women's remarriage possibilities decrease after their 30s, while men's chances improve. Low income, for men, and the presence of children, for women, decrease the probability of remarriage. Demographic factors (many more surviving women than men) give Black women an even lower rate of remarriage than White women.

There is a small, but statistically significant, difference in favor of first marriages being happier (Aldous, 1978), although Hetherington, Cox, and Cox (1976) found the only differences to be lowered self-esteem and sense of competency with the opposite sex on the part of remarried individuals. When Spanier and Furstenberg (1982) compared remarried with still divorced individuals, they also found few distinguishing characteristics. Neither the presence of children nor age nor sex seemed important factors in determining who remarried or how happy they were.

The Never-Married

Since present cohorts of Americans—at least those over 30—are probably the most married in human history and in the world today, those adults who have never married are rare and atypical. While single young men and women are not strikingly different in their goals and characteristics, middle-aged singles are. Bernard (1973) uses the graphic terms "cream of the crop" for never-married women and "bottom of the barrel" for never-married men. Women able to be self-supporting and successful in a chosen occupation can be particular about whom they marry. Men unable to attract a wife tend to be poor providers or unfit in some way.

When Peter Stein (1978) interviewed men and women who remained single into their 30s, the men seemed less comfortable than the women, saying that they felt intense family and social pressure to marry and were not sure they liked their jobs or their living arrangements. People over 65 who had never married were described by Gubrium (1975) as lifelong isolates. Because they had not experienced the loss of a spouse, as older widows and divorced people had, they were generally as comfortable as older married people. They tended to be autonomous and resourceful, and while they may have missed a lot of the "good" parts of life, they had also missed a lot of the "bad."

Many more Black men and women than Whites never marry, by something like a 3:1 ratio. One reason given by Black singles (Staples, 1977) was that they did not have a place where they could meet possible mates. Since numbers are in their favor, however, other factors need to be considered.

New Forms of Marriage

Many forces in today's world operate to weaken the appropriateness and satisfaction of traditional monogamous marriage. Let's examine just a few. First, increasing life expectancy makes "till death do us part" a much heavier commitment than it was when 20 or 30 years of marriage, rather than 40 or 50, was the rule. Second, overpopulation makes the bearing of many children "bad" rather than "good." Third, decreased infant mortality makes it more likely that each child born will grow up; thus, a large supply of children becomes less necessary to ensure family continuity and help. Fourth, much new technology does not require physical strength, and most jobs today can be done equally well by women or men. Women who can get jobs as easily as men can do not need to depend on husbands for economic benefits. Fifth, the supplementation and substitution of home services makes a professional housewife an option instead of a necessity for each man. Sixth, increased mobility has led to superficiality in human relationships and to the absence of socialization for deep commitment and involvement.

Writers such as Toffler (*Future Shock,* 1970) and Bernard (*The Future of Marriage,* 1973) have pointed out the irrelevance or imperfections of old forms of marriage and have suggested possible new forms. So far, however, the radical new styles that have received most attention have been rare and transitory. Some of the more popularized variations, described by such writers as Bartell (1971) and Constantine and Constantine (1973), are rarely heard of a decade later. These include swinging, intimate networks, ménage à trois, group marriage, and communes. Homosexual partnerships have received some notice recently; they seem to be more stable among women than among men. The most common pattern remains monogamy or serial monogamy, with divorce followed by remarriage. When children, grandparents, and former and present in-laws are considered, family systems can become very complex, as will be noted later in the chapter.

The 1980 census showed several striking changes in household membership (Death of the family, 1983). The number of people per household has decreased. The number of children being brought up by a mother alone has increased. The number of cohabiting couples has also increased. As noted earlier, intensive studies of cohabiting couples suggest that it is better to view them as a stage toward marriage than as an alternative to marriage (Glick & Spanier, 1980). Most young members of such couples plan to marry eventually, though not necessarily their current partner. Older members tend to be those for whom marriage is less possible: once-married women and financially unstable men.

Generations in the Family

The rhythm of development within the family has altered over the past few generations; indeed, over the past two centuries. Before 1900, only about 40% of American women went through what was later considered the "ideal" family cycle of leaving home, getting married, having children, launching children, and surviving with their husbands into old age (Hareven, 1977). The rest (60%) never married, never reached marriageable age, died before childbirth, or were widowed while their children were small. More people today live out their full life spans, and more parents limit the number of their children.

The grandparents of today's young adults, who married early in the 20th century, were married longer before they had their first children than were the next two generations. However, they had children at closer intervals and continued having children for a longer period of time. Table 5-1 shows that, in spite of all the talk of enormous change in family structure, what actually seems to have happened is a slow change away from turn-of-the-century norms—interrupted by the decade of the 1930s, the Depression—followed by a return. Thus, the vaunted delays in marriage and childbearing of the late 1970s and 1980s look very much like what our grandparents and great-grandparents were doing, although perhaps for somewhat different reasons. Note that the more recent figures are only estimates, because recent cohorts have not completed their family careers.

The American family profile has also been changing. In 1960, the percentage of children remained about the same as in 1900, but there were fewer family members between 20 and 35 and more older people. In 1980,

Table 5-1. Estimated median age of mothers at selected points of family careers

Stage of the family life cycle	80-year average	Decade of birth of mother							
		1880s	1890s	1900s	1910s	1920s	1930s	1940s	1950s
		Decade of first marriage							
		1900s	1910s	1920s	1930s	1940s	1950s	1960s	1970s
Median age at:									
First marriage	20.9	21.4	21.2	21.0	21.4	20.7	20.0	20.5	21.2
Birth of first child	22.6	23.0	22.9	22.8	23.5	22.7	21.4	21.8	22.7
Birth of last child	31.3	32.9	32.0	31.0	32.0	31.5	31.2	30.1	29.6
Marriage of last child	53.5	55.4	54.8	53.0	53.2	53.2	53.6	52.7	52.3
Death of one spouse	62.8	57.0	59.6	62.3	63.7	64.4	65.1	65.1	65.2
Difference between age at first marriage and:									
Birth of first child	1.7	1.6	1.7	1.8	2.1	2.0	1.4	1.3	1.5
Birth of last child	10.4	11.5	10.8	10.0	10.6	10.8	11.2	9.6	8.4
Marriage of last child	32.6	34.0	33.6	32.0	31.8	32.5	33.6	32.2	31.1
Death of one spouse	41.9	35.6	38.4	41.3	42.3	43.7	45.1	44.6	44.0
Difference between:									
Age at birth of first and last children	8.7	9.9	9.1	8.2	8.5	8.8	9.8	8.3	6.9
Age at birth of and marriage of last child	22.2	22.5	22.8	22.0	21.2	21.7	22.4	22.6	22.7
Age at marriage of last child and death of one spouse (empty nest)	9.3	1.6	4.8	9.3	10.5	11.2	11.5	12.4	12.9

Source: U.S. Department of Commerce, Bureau of the Census, 1976.

the middle generation—particularly people in their 40s—was a smaller percentage, overpowered by both younger and older generations.

It does not require much imagination to see the consequences for family life of different family compositions. For instance, if a large number of children must be cared for by a small number of adults, more work and responsibility will be delegated to older children. A smaller adult/child ratio is also more likely to be associated with authoritarian practices, because there is little time or energy for parents to consider the individual needs of particular children at particular times. More older people means that the generation in the middle can be described as "squeezed" between the care of parents and of children.

Adults today are not all of one generation—as they tended to be at the turn of the century—but are of three or even four generations (for example, parents, grandparents, and great-grandparents). Therefore, adult interrelationships are more complex and provide a variety of models for the growing children. If there are more children than adults in a family, children have much less value than if there is one child on whom several generations of adults focus hopes, wishes, and attentions. Husbands and wives who have only one or two children are freer to pursue activities other than child rearing and to examine their own relationships. They are also likely to be less upset when their children grow up and leave home.

The three generations of Minneapolis families studied by Hill and his associates (1970) interacted with each other continually. They shared activities, visited back and forth, and helped each other in many ways. The middle generation (parents of married children) was the lineage bridge between the older and the younger generations. This generation helped and was involved with both other generations. Each generation turned to the kinship network for the help it needed: grandparents for care in illness and household management, middle-aged parents for emotional gratification, and young married couples for assistance with finances and child care. Table 5-2 shows the percentages of help given and received by all three generations over a year's time. The family is both major donor and major recipient of help. The popular notion of the modern family as a vulnerable, isolated, nuclear unit of husband, wife, and young children is not supported. Instead, generational units form a modified extended family with a rich network of interactions.

A Developmental Interpretation of Parenting

The development of parent/child dyads (mother/child and father/child) may follow a pattern similar to that postulated for the husband/wife dyad earlier in this last chapter. We can look at combined effects of separate development of each parent and his or her child. Or we can look at the development of

Table 5-2. Comparison of help received and help given by generation for chief problem areas

| | Type of crisis | | | | | | Type of crisis | | | | |
| | Economic | | Emotional gratification | | Household management | | Child care | | Illness | | |
	Gave (percent)	Received (percent)	Gave (percent)	Received (percent)	Gave (percent)	Received (percent)	Gave (percent)	Received (percent)	Gave (percent)	Received (percent)
Grandparents	26	34	23	42	21	52	16	0	32	61
Parents	41	17	47	37	47	23	50	23	21	21
Married children	34	49	31	21	33	25	34	78	47	18

Note: Percents may not total 100 because of rounding.
Source: Hill, Foote, Aldous, Carlson, and Macdonald, 1970.

133

each of the parent/child dyads as systems. Or we can consider the family (mother/father/child or children) as the system. Or we can look to even larger units.

Most family-development descriptions so far have followed the first approach. The development of the child has been followed along one track and that of each of the parents—although usually only the mother—along parallel tracks. Much research has focused on the attachment of infants to mothers, starting with the work of Ainsworth (1969) and Bowlby (1969). Hartup and Lempers (1973) pointed out that attachment is probably mutual. The parent becomes attached to the infant as the infant does to the parent. Because most longitudinal studies on relationships have not gone beyond infancy and very early childhood, we must wait for future research to help us understand the nature of social bonds and social networks over the life span.

The dyadic or family system makes strenuous efforts to maintain stability, or homeostasis, in the face of the enormous changes accompanying the development of a child. The presence of a child or children in a family may make it imperative for the family system as such to develop *or else*. Divorces may reflect not just the failure of the husband/wife system to deal with change. It may also reflect the failure of the total family system to function.

Mothering

The American mother—particularly the American urban middle-class mother of today—is supposed to be the primary child rearer. This has been the norm since the middle of the 19th century (Hareven, 1977). Before then, the separation between job world and family world was smaller, particularly for working-class families. Family members were more likely to function as a unit, both on the job and in what are now called "family matters."

The burdens on the housewife/mother of today, according to Lopata (1971), are many. It is difficult to learn and carry out complex child-rearing and housekeeping procedures without training. There is the belief that mothers alone should be responsible for raising their children. There is the notion that if mothers are sufficiently competent, they can—and must—raise superior children; if the children are less superior, it is the mother's fault. There is a belief that all problems should be handled rationally, systematically, and calmly— which is almost impossible in the highly emotional milieu of infants and children. Finally, social change and social heterogeneity present conflicting norms.

The belief that the mother is the primary parent pervades our culture so thoroughly that both new mothers and new fathers acknowledge it. Shapiro (1978) reports that first-time mothers admit that they want to be credited as the parent. They tend to denigrate their husbands' parenting competence in order to highlight their own tenuous successes. A new father in one of my classes admitted that he would not pick up the baby when the infant cried at night without first getting his wife's permission. He had to "go through channels." H. Feldman (1971) found that more of the fathers he studied would have been willing to participate in care of their infants than were allowed to by their wives.

Being a mother and knowing how to be a mother are so much part of a woman's self-affirmation that the events of pregnancy and childbirth are highly charged. Another side of this coin, unhappily, is the fact that most new mothers are profoundly ignorant about details of what to expect from their babies and what to do for babies. Yet pediatricians—male, particularly—seem to assume that mothers *must* know about such things because, after all, they are mothers. What they learned in early biology classes—that there is no "maternal instinct" that includes specific, built-in knowledge of how to nurse, diaper, and care for babies—seems to have made no impression.

In part, the physicians themselves may be ignorant of these everyday details, which aren't likely to be taught in medical school or observed in hospital wards. It is no wonder that publishers profit from the multitude of "how-to" books on mothering and that the media in general find parenting advice a good way to get large audiences. Women from tightly knit kin networks such as those described by Bott (1971) find mothering much more familiar and comfortable (Aldous, 1978). After all, they have probably assisted aunts, mother, older sisters, or cousins in these jobs, and they also have all these relatives on hand for advice and help.

Facilities that might supplement maternal care, such as community child-care centers, are not providing the quality care they promised a decade ago or that similar facilities provide in other countries. More options for the care of infants and preschool children, including trained child-care workers and foster grandparents, could make this relatively short period of intensive maternal stress one that approaches the ideal that having a baby is a joy. The country does not seem to be moving in that direction, however. College students, both women and men, expect that they and their spouses will work at the same time as they raise children. They do not often think about how they will manage child care.

Pregnancy

Pregnancy is a psychobiological/social event, a period of conflicting feelings and experiences. To begin with, it is an event with extreme age proscriptions. It is not supposed to occur either too early or too late. There is a prevalent dictum that the first child should be born before the mother is 30. This dictum has become so firmly entrenched that many women who are not married, or who have not had a child by then, go through a "29-year-old crisis."

This rule is supported by the medical profession, which warns of the increased probability of birth defects beyond this age. A look at Table 5-3, however, shows that such warnings may exaggerate the risks of births to mothers over 29, particularly for White women. Until they are over 40, their risk of having a terminated pregnancy—part of that age group's presumed decline in capacity to reproduce—is lower than the same risk for women pregnant before the age of 15. Black and other women have a higher risk of not carrying a pregnancy to term than do White, and this is true at all ages. However, the pattern of decline with age is similar in both groups.

As for risk to the child, it can be seen in Table 5-4 that the risk of Down's Syndrome, usually cited as a sign of aging maternal capacity to reproduce effectively, is still only 1 in 280 between the maternal ages of 35 and 39. While it is clear that the risk increases progressively in mothers from 29 on, this risk may be worth taking for couples who have good reason to delay childbearing. Taking time to become ready emotionally, socially, and economically could logically justify the odds (still favorable) for childbearing in the 30s, particularly since amniocentesis and even better techniques now permit the detection of some of the most common birth defects in utero, with the option of abortion.

Pregnancies at very early ages—under 19—are fraught with at least as much risk as those after 29. At least they are accompanied by higher rates of low birth weight, prematurity, and birth defects. It is true that many of these abnormalities may stem from socioeconomic factors, since teenage pregnancy is commonly found among low socioeconomic groups.

First-time pregnancies are different from later pregnancies in more than one way. They are unknown and ambiguous; it is not surprising that many primiparous (first-birth) women are anxious (Shapiro, 1978). The first-pregnancy women whom Shapiro interviewed were less likely to express their

Table 5-3. Distribution of fetal deaths, by age of mother, per 1000 live births for group: White and "all other"

Age of mother	White	All other
Under 15	17.7	25.1
15–19	9.5	14.4
20–24	7.5	13.2
25–29	7.4	13.9
30–34	8.9	17.5
35–39	13.7	27.1
40 and over	26.4	48.1

Source: U.S. Department of Health, Education, and Welfare, National Center for Health Statistics, 1978.

Table 5-4.   Risk of Down's Syndrome as a function of mother's age

Age of mother	Risk of Down's Syndrome
Under 29	1/3000
30–34	1/600
35–39	1/280
40–44	1/70
45–49	1/40

Source: Nagle, 1984, p. 110.

anxiety than those who had been pregnant before, however. They may have been too defensive to admit such feelings, even to themselves.

Interviews with 67 couples in the 8th month of pregnancy (Soule, 1974) indicate that much of the pregnancy experience is shared by both parents. It is a "couple experience," although it is physically more *direct* for the woman than for the man. Many women are unhappy about their appearance at this time (H. Feldman, 1971) and feel uncomfortable in public; others are proud and pleased with the way they look.

Childbirth

During the 1960s and 1970s, perhaps because of the various "movements" of the time, a variety of new or renewed childbirth practices were tried. So far, little systematic evaluation of these methods exists. In general, however, these "radical" approaches point to the importance of childbirth for many couples.

The thrust of these new practices has been to remove pregnancy and childbirth psychologically from the medical realm, which tended to automatically classify such events as "diseases." Anderson and Standley (1976) feel that when a wife in labor talks to her husband, she is less likely to feel pain. The new methods change the frightening and impersonal labor- and delivery-room atmosphere to a more familiar, more personal, and socially more open experience. This change may lessen tension and pain no matter what else occurs.

Support for the idea that fear of the unknown may contribute to childbirth pain comes from differences in experience between first-birth and later-birth women. It is true that a first birth, particularly in a very young woman, may be more difficult physiologically. Yet primiparous mothers describe feeling strange, distant, and unfamiliar, even in their attitudes toward their babies (Robson & Moss, 1970), and later-birth mothers are much more comfortable. This difference suggests that the psychological component is important. Shapiro (1978) reported that the first-time mothers found labor and delivery so fatiguing and stressful that they "distanced" themselves from the experience, were numb or in shock, or were simply worn out. They felt a discontinuity between the pregnancy and the birth.

In contrast, the second-time mothers, regardless of medication, said that they were more able to attend to and enjoy the experience and felt more available to make contact with their infants moments after birth. In general, the new mothers felt that the labor and delivery experience marked both a painful separation from the pregnancy and the infant within themselves and a new kind of attachment to the infant outside themselves. This pattern was particularly true for nursing mothers. Incidentally, those women who had difficulty breast feeding reported not being well taken care of and helped by their own mothers when they were children. The second-time mothers breezed in and out of the hospital and saw the period as a brief respite, followed by "business as usual." They also were more able to consider their own needs for rest and solitude and were less likely to want to room in with or to spend all their time with their babies.

The Mothering "Instinct"

Are women biologically primed for motherhood? Do they have built-in mechanisms that make them more natural or more desirable parents than are men? If so, at what point does this priming take place? These questions are central to several current theories. Psychobiologists would answer yes to the first two questions. And most would claim that hormonal mechanisms were involved. Thus, puberty would "turn on" maternal feelings, and menopause would turn them off.

Gutmann (1975) hypothesizes that a more socially derived "parental imperative" pushes men toward stereotypically masculine traits and women toward stereotypically feminine traits—that women become more "maternal" at the end of adolescence, and less "maternal" when their children are grown, at the time of the "empty nest."

A third theoretical perspective is that of social-learning theory, which suggests that both men and women are socialized to an interest in babies when they become parents. They lose this interest when they are no longer parents of babies. Shirley Feldman and Sharon Nash (1978, 1979) devised an ingenious set of experiments at Stanford University to test these hypotheses. In one study, young adults who were either cohabiting, married and childless, pregnant, or parents of infants were confronted with an infant and mother in a waiting room. They were also given some tests involving pictures of people of various ages, including infants.

The results showed marked sex differences. On most measures, women showed much more sensitivity to infants than did men, but this was not true of all women, only those who were themselves mothers of infants. In fact, the pregnant women conspicuously ignored the babies. Fathers of infants were more interested than other men, but tended to focus their interest on their own children. A second study by the same investigators used the same situations and measures, but with older men and women: with parents of adolescents, with empty-nesters, and with grandparents. The grandparents—the only ones who were personally involved with babies—were much more "tuned in" to the babies in the waiting room.

Essentially, neither the sociobiological nor the parental-imperative theory was confirmed. However, the grandfathers' behavior is what Gutmann would predict. The social-learning theory is the closest to explaining the mothering effect in the study. Having a baby makes one interested in babies. It makes women interested in all babies, but men, apparently, only become interested in their own. This difference is harder to explain than is the "simple" increase of interest.

Fathering

Complicated as the mother/child relationship is, the father/child one may be even more so. Many people believe that fathering is at best an indirect activity, that a father's main function is to support the mother economically and emotionally so that she can carry on her job of bearing and raising children. There are, however, direct functions in the fathering role, even at its beginning.

For those who look to primate behavior for clues or support for human behavior, it should be noted that there is wide diversity in the behavior of adult primate males toward the young. Behavior can range from extreme hostility to extreme nurturance (Mitchell, 1969). Pleck (1975) concludes that, although hormones may facilitate the development of parental behaviors (presumably only in mothers), such behaviors can also develop in the absence of hormones, even if more slowly.

Observers of couples during pregnancy have not noticed much difference between the attitudes of the father-to-be and the mother-to-be toward the coming event (Soule, 1974). In general, the 67 husbands studied by Yarrow, Waxler, and Scott (1971) were less ambivalent about the pregnancy than were their wives, and they anticipated fewer life changes in the immediate future. In a way, this expectation was realistic. The ten first-time fathers studied by Shapiro (1978) felt intensified financial pressure, but it was their wives who made drastic lifestyle changes.

First-time fathers described themselves as elated during and after the first birth. Those going through a second birth were still pleased, but not as emotionally involved. After the first birth, they said that they had felt physically excluded during the pregnancy. They enjoyed the moment of birth because the baby became directly available to them.

There is no evidence, incidentally, that the presence of the father at birth facilitates father/infant bonding (Greenberg & Morris, 1974). Some men who participated at the births did not develop strong attachment to the babies; others did. The fathers in Shapiro's sample had different responses to their wives' efforts to exclude them from the care of the newborns. Some were relieved, some withdrew from the scene altogether, some were angry, and some actively competed for contact with their babies. Yet most fathers felt much more removed from their babies' crying and were able to tune it out or ask their wives to do something about it. Not until the second month did most fathers report feeling "hooked" on parenting. At this time, they spent more and more time with their infants, primarily in play.

A series of studies by Parke and his colleagues (Parke & O'Leary, 1975; Parke & Sawin, 1975) found that both first-time mothers and first-time fathers were eager to hold and interact with their newborn babies. The one notable difference was that fathers did not smile at their babies as much as mothers did. Also, most infants form relationships with both parents at about the same time (Lamb, 1978), although they show clear preference for their mothers at about one year of age.

An interesting indirect effect of fathers was observed by Parke and O'Leary. Mothers seemed more interested in their babies when the fathers were around. This pattern was particularly true for mothers of boys, who touched them much more when the fathers were there. Some of these research findings on fathers' influence in infancy may, of course, be a cohort effect, influenced by the movement toward joint parenting. When men try to participate in family work, they are more likely to accept child-care responsibilities than other household work (Pleck, 1975).

A study of the importance of parenting to a group of fathers (Heath, 1978) found that less than half of the fathers showed very strong parenting desires or effects. Those who were affected by becoming fathers were described as better adjusted and more mature adults. H. Feldman (1971) reported that men said becoming fathers had made them less selfish. It may be that the age and maturational point at which a man becomes a father are more important to his reaction than they are for the mother. As noted earlier, the high school fathers in De Lissovoy's (1973) study seemed to remain boys, busy at school and with friends. Nydegger (1973) reported from a study of older first-time fathers that "late fathers are great fathers." They tended to be less "physical" but more involved and concerned.

Even though both first-time mothers and first-time fathers are eager to hold and interact with their new babies, according to Parke and O'Leary (1975), mothers are far more likely to feed the babies, even if they are bottle-feeding. And mothers are more likely to assume all the other work, too. Shapiro's first-time mothers were highly sensitized to the babies' cries. During the first month, at least, the mothers felt that crying put a demand on them and indicated that they were not sufficiently competent. Feldman's (1971) longitudinal data show that those couples that said their babies brought them closer together were the ones who at one month had been able to handle the crying or not feel threatened if they could not stop it. They were also likely to feed the children according to the children's needs instead of their own. Babies who cry less and smile more, who respond nicely to cuddling, and who coo on schedule are more likely to induce mothers' feelings of well-being and competence than are babies who are fretful, ill, or developing poorly (Robson & Moss, 1970).

The way fathers play with their children tends to be different from the way mothers play (Lamb & Lamb, 1976). Fathers, particularly young ones, are more vigorous and use unusual and unpredictable movements. Babies enjoy playing with their fathers more than with their mothers.

After the child is about 1 year of age, fathers tend to play mostly with their sons. Much of the sons' sex-role modeling, however, depends on the way mothers picture fathers to their sons, particularly if the father is not around much. There is a difference between saying "Daddy is away on a trip, but he misses you" and "You behave just like your father!" (Lewis & Feiring, 1978). Fathers' absence, which used to be considered harmful to sons, may sometimes lead to greater cognitive development. Or maybe the fathers who are away more are brighter and have brighter children. Cognitive distancing, considered a sign of more analytic thinking, is more common in middle-class families. According to Sigel (1970), such distancing results from intermittent object presence. Brooks and Lewis (1981) found that infants label pictures of their fathers earlier than they label pictures of their mothers, just as they say "Daddy" before they say "Mommy."

Late fathers—those whose first children are born when they are about 40—tend to remain involved with their babies longer than do young fathers, perhaps partly because of greater economic security. They see their role as a model and a transmitter of qualities they value, and they are more dispassionate, objective, and accepting of differences. Early fathers are more likely to see their role as a teacher of skills, a problem solver, or a buddy (Nydegger, 1973).

The effects of education and social class are marked in fathering, as they are in mothering. Lower-status fathers are perhaps less involved. Having a child may be seen as a sign of potency, and the duties of a father may be seen as symbols of physical security. Although there has been some cultural shift away from paternal authoritarianism, lower-class fathers are still likely to follow this pattern. Furthermore, Veroff and Feld (1970) believe that the less education a father has, the earlier his discomfort with fathering, because his child will find out earlier that he has lower status than do other people the child meets. In this respect, college-educated fathers are better off. Grade school-educated fathers become uncomfortable when their children are in grade school, high school-educated fathers when their children are adolescents, and college-educated fathers when their children are grown.

Parents of Older Children

Parents of older children often express negative feelings toward schools and teachers (Klein & Ross, 1958), presumably because they feel rivalry with them, analogous to the effect noticed by Veroff and Feld (1970).

Since in most American families mothers are the primary child rearers, even if they are employed, their own development during the years of active mothering should be heavily influenced by the development of their children. To a lesser extent, this should be true of fathers also. A few writers in the field say this, but so far the research to back up these assumptions is almost nonexistent. Developmental psychologists have been turning their attention to parent/infant interactions that give equal attention to the behavior and feelings of mother, father, and infant, but once the child is 4 or 5 years old, and particularly once the child starts kindergarten, parents are ignored or treated as mechanisms for producing the children being studied. Questions are phrased in terms of the relative influence of authoritarian versus democratic practices on the child's cognitive development, for example, rather than in terms of the effect, say, of the child's cognitive development on parental feelings.

Several themes can be found in the current research on this topic. The first is the concerns of parents—mostly mothers—as a function of a child's progress through the years of childhood. An early study (Klein & Ross, 1958) reported that mothers' concerns changed over the weeks before and after their oldest child entered kindergarten—a turning point acknowledged as one of the most significant in parental feelings as well as family interactions. Before school began, mothers said their chief worry was about the child's safety, to and from school and in school. Later, they worried about whether they had been good parents, whether the teachers would see that they had not "done their job" well. From these feelings, an adversary relationship between teacher and parent is likely to emerge. Teachers often "get their kicks" from feeling that they can undo the errors of the parents or improve upon their upbringing; parents feel that the teachers are trying to take their children away. This is not helped by the children's coming home with stories in which the teachers are clearly cast as the authority figures, a role once monopolized by the parents. About this time, mothers worry about getting the children to school on time, seeing that they do their homework, and at the same time, seeing that they get enough sleep. New family interaction patterns result, with more input from the children.

Veroff and Feld's (1970) survey of parental attitudes showed mothers feeling most negative before the children started school. They felt particularly restricted in their own lives at this time. However, they said they had the most child-rearing problems when the children were of school age. This was even more true for fathers. Overall, one-fourth of parents made negative statements about preschoolers and one-fourth about adolescents.

A second theme deals with communication patterns, primarily with preschool children (Schmidt & Hore, 1970). For example, there is more physical contact between parents and children of low socioeconomic status (SES). "Looking at" was more common in high SES families; children's looks toward parents were less reciprocated by parents in low than in higher SES families. A different kind of study of parental responsiveness (Yarrow, Waxler, & Scott, 1971) reported that parents returned to interact again with those children who had responded more in previous interactions.

The sex of the child affects parent/child interactions. Rothbart and Maccoby (1966), for example, found that parents are more permissive toward children of the opposite sex—mothers to sons and fathers to daughters. There has recently been much interest on the part of developmentalists in the subject of fathering. Lamb and Lamb (1976) conducted one of the leading investigations in this field. One of their observations is that mother/child interactions are more dyadic than father/child. Unless the father is a primary caretaker, his interactions with his child or children are embedded in the network of all family relations, and his role is often defined by the mother.

Finally, much of parents' social life is determined by their parenthood. Their participation in voluntary organizations such as PTA and Scouts, for example—prominent during the primary grade years and adolescence—form a large part of their social or community activities (Babchuck & Booth, 1969) and lead to formation of many of their friendships.

Adolescents are notably difficult for their parents. They interfere with parents' privacy (Hoffman & Manis, 1978). They stay up later at night, join their parents' conversations, and are attuned to their parents' sexuality. They seem to take over the house. The middle-aged mothers in the San Francisco study (Lowenthal et al., 1975) mentioned conflict over tidiness, study habits, communication, and lackadaisical attitudes. The same parents who complained also praised, however. And very few parents would ever consider separating from their children, even their adolescent children. Both parents and adolescent children, in fact, will go to great lengths to maintain their family ties. Hagestad (1981) found the use of "demilitarized zones"—pacts concerning what *not* to talk about. Troll (1972) observed an analogous strategy of being careful about what they fight over. Both college students and their parents said they fought over hairstyles and clothes—relatively trivial issues—but not over serious moral or core values.

Often the demands and burdens of child rearing are so immediate and overwhelming that mothers do not look ahead to their inevitable ending. Most women who are approaching the "empty nest," however, do not view it as a disaster. They are more inclined to look forward to greater freedom and a new phase of life. Anyway, mothering rarely ends with the departure of the children from the home. For most, ties continue throughout life.

Parents of Adults

Most studies have found that more than 80% of present-day middle-aged and older people who have ever married have living children (for example, see Murray, 1973). It is intriguing to realize that about 10% of those over age 65 also have children who are over 65.

Parents are supposed to "launch" children when they are through raising them. In our society, this time comes when children complete their education or training for economic self-sufficiency. Working-class families generally expect their children to leave when they finish high school, middle-class families when they finish college or sometimes graduate or professional school. According to nuclear-family norms, parental cords should then be cut, and only formal relations should continue.

These expectations seem to be more norm than reality, however. Ten years ago, more than half of American young adults between 18 and 25 who were not married lived with their parents. This figure fluctuates with economic conditions, which either permit or disallow separate households.

In one study, of rural Pennsylvania families, both mothers and fathers reported a mixture of loss and gain in launching their children (Barber, 1978). The mothers tended to be more extreme, some reporting more loss than did any men and some reporting more gain.

The gain was an increased sense of personal freedom and relief from parental responsibilities. The loss of the children in the home was often exacerbated by concurrent biological changes (menopause for women) and career changes (reported more by men). Women tended to have anticipated this event more than did men and thus to be better prepared. Some men were faced with the independence of their children just when they were ready to get close to them.

Barber's sample may not represent the majority of launching parents. A national survey (Borland, 1979) found no evidence for the idea that the empty nest was a crisis or even a time of loss. Other research (Hagestad & Snow, 1977) reports that most parents interviewed saw this event as a distinct gain. They gained freedom, and they also gained a new set of resource people: their children. This latter gain was different for mothers and fathers and different for sons and daughters. As with most findings, the mother/daughter dyad was unique in many ways.

Some research has suggested that the departure of the children from the home (the empty nest) does not seem to affect fathers to the same extent that it affects mothers. However, Lurie (1972) points out that the joys as well as the difficulties of parenthood reside in interaction with children. When the children have left home and founded their own families, fathers find less conflict with them, of course. But they also derive less pleasure from them.

The oldest group of fathers in the San Francisco study (Lowenthal et al., 1975) expressed as much concern over their sons as did the oldest mothers. Of course, mothers also were concerned about their daughters. Curiously, middle-aged women were not as pleased with their mothers as they were with their fathers.

Because adult-parent/adult-child interaction appears to be carried on more through the female linkage than through the male, the father of adult children may assume an even more peripheral role than he had when his children were small.

An ongoing study of fathers aged 45 to 80 (Nydegger & Mitteness, 1979) shows developmental changes in fathering even after their children become adults. According to the investigators, these changes are transformations, rather than losses. The number of functions fathers perform drops from eight or nine when their children are preadolescents to one or two when they are adults. No new functions are added. The first function to drop out is authority, followed by protecting, teaching, providing, and last, if at all, counseling. The one function that remains, and that is developed, is friendship. These findings thus are in agreement with those of Hagestad and Snow (1977), whose middle-aged women respondents said their daughters had become their friends.

Three-fourths of the mothers and one-third of the fathers interviewed by Hagestad and Snow admitted that their children had tried to change them in some way, with at least partial success. Mothers reported influence in activities outside the home—in work, education, or leisure. In fact, several mothers reported that their children had been a major influence in the mothers' returning to work or to school. Fathers were influenced in views on current issues and also on improving their physical appearance. One father said "You know, not infrequently, I find myself in situations where I ask myself how Steve might handle it if he were me" (Hagestad & Snow, 1977, p. 4). In general, mothers were more open to being influenced than were fathers. Perhaps mothers had stronger emotional ties with their children. Although mothers were influenced more and had more intense interactions with their children, there was no sex difference in support received from children.

The mother/daughter dyad was perceived by Hagestad and Snow (1977) as the most balanced or reciprocal. The father/daughter dyad was seen as the most imbalanced, with the daughter giving much more than receiving. Mothers and daughters also saw their relationships in the same way. Their consensus was stronger than for other parent/child dyads. Practically all the mothers and fathers felt that their now adult children were sensitive to their feelings and moods. However, mothers were about three times more likely to discuss personal problems with children than were fathers.

Intense feelings, on the part of both parents and children, can continue to swing back and forth if grown children continue to live at home. "Although years of separate residence and greater self-knowledge may erase some of the minor difficulties and blunt the edge of some of the major ones," observe Hess and Waring (1978), "struggles for control, patterns of blaming, disappointments about achievement and such, may linger to undermine the possibility of a comfortable relationship between parents and children in the later years" (p. 251).

Times of crisis can reawaken conflict. One might say there is a continual push and pull of attachments throughout life. Most middle-aged and older parents admit they prefer "intimacy at a distance." Their feelings of closeness carry with them a need for some separateness.

Although friends sometimes substitute for lost siblings, they rarely substitute for missing children (Rosow, 1967). The reciprocal is also true. Dobrof and Litwak (1977) found that adult children who had placed their parents in nursing homes felt strained, guilty, and bereaved. Such a decision represents a crisis in the family (Tobin & Kulys, 1979) and reawakens many old issues. It is not uncommon for the sibling who has been least loved by the parent to emerge as the caretaker because of that sibling's wish to try for that love one more time, even at the cost of much sacrifice.

Mothers and Daughters

Allied to the female linkage of family household units is the preeminence of the mother/daughter dyad throughout life, particularly throughout adult life. We have noted that mothers find it easier to handle infant daughters than infant sons—but that daughters are more likely to achieve if mothers are more demanding and punitive. As children, daughters are kept closer to home and mother; as adults, daughters are more likely to live closer to mothers, to visit them more frequently, and to exchange help with them more frequently than sons. It is debatable whether daughters are more like their mothers than their fathers or more like their mothers than sons are (Troll, Neugarten, & Kraines, 1969; Troll & Bengtson, 1982), but, as adults, most studies show that they report more attachment to each other than to fathers or than sons do to mothers (O. Haller, 1982; Walker, Thompson, & Morgan, 1982). A book called *My Mother, Myself* (Friday, 1981) made the bestseller lists and evoked much discussion among women, both professionals and women at large.

Recent research has been pointing to the corollaries of parent/child closeness, and they are not all positive, just as close relationships in general can be either love or hate, shifting from one to the other over time. Hagestad (1977) found that middle-aged mothers expected a lot from their young adult daughters, but usually gave them no credit when they fulfilled these expectations. The same mothers expected little from their sons and were lavish with praise when they did something for them. A study of the feelings of gerontologists toward their aging parents (Turner & Huyck, 1982) reported that the women were more bothered and upset by their parents, more resentful, and less satisfied with the relationship than were the men. (Most of the old parents were mothers.) More than 50% of the female respondents complained. One-third of the women further described their mothers as critical, controlling, or demanding. At the same time, they also noted that their mother's love and affection was the most rewarding part of the relationship.

Two other variables have been investigated, and for both the factor of age is an intervening variable, suggesting that mother/daughter relationships, at least in some respects, fluctuate over the life span. Some investigators find that daughters become close to their mothers again after they are married and themselves mothers, but that the early years of independence are accompanied by distancing from mothers (Bengtson & Black, 1973; Baruch & Barnett, 1980). Others, however (O. Haller, 1982; Walker & Thompson, 1983), find that unmarried young women are closer to their mothers than those who are married or married with children. The marital status of older women, however, does not seem to make a difference in either generation.

Mothers and daughters give each other lots of help of different kinds (Troll, Miller, & Atchley, 1979), but this flow of help is not always balanced. When young women get more help from their mothers than they give, relationships are less intimate than when aid is balanced. But the reciprocal is not true. When middle-aged daughters give lots of help to their sick old mothers, neither they nor their mothers report less attachment (Walker, Thompson, & Morgan, 1982).

Social Class and Ethnicity

Patterns of child rearing vary among different social classes. But what is middle-class behavior in one era may become working-class behavior later. Less educated mothers feel particularly negative about their parental role. They are less likely to have planned their maternity, are more often raising their children without a husband, and are likely to have more children than they want. Yet college-educated mothers don't come off much better, for they have higher standards for achievement all around. They must be perfect mothers, and their children must be outstanding children.

Variations among Black, Anglo, and Hispanic groups in the United States complicate the social-class patterns to which they are tied. More middle-class Black and Hispanic families live in separate dwellings and provide help down the generational line than do lower-class and poorer families (Jackson, 1977; Cantor, 1977). Furthermore, the more "manual" the work done by the Black family, the stronger its female generational linkage. What poorer Black families can provide for their young-adult children, such as more education, more often goes to daughters than to sons. Cantor's study of New York City elderly found that the Spanish were the most likely to have ongoing contact with at least one child, as compared with White and Black residents. A smaller study of Hispanic families living in Kansas (Bastida, 1978) used more dis-criminative measures of ethnicity. This study found that more "ethnic" fam-ilies—those with no intermarriage, who spoke Spanish, who shared values, and so on—were most likely to maintain cross-generational association. It is interesting to note, however, that almost none of these families lived in joint households. In the absence of ill health and poverty, the American pattern of independent households prevails. It also mattered which sex had married out-side the group: if women did, there was less change in family behavior than if men did.

Grandparenting

The word *grandparent* suggests an old person. Yet many grandparents are not old; and the important information about old people is not usually that they are grandparents.

Grandparenting has become a phenomenon of middle age rather than of old age. Earlier marriage, earlier childbirth, and longer life expectancy over several cohorts have produced a generation of grandparents as young as their 40s. The increase in teenage parenting has made many people in their 30s grandparents as well. These grandparents, because their children tended to be closely spaced, are truly grandparents in identity. They are not, at the same time, parents of young children. The increasing number of families that have three, four, and even five generations has made many grandparents the second or third generation in the family, rather than the first. That is, they are not the oldest living generation. Furthermore, grandmothers as well as grandfathers now tend to be employed. The rocking-chair image is obsolete, and its dis-appearance may have far-reaching consequences for child and adult sociali-zation as well as family interaction. A woman of 50 or 60 can be caring for an elderly mother of 70 or 80 and can simultaneously be involved with her children and grandchildren. She is bound to be divided in her loyalties toward the various generations in her family.

Four general conclusions can be drawn from recent reviews of the literature on grandparenting—as distinct from that on aged family members:

1. Grandparents are not absent from central family dynamics, but often play an important part in them, even though they usually play a secondary role to the parents;

2. Grandparental interactions and roles are diverse—much more diverse than parental ones—varying in part with social class, ethnicity, and sex, but largely, it seems, with individual feelings, preferences, and life circumstances;

3. Developmental status of both grandchild and grandparent influence their interactions and their reciprocal feelings;

4. The most important role of the grandparents may be that of maintaining the family system as a whole.

From deeply and heavily involved grandparents at one extreme to minimally involved ones at the other, the importance of grandparents in family functioning is beginning to be recognized. Although their influence is not always seen as beneficial by some theorists, there is increasing evidence that grandparents play an important role in promoting the well-being of one-parent child-rearing units, particularly those of teenage mothers (see review by Tinsley & Parke, 1983). Similarly, Hetherington's study of divorce (Hetherington, Cox, & Cox, 1976), mentioned earlier, found that the contributions of grandparents were highly related to the quality of the mother/child relationship in that majority of cases in which mothers were the primary child rearers.

Grandparental influence is more probable today because increases in life expectancy produce more generational overlaps between younger and older generations in the family. Grandmothers in particular, can see their grandchildren develop well into their adult years. Reciprocally, most young children can get to know their grandparents and even great-grandparents.

Not only is contact constant in most families, but reciprocity of help and services is, too. Few grandparents wish to return to parenting with their grandchildren (see Lopata, 1973; Cohler & Grunebaum, 1981), but they do remain alert to what goes on. If they think all is well, they prefer to remain formal or distant or indulgent grandparents, visiting their children and grandchildren as one part of their regular life activities, but otherwise enjoying their own life. It is more interesting to be with their peers, who are likely to share more recreational interests, than helping out with needy children who remind them of their lack of success in parenting. It is nice to be free of worry about the adequacy of the socialization of their descendants and the "carrying on of the torch." If there is trouble, however, they give up much of their personal, nonfamily life to meet the needs of the family. This means double suffering for them—deprivation as well as concern.

In my ongoing three-generational research, I have found that grandparents refer spontaneously to their grandchildren 27% of the time but grandchildren refer to their grandparents only 10% of the time. One interpretation of this difference may be that grandparents monitor the status of their grand-children more than grandchildren monitor their grandparents.

That grandparenting is not a renewal of parenting undertaken by empty and possessive elders is seen in the contingent nature of the relationship. Both Cumming and Henry (1961) and Lopata (1973) have stressed this point: grandparents don't want to start over as parents of young children. Gilford and Black (1972), analyzing the University of Southern California's three-generation sample, found that grandparent/grandchild interactions and feelings depended upon the attitudes of the parents toward their own parents. Hagestad and Speicher (1981) found that the middle generation of parents remain as mediators of the older and younger generation's interactions even when the grandchildren are adults. In other words, there is replication of the "lineage bridge" phenomenon seen by Hill and his colleagues in their Minneapolis study (Hill et al., 1970).

Diversity

It is often assumed that grandparenting is a role-less role because there are no overtly prescribed functions. Parents of young children generally know what is expected of them in raising the children; grandparents do not, at least not in the same way. The diffuseness of their script can be seen in the wide diversity of grandparenting styles reported by most observers since the now classic study of Neugarten and Weinstein (1964). Efforts to categorize this wide array of styles and behaviors are reflected in the five styles noted by Neugarten and Weinstein: formal, fun seekers, surrogate parents, reservoirs of family wisdom, and distant figures. A four-part typology is used by Wood and Robertson (1976), based on the two dimensions of personal orientation toward grandparenting and conception of the social or normative meanings attached to grandparenthood. Their four resultant types are: remote, symbolic, individualized, and apportioned. More recently, Kivnick (1981) developed a third typology, using five categories: centrality, valued elder, immortality through clan, reinvolvement with personal past, and indulgence.

So far, no systematic study has been made of the relationship between amount of involvement and such external variables as social class and ethnicity. In general, of course, family studies have found that poverty and ethnic- or linguistic-minority status are associated with clumping of relatives, either under one roof or in close geographic proximity. The increase in the number of grandparents living in independent households during the 1960s and 1970s, frequently interpreted as evidence for the breakdown of the family, is probably more a sign of economic affluence.

Developmental Issues

When we consider that the ages of grandparents may be anywhere between 30 and 120 years and of grandchildren anywhere from birth to 80 years, we realize that the respective ages of members of the two generations must be significant in their relationship. Although chronological age per se is a treacherous and inadequate index of developmental status, there can be no question but that there are wide variations in development in all generations. Some grandparents are vigorous, youthful adults, but some are feeble and badly in need of help themselves. Some seek lots of excitement and stimulation in their life; others want a quiet, predictable routine. Conversely, some grandchildren need infinite nurturance and protection, while others are ready to move out into heady encounters with the world outside the family. Still others may be settled into the responsibilities and restrictions of raising their own young.

These gross developmental differences are reflected in wide differences in styles of grandparenting, as well as in the kind of grandparents their grandchildren want. Neugarten and Weinstein (1964), for example, found that younger grandparents had more diverse styles than did older ones. Some young grandparents were fun seekers, and some were distant figures; that is, some enjoyed playing with their grandchildren, and some sought enjoyment in other spheres. Older grandparents, though, were almost always formal and distant, perhaps absorbed in their own failing health.

In my ongoing three-generational study mentioned earlier, grandparents in their 50s, 60s, and 70s were more likely to say good things about their grandchildren, whereas those in their 40s and 80s were more likely to be critical. It could be the 50-, 60-, and 70-year-olds were much more comfortable about being grandparents than those who felt they were too young or too old (see Neugarten, Moore, & Lowe, 1965, who found clear age designations for when it was appropriate for different life events to occur). Both Kahana and Kahana (1970) and M. Clark (1969) report that younger grandchildren are more appealing to older grandparents. There may be an upper limit to this effect, however, with very old grandparents finding highly active preschoolers a trial.

Children change rapidly and dramatically throughout the first two decades of life. According to Kahana and Kahana (1970)—the only systematic study so far on age differences of grandchildren and their attitudes toward grandparents—children under 10 feel closer to their grandparents than do older children. Their 4- and 5-year-old respondents said they liked their grandparents to be indulgent, the 8- and 9-year-olds liked them to be fun, and children older than that preferred that they keep their distance. The wish for distancing may be temporary, if true, because several studies of young adult grandchildren (for example, Hagestad, 1978; Gilford & Black, 1972; Robertson, 1977) found that all these grandchildren said their grandparents were important to them.

In spite of supposed changes in sex roles, traditional differences do seem to be maintained in grandparenting, as they are in parenting. Hagestad (1978, 1982) found that grandmothers are more likely to have warm relationships with their grandchildren—and their children—than are grandfathers. Further, most of these warm relationships are down the maternal line, the mother/daughter tie being a particularly strong one. Influence of grandparents is not, however, restricted to grandmothers. Neugarten and Weinstein (1964) note that although grandmothers are more likely to be surrogate parents, grandfathers are more likely to be the reservoirs of family wisdom. Hagestad's (1978) respondents, on the other hand, indicated that both grandmothers and grandfathers are reservoirs of family wisdom, but that they operate differently and in different domains. The grandmothers were more generalized in their advice giving, making much less distinction than the grandfathers as to whether they were influencing their granddaughters or their grandsons. The grandfathers usually confined their influencing to grandsons. The topics discussed were also differentiated according to sex. Grandmothers tended to discuss interpersonal and intrapersonal topics: how to relate to others, dating, and the relative importance of family and friends. Grandfathers concentrated on areas outside the family/personality domain: work, education, money, the management of time, and wider social issues.

The possibility of cohort or period changes in sex differences is suggested by the fact that the grandchildren said they did not restrict their influencing attempts or their advice seeking by either subject matter or sex of grandparent. Whether this less traditional sex stereotyping by the grandchildren will stay with them when they become parents and grandparents is yet to be seen.

Laboratory or home observations of family interactions that include grandparents are scarce. In one early study, Scott (1962) watched an interaction sequence among both parents, a teenager, and a grandmother. She reported that the grandmother was not an active participant in the interaction. Field and her colleagues (Stoller & Field, 1981) videotaped interaction sequences in the participants' homes. Their subjects were Black teenage mothers in Florida, their infants, and their mothers. Like Scott, they found that the grandmothers mostly sat back and watched the young mother with her baby.

A different sort of evidence for grandparent involvement is provided by the ingenious research of Feldman and Nash and their colleagues at Stanford University (Feldman & Nash, 1978), mentioned earlier in this chapter. They found that grandmothers of infants were more responsive to the infant in the waiting room than were mothers of adolescent children or "empty-nest" mothers. Grandfathers of infants were more responsive than men in any category except fathers of infants.

Siblings

Most American families over the past century that had children had more than one child. Therefore, 80% of all Americans have at least one brother or sister.

The sibling relationship changes structurally over the years. In childhood it is one of daily contact and the sharing of most experiences. This closeness thins during the school years and adolescence, as siblings begin to have different school and friendship experiences, but they still share home experiences. Separation is most extreme during early adulthood, as each sibling establishes his or her own home. However, many siblings follow parallel paths and find communication easy and meaningful when they do get together. The obligations of caring for aging parents can bring brothers and sisters closer again. But with the death of their parents, further interactions are determined by the siblings' personal preferences, rather than by family ritual or need.

Studies of geographic proximity and frequency of contact between siblings generally show declines over the later years. Rosenberg and Anspach (1973) found that 75% of blue-collar workers in Philadelphia between the ages of 45 and 54 had at least one sibling in the metropolitan area. Of those between 55 and 65, 64% did.

Adams (1968) found, as might be expected, a relation between distance and frequency of contact. Of siblings who lived within 100 miles of each other, 65% visited monthly or oftener, and 69% of those in the same city saw each other at least weekly. Rosenberg and Anspach had similar results. Of those who had siblings in the greater Philadelphia area, 68% in the 45–54 age range had seen each other in the week preceding the interview, 58% in the 55–64 age range, and 47% of those over 65. Cicirelli (1980b) found that siblings who neither visited nor telephoned each other did keep in touch by writing letters. Only a few of his 300 respondents had actually lost touch with siblings.

What we know about relationships between siblings in childhood points to two contradictory attributes: solidarity and rivalry. Perhaps all solidarity among people has a rivalry component, and all rivalry a solidarity component. And perhaps nowhere is the contradiction so intense as between siblings. "Loving" 2- and 3-year-olds go about planning the destruction of a newborn sibling with remarkable ingenuity. And 20- and 30-year-olds may be impelled to succeed in the world not so much because of parents' expectations as because of a desire to outdo siblings.

There may be some basis for these childhood resentments, as shown by data on differential treatment in childhood according to birth order. Mothers show more affection and approval toward first-born children and show more restrictiveness and severity to later-borns. First-born children, however, are treated as if they were older than their chronological age; they are expected to be more mature and to reach higher goals. College students who were oldest children admitted to being bossy. And those who were younger children said they tended to appeal for help against their older siblings to parents and other older siblings (Sutton-Smith & Rosenberg, 1970).

In their study of 64 adult siblings, Bossard and Boll (1956) reported that rivalry and conflict were minimal and that loyalty to each other was more important. Their respondents remembered being fairer to each other when they were children than their parents had been to them. In the large families that constituted their sample, the emphasis was on sacrifice—on the group rather than on the self.

A general conclusion from most studies is that the following family-structure variables are the most important: (1) ages of all the siblings, as well as the number of years between them; (2) sex; (3) number of children in the family; and (4) strength of the parental dyadic bond (Schvanaveldt & Ihinger, 1979).

Cicirelli (1980b) concludes that when adults first leave their parents' home, they retain earlier feelings toward siblings. His study of college women (Cicirelli, 1980a) showed strong positive feelings for at least one sibling. Their feelings about their "closest" siblings were as strong as those toward their mothers, and they were closer to their closest siblings than they were to their fathers. Later-born women felt closer to their siblings than did earlier-born women. "Closest" siblings were likely to be those near them in age.

In another study, Cicirelli (1979) found that 65% of older people felt "close" or "extremely close" to the siblings with whom they had the most contact. Only 5% said they did not feel close to any sibling. Another study of older people (Allan, 1977) found that, even when contact was limited, involvement with siblings continued. They kept in touch with each other's location, activities, and circumstances, even if the information was gained indirectly through the family network in some cases. When negative feelings toward siblings' spouses kept them from closer interaction, they usually managed to maintain some kind of relationship. Frequent close companionship was more common among working-class families than among middle-class families. The general finding that working-class families live closer to each other and have fewer outside social contacts may apply here.

Adams's (1968) North Carolina respondents said they felt even closer to siblings in adulthood than they had in childhood. Adult-sibling solidarity seems to be enhanced by similarity of interests, residential proximity, common obligations to aging parents, and the absence of invidious comparisons (Aldous, 1978). Apparently living near each other is a necessary though not sufficient requirement for sibling closeness, as in grandparent/grandchild relations. The geographic requirement held least for sisters, who tended to keep in touch by letter even when they did not live near each other. Of Adams's respondents, 70% said they kept in touch with their brothers and sisters because they enjoyed the contact. Family ritual occasions such as holidays, birthdays, weddings, and so on help to maintain sibling contact. The fact that one sibling may "make good," and another may not, does not irrevocably cut their ties. The successful one enjoys his or her success more through comparison with a less successful brother or sister; the less successful ones may bolster their pride by "name dropping."

The death of parents can mark the breakup of sibling ties. Old rivalries can come to the fore as siblings settle parents' financial affairs. Common concerns are removed, too. Using age as a measure with a working-class sample, Rosenberg and Anspach (1973) reported that two-thirds of people under 55 stayed in touch with siblings in the area but only half of those over 55 did. Older sisters sometimes took over the kin-keeping functions of their mothers and kept the family together by communicating with all brothers and sisters and maintaining ritual family get-togethers.

As in other family interactions, the female linkage is prominent among siblings. Most studies find the closest bonds between sisters, next between brothers and sisters, and least between brothers.

Lowenthal and her associates (1975) found that older respondents said they liked their cross-sex siblings more than did the younger ones. Even though sisters were close, they also were most rivalrous. Closeness and rivalry are not mutually exclusive. There can be frequent quarrels about the care of aged parents. Relationships can remain stable over many years of minimal communication but can change when interaction becomes vigorous again, as often occurs when siblings must cooperate to deal with aging parents.

There is a good deal of mutual assistance among siblings (Adams, 1968), although nowhere near as much as between parents and children: 20% as compared with 80%. Lopata (1973) describes the intermittent and temporary nature of sibling assistance in the case of widowhood. A brother may come to help with funeral and financial arrangements. A sister may come to console and help with housework and child care. But both return to their own homes as soon as they can.

Aldous (1978) notes that unmarried siblings may move near each other or may even continue to share the family home after their parents die. Their married siblings, particularly sisters, often try to help them. Shanas and her associates (1968) found that those who have never had children are more likely to give than to get. They are the generous bachelor uncles or aunts who contribute gifts, educational funds, and so forth.

In Black families, according to Hays and Mindel (1973), kinship systems are organized around siblings and other relatives more than around the parent/child relationship. At the present early stage of research on Black family relationships, this finding is hard to interpret. How much it derives from remnants of the extended-family cultures of Africa, how much from the large percentage of teenage unwed mothers and consequent child rearing by grandparents and aunts, and how much from as yet unknown causes we are in no position to judge (Staples & Mirandé, 1980).

Other Kin

The same principles that operate with respect to siblings apply to other collateral kin such as cousins, aunts, uncles, nieces, and nephews. First, these relatives serve as a reservoir from which replacement and substitutions for missing or lost closer kin can be obtained. Second, ties are based on individual characteristics more than on degree of kinship. The scattered bits of research about such kin seldom ask about "favorite cousin" or "favorite uncle or niece." Instead, they ask about "best-known cousin" (Adams, 1968); or a male cousin, or mother's oldest brother, or father's oldest brother (Klatsky, 1972); or "extended family" (Brown, 1974), to cite a few examples.

In general, extended kin have served an important function in the migration history of our country. Most migrants, whether from across the oceans or out on the farm, moved toward areas where other relatives had already settled (Hareven, 1976).

For most people, extended kin become temporarily important at family ritual occasions such as weddings, funerals, reunions, and some holidays. The symbolic significance of such events can override interpersonal feelings, which are likely to depend on personal characteristics and history. Positional symbolic representation can be in terms of a particular family line ("one of the Smiths") or generation ("my grandmother's cousin"). Relatives may be invited to a wedding to represent the bridegroom's paternal family or the oldest living generation. When grandparents die, great-aunts or great-uncles are invited to give the family a more rounded presence, even if they have not been included for many years.

Involvement with extended kin can sometimes be overwhelming. For example, Cohler (1979) found that Polish-American and Italian-American women, particularly those who are middle-aged and older, have such heavy involvement and such close contact with many relatives that they are "at risk." It is easy for them to become overwhelmed by demands. Hess and Waring (1978) say that too much involvement with family is as bad as too little.

Middle-class people visit their distant relatives (in kinship terms) more than working-class people do, if geographic distance is controlled. Middle-class kin also tend to be more dispersed geographically than are working-class kin. Thus, middle-class families maintain contact in spite of greater distances.

In-Laws

Limited attention has been devoted to the in-law relationship in the later part of the family life cycle. Most writers refer only to the in-law problems of young married couples; few note the adjustment problems of middle-aged parents and even grandparents to the new families introduced into kin networks by each new marriage in the family. One study of in-law relationships (Duvall, 1954) found that wives reported that they had the most problems with mothers-in-law and the second most problems with sisters-in-law.

Adams (1968) found that middle-class wives wrote to both sets of parents, while working-class wives concentrated on their own kin. Turner (Troll & Turner, 1979) found that her female college students were writing to their lovers' parents and had taken over the female kin-keeping functions far in advance of marriage, or even when eventual marriage was doubtful.

Summary

Adult development is played out on the family stage. Almost all American adults have a spouse (or ex-spouse), children, and siblings, and many also have grandchildren. Most have living parents and a few, living grandparents. Contrary to popular myths, family relationships and family systems *are* important, and are far from dying out. Some family relationships are old: one has known one's parents, grandparents, and siblings all one's life. Others are created new in adulthood: one must develop relationships with one's spouse, children, and in-laws from scratch. The effects of age at which one marries or becomes a parent are thus easy to understand: the more mature one is at these times, the wiser one's approach.

Sex differences pervade all family relationships, from behavior and meaning in courtship, to household division of labor and role differentiation in marriage, to parent/child and sibling relations, to grandparenting behavior. The choice of a husband is more serious than the choice of a wife. Women—even "liberated" women—are the ones responsible for house and children; if they are employed they are dual-career people. Fathering is less central to men's lives than mothering is to women's. Divorce and widowhood place economic, labor, and emotional burdens upon women, although men may be devastated for a while by the loneliness. The mother/daughter tie is a particularly powerful one throughout life, even though it may be full of conflict at times.

Significant as marriage is for the man and woman involved, becoming parents is even more powerful in changing lifestyle and relationships, particularly for mothers. The focus of the couple shifts to the children, and the "fit" between husband and wife may decrease. It is not clear whether the "empty nest" is the "second honeymoon." Diversity of post-child-rearing patterns probably exists, especially now with the increase in length of this period. Parent/child relations do not end with the adulthood of the younger generation, but continue throughout life, particularly after the younger-generation members become parents or the older-generation members become feeble.

While sex holds first place in the love of newlyweds, it drops in salience as other aspects of the relationship become important. For those couples who continue to enjoy it, though, sex remains a significant marital activity into old age.

Some family relationships of adults attest more to the strength of the family system than to their particular roles. Grandparents are prime examples. They remain central in the lives of their children and grandchildren and help when needed—as with teenage parents or divorced mothers—but are not primary child rearers.

Chapter Six

Development
in the Job World

Kinds of Job Development

Most of our lives are organized by the world of jobs or by our position in that world. Where we live, the kind of home we live in, the kind of clothes we wear, the hours we wake up and go to bed, the kind of food we eat, our friends, our recreation and social life, our participation in organizations, even our self-esteem and health are related to the kind of job we or some member of our immediate family holds.

Adulthood itself is defined by participation in the world of the job. It begins with entry into a first job and ends with retirement from a last job. Both Freud and Erikson recognize the salience of work in their concepts of maturity and mental health. A good man, to Freud, is one who is able to love and to work. For Erikson, the stages of Intimacy and Generativity define adulthood—again, love and work.

From early childhood, we plan the kind of job we are going to hold "when we grow up." We may have many different ideas that fluctuate a great deal before they gradually consolidate into a small number of possibilities that we can try out for size. We are prepared to educate and train ourselves to reach an acceptable level of proficiency for entry into our first job and then "work up" to the top.

But what if we can't get the right first job, the one that leads up the ladder to success? Or what if that job evaporates as the company folds or is absorbed by a larger corporation or moves to another part of the country? What if our skills, which we worked so hard to perfect, become obsolete in ten years as a group of younger people grow up with newer skills, and we are declared outmoded? Or we get bored with doing the same thing all the time and want to try our hand at something new? What if we don't get hired, or we get fired or get lower pay or get subtle kinds of unpleasant treatment because we are not the right color, age, or sex? Finally, what do we mean when we talk about development in the job?

It is harder to conceptualize development in work than development in other areas of life, such as intellectual abilities, personality, or the family. An uncomplicated definition would merely refer to any systematic changes with age (Neugarten, 1968). For example, at least from cross-sectional data, job satisfaction increases with age as job mobility decreases with age. We could then say that job development during the adult years consists of settling into a job and growing to enjoy it more (or finding a job that is liked and settling into it). This would be the only kind of development possible in the vast majority of jobs, in which the workers have little autonomy and where their primary motive for working would have to be money.

Another way to define job development is in terms of directional movement along a path. For example, some people—although probably no more than 30% of workers—move up systematically in the status hierarchy of bureaucratic organizations, from a bottom position at the time of entry to a higher position after a suitable number of years. Wilensky (1961) would call this progression an **orderly career.** In some cases, such a progression is simply additive, involving a given number of years at each step in order to qualify for promotion to the next step, as in the army or the civil service. In other cases, a certain amount of qualitative transformation in cognitive or personality structure (see Chapter 2) is expected to take place during the process. The junior executive is supposed to gain in expertise and wisdom as he or she gains experience, thus becoming a different kind of executive, before he or she moves into a senior post.

In the additive (ladder) model, the additions may be steps along a route to a predetermined goal—whether that goal be money, status, or a particular position, such as president of the company or the country. Goals like these are usually extrinsic characteristics of jobs; that is, the actual work done day by day has less meaning than reaching the goal, although this does not mean that the work itself cannot be enjoyed, too. In the transformation model, the focus is more likely to be internal rather than external. There might be stages or sequences along the way instead of rungs on a ladder. Artists or artisans can enjoy this kind of job development, provided they measure progress not quantitatively—for example, so many pictures or books each year—but qualitatively, by improvement in the pictures or books as one follows the other.

All the models described above deal with development of individuals or their products. We might also consider development of the work group or of the productive society. From the time such a group assembles, it can continue to grow, in both complexity and coping power. It can learn to work more smoothly with fewer overt communications and to differentiate into a variety of functional positions that are integrated into a more effective unit. Perhaps, in a society moving toward more rapid job changes to meet changing conditions, the benefits of this kind of production-group development, which can come only with stability over time, are lost.

Most of the empirical and theoretical literature on jobs, work, and careers has been concerned with industrial settings—and with men. Only a few studies have dealt with development in such nonbusiness careers as art, science, homemaking, and the helping professions (for example, H. S. Becker, 1951; Becker, Geer, Hughes, & Strauss, 1961; Henry, Sims, & Spray, 1971; Lopata, 1971; Roe, 1961). And only recently, as more and more women are entering the labor force, are studies of the vocational development of women accumulating (for example, Kanter, 1977).

Most adult men and half of all adult women either have a job or are trying to find one. They are thus technically included in the labor force. A job usually takes a person outside the home, has a regular schedule, involves specified activities, and provides money. If this job is related to the person's training, to previous jobs, and to future anticipated jobs, it can be considered part of a career.

Why People Work

Anyone talking about the subject of working should begin by reading Studs Terkel's charming book called, simply, *Working* (Terkel, 1972). Work, he says, is "a search for daily meaning as well as daily bread, for recognition as well as cash, for astonishment rather than torpor; in short, for a sort of life rather than a Monday through Friday sort of dying. Perhaps immortality, too, is part of the quest" (p. xiii).

Work has different meanings for different people. For some, it may be a source of prestige and social recognition, a basis for self-respect and sense of worth. For others, it is an opportunity for social participation or a way of being of service. For still others, it is enjoyment of the activity for itself or for creative self-expression. Or work may be merely a way to earn a living. There are age differences and age changes in such job orientations. There also seem to be family similarities and lifetime stability in at least some aspects of job orientation.

Baruch, Barnett, and Rivers (1983) differentiate two components of well-being in adults: mastery and pleasure. These components can be met in one or more spheres of life involvement. If one sphere is abundant, it may be sufficient. There are men and women whose job provides both; others whose family provides both. Most people distribute their activity and involvement over several spheres.

Frequent references have been made in this book to the Berkeley and Oakland longitudinal studies. The men and women of the Oakland study were reinterviewed in their 40s, and Glenn Elder (1974) looked particularly at the effect of the Depression upon their later lives. Some of the subjects had experienced considerable deprivation during their teens (the 1930s); others had not. The effect of deprivation on orientation to work in general can be seen in Figure 6-1. The deprived men were compared with the nondeprived men, and with all the women, who were not separated here by early experiences of deprivation. Four arbitrarily chosen spheres were considered: work, family, leisure, and community. Obviously, both sex and early deprivation show enduring effects. First, regardless of deprivation, men in this cohort overwhelmingly chose work as their most preferred activity; many fewer women did. Women overwhelmingly chose family as their most preferred activity. The men who had originally been deprived were much more involved with their families than the nondeprived men, though. The nondeprived men, in fact, were more involved with leisure activities than with family.

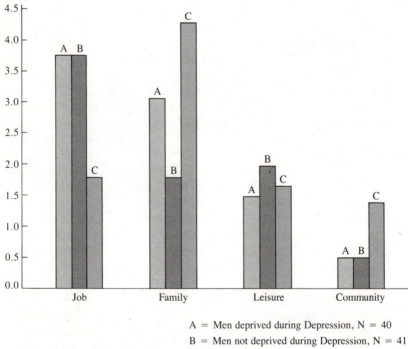

A = Men deprived during Depression, N = 40
B = Men not deprived during Depression, N = 41
C = Women, N = 52

Figure 6-1. Activity preferences of Oakland (California) men and women in their 40s. (Adapted from Elder, 1974, Table 7 and Figure 8.)

Elder's data were collected 20 years ago. Recent studies show shifts in these patterns. Men in general are valuing work less and leisure more; women are approaching the patterns of men. Two studies at the University of Michigan found the former (Veroff, Douvan, & Kulka, 1981; Quinn & Staines, 1979); Baruch, Barnett, and Rivers (1983) report the latter. Veroff and his colleagues studied two large representative national samples, one in 1957, the other in 1976. Their findings about job commitment are shown in Table 6-1. Over this 19-year period, most categories of workers reported less job commitment—more desire to have a different job. Curiously, farmers were most committed in 1957 and increased the most in commitment during this period of time. In 1957, clerical workers wanted to change the most; in 1976, machine operators held this place. Both these categories, incidentally, are low in decision making and high in stress, as will be discussed later.

What we cannot say, because there is no specific research on the subject, is whether this kind of generalized job commitment remains stable over any person's life. There are no longitudinal data available. For achievement motivation, however, both longitudinal and family generational studies show stability over time. In both men and women, achievement striving in adulthood correlated with observed achievement behavior in middle childhood and early adolescence (Kagan & Moss, 1962). In this Fels Research Institute study, achievement behavior was one of the most consistent behaviors over time.

One of the earliest studies of family background and work orientation is that of Reuben Hill and his colleagues in Minneapolis, who studied 100 three-generation families during the late 1950s, each including three sets of couples (Hill et al., 1970). They found that in 47% of the male lineages, grandfather, father, and son all remained in the same general occupation and had the same orientation toward work. The fact that half of these families kept the same kinds of jobs and attitudes toward jobs over the generations during a time of rapid industrial change when youth were supposed to find new paths

Table 6-1. Percent of men who are committed to their present job

Category of present job	1957 survey	1976 survey
Professional	65%	56%
Manager	72	62
Clerical	39	45
Sales	53	56
Skilled trades	55	39
Operatives	55	40
Service	57	52
Laborer	66	41
Farmer	79	87

Adapted from Veroff, Douvan, and Kulka, 1981, Table 6-36.

is remarkable. Two separate studies under my direction found significant correlations between parents and their children in how much they valued achievement (Troll, Neugarten, & Kraines, 1969; Troll & Smith, 1972), again showing family transmission in the work area.

Most studies report sex differences in what people want from their work. Women are seen to be more interested than men in the interpersonal and extrinsic factors of jobs and less interested than men in the status and achievement factors. They are less inclined than men to say that they would continue to work if they were freed from economic necessity; only 57% of the women would work if they did not have to, but 75% of the men would (Crowley, Levitin, & Quinn, 1973).

In the Lowenthal, Thurnher, and Chiriboga study (1975), the working women (lower-middle class) were not highly committed to their work. Getting jobs was for them secondary to their primary activities as wives, mothers, and homemakers. Lillian Rubin (1976) found the same thing when she interviewed working-class women. These women were satisfied with financial rewards that were lower than those of men because they were just adding to their husbands' income in order to maintain their families' lifestyles. They said they would pass up chances for advancement if it meant increased obligations that would drain their energies and leave less for their family roles. They never really tried to succeed in their jobs, and retirement did not have the significance for them that it had for men in the sample. However, remember that these women were part-time, often temporary workers. Those middle-aged women in the same study who had worked steadily for years said that their work *was* important to them. In fact, they wondered if it was more important than it should be.

Although the Fels longitudinal sample showed impressive stability in achievement motivation from childhood to early adulthood, comparison of men's and women's age differences through the adulthood years shows some interesting differences (Troll & Schwartz, in press). Young men, in their teens and 20s, were rated highest in achievement motivation among the men; men in their 30s were somewhat lower, and older men lower yet. Adolescent girls were particularly low, but women in their 20s and 30s were as high as the young men. Older women were more variable. Very high-achieving women, though, were almost as likely to have high-achieving daughters and granddaughters as high-achieving men were to have high-achieving sons and grandsons.

A 20-year longitudinal study of AT&T executives (Bray & Howard, 1983) found that the more successful men, measured by job status level, increased in their need to accomplish difficult tasks and to solve difficult problems, and that this major shift occurred during the first eight years on the job. The success of their early efforts led to increased desire for success. It also led to a gradual move from extrinsic to intrinsic achievement motivations. Kanter (1977) reports similar trends from other studies. When early efforts do not meet with success, however, perhaps because of the luck of early job placements, men with high achievement needs may look to other arenas to satisfy these needs.

Cross-sectional studies have repeatedly found age differences in men's orientation to work. Older men differ from younger ones in wanting to control and manage more and to do their work their own way—to be more independent (Veroff & Feld, 1970; Friedmann & Havighurst, 1954).

Are women working because they need money, or because they are lonely? Are they more concerned about interpersonal relationships than accomplishments? From their survey of the literature, Stein and Bailey (1973) conclude that, in fact, women are as motivated as men to achieve, but that the areas in which they achieve are different. They have a more social pattern of achievement behavior than do men. Furthermore, the reason they direct their achievement behavior to social areas is that they receive more social approval for doing so than if they try to achieve in areas that are classified as masculine. Remember the discussion of achievement in Chapter 4.

Becoming a Worker: Pre-Job Development

The foundations of occupational development, like those of family development, are laid down long before adulthood. Before we start thinking about a choice of vocation, we have a well-established orientation toward the importance of work in life, we know the general kind of work we should aspire to, and we have rehearsed the way we should behave as a worker (see Chapter 4). Furthermore, our sex, social-class background, ethnic identity, and school experiences all have a profound influence on the options available to us in the job market. Some positions require such specific training that they can be filled only by people from particular schools or firms, to which access is regulated. Some jobs are filled only from the lower ranks within an organization, others only from outside an organization. Obviously, we cannot even consider a job unless we know of its existence, and this knowledge may be restricted.

Job preparation and training proceed on many levels. In a broad sense, the whole educational progression from kindergarten on up is a process of vocational selection and training—and not only for middle-class occupations. University curricula are broadening to include specific training for a variety of careers whose preparation was once handled in technical schools or on the job. Many of these new training programs are directed to occupations that did not exist a few years earlier.

Our educational system is our primary occupational training ground, not only developing skills but also separating children according to their future occupational tracks. Johnny becomes recognized as good in mathematics and is encouraged toward scientific occupations. Billy is a "natural leader" and is helped to dream of politics or executive status. George is "good with his hands" and is sent to technical or trade school.

Job Initiation

Not all job selection and training can precede entry into the job world. Inkeles (1968) points out that the family can be of only minimal help in training because children don't always enter the same occupation as their parents—in part because social change makes the parents' occupations obsolete (Toffler, 1970). The school cannot help completely because, in many cases, occupational choice—or job availability—is not determined until the end of schooling. There may also be a lag between training programs and job-market changes. Therefore, the first years in the labor force are typically a time of trial and error for the new worker.

The first year on the job—like the first year of marriage or parenthood—can be seen as a critical period. In some ways, it is a period of initiation, accompanied by fears about one's competence and self-worth and by the use of such coping strategies as rehearsal and strict adherence to rules (Becker, 1964).

Several recent longitudinal investigations of men's occupational development find that the first few years on the job are strategic so far as later job attitudes and behavior are concerned. Elder's (1974) study of the Depression cohort, Bray and Howard's (1983) report on AT&T executives, and Kanter's (1977) study of corporations all find that these first few years can wipe out earlier distinctions, such as economic deprivation, or separate men who started out alike.

In some ways, the process of vocational development could resemble that of family development. In both cases, there would be a matching for maximal fit and a progressive shift from extrinsic to intrinsic criteria. Just as, ideally, the premarital period is the time for preparing oneself and for finding the best-matching spouse, so ideally the period before the first job would involve preparing for and finding the best-matching occupation. Just as the spouse-selection process ideally moves from emphasis on extrinsic criteria such as physical attractiveness and popularity to emphasis on intrinsic criteria such as mutuality of values, backgrounds, and interests, so the job-selection process moves, ideally, from selection on the basis of extrinsic factors such as pay, fringe benefits, and status to selection on the basis of intrinsic factors such as congruence of values, expectations, and performance.

Vocational psychologists such as Roe (1961), Veroff and Feld (1970), and Holland (1973) stress the matching of personality characteristics such as interests, motives, and orientations to analogous characteristics of the job under consideration. Such matching is seen to be a conscious activity prior to job search that is best assisted by vocational counselors trained in the use of a variety of tests and coding devices for assessing personality as well as job characteristics. In Holland's scheme, this kind of conscious matching is seen as appropriate throughout adult life, because of constant change both in workers themselves and in job requirements.

Moving Up

When an acceptable level of proficiency has been reached, individuals are expected to enter their first job and from there "work up," hopefully to the "top." This level of proficiency may be no more than knowing how to carry a load and sign a paycheck. Or it may involve elaborate accumulation of knowledge and skills.

This kind of development may depend on all kinds of informal and subtle in-service training (Becker & Strauss, 1956). Co-workers already on the job may teach new workers some of their trade secrets, but not until they feel the new people can be included in their group. Superiors may serve as sponsors or mentors and may arrange for certain kinds of experiences that will train for what they know will be the next step ahead—a step that they may, in fact, maneuver at the appropriate time.

Kanter (1977) refers to "fast trackers"—workers who are marked out almost at the beginning of their careers for rapid advancement. The opposite are "dead-enders." Female executives interviewed by Henning and Jardim (1976) all reported mentors who were men, incidentally. One must learn the right amount of time to stay at one level and how to grasp opportunities as they arise.

Because the work group is important to how people feel about their jobs—and because people's careers are interdependent—awkward and delicate situations occur when subordinates or colleagues move ahead. Different people can be important at different stages of a career. At one point, age mates are crucial, even if only as competitors. At another time, it is superiors who are most important. Because those who fail usually disappear from the scene, the longer people remain in jobs, the more likely they are to interact only with those who are also succeeding. One effect of length of stay on a job is the formation of a strong and cohesive job culture. In fact, loyalty to such a group can work against job mobility.

When Elder (1974) analyzed the factors that led to occupational status of the men who had gone through the Depression in their adolescence, the most important was access to higher education. Although the most successful members of that cohort were higher in IQ and family status than the less successful, these factors were important primarily because they contributed to educational opportunities.

Kanter (1977) lists three ways in which opportunity can be blocked to produce "dead-enders": being in low-ceiling occupations, failing to reach the high ceiling possible, and taking the wrong route to a high-ceiling job because of poor background. These three ways, she feels, have different consequences for the attitudes of the workers involved. Men in a low-ceiling occupation, because they don't expect to be able to climb, are not generally disaffected and usually turn to other sources of enjoyment in working, such as association with colleagues. Individuals who fail feel very bad and turn for their social life to people outside their organization, who may not know of their job failure. Those who have taken the wrong route are intermediate in disaffection. They tend to turn to subordinates or less advantaged people for social companionship.

Great opportunity, states Kanter, breeds competitiveness, an instrumental orientation toward personal relationships—"using friends"—and being excessively absorbed in work. All these characteristics are noted by Bray and Howard (1983) in successful AT&T executives. Thus, Kanter suggests that too much opportunity may run counter to many human and humane values. It also turns people away from intrinsic enjoyment of their jobs toward an emphasis on extrinsic rewards, thereby making the most successful people more like the least successful in job attitudes.

The importance of social skills and social interaction in getting ahead in the managerial world is also documented by Kanter (1977). British executives spent 80% of their work time talking, with less than a quarter of this making decisions.

Corporations demand from their executives a personal attachment and a generalized, diffuse, unlimited commitment that extend way beyond stated working hours and that include entertaining and being entertained at home as well as outside the home. A survey of sales managers showed that they placed loyalty highest of all their job strengths, much higher than ambition. Frequent geographic transfers that cut down on personal ties and commitments only served to increase such diffuse company loyalty.

An interesting example of transformational job development is described by Henry, Sims, and Spray (1971) in their study of mental-health professionals—psychiatrists, social workers, and clinical psychologists. At some time during their training years and subsequent therapeutic work, they underwent marked changes that turned them all into psychotherapists. This led them to share beliefs and ways of behaving and to share a common ideology that superseded the beliefs of any specific school of psychological thought. Although they started out with very different educational backgrounds, they ended up similar in their use of work and leisure time, in their patterns of interests at work, in their social interactions both at work and at home, in their systems of belief and explanations of behavior, and in the kinds of people they met as patients.

A different kind of development was seen by Kohn and Schooler (1979), who observed that intellectual flexibility led to jobs with substantive complexity, which reciprocally led to greater intellectual flexibility. This is another illustration of positive feedback (in the physics sense), like the one cited in Chapter 5 of well–communicating couples becoming even better and poorly communicating ones becoming worse over time.

There is increasing disparity between men and women as they progress along their career paths. Even if they have been pursuing careers to the same extent, in the course of time men earn higher salaries, reach higher positions, and reach them more easily.

Working Women

Although some see women's employment as a new and remarkable event, it is not. Women have always worked. As the old proverb says, "A woman's work is never done." Women have also worked outside their homes. In fact, in the early years of the Industrial Revolution, whole families worked together in factories—husbands, wives, and children of all ages. Migrant-worker families today still work together in the fields. One of the first acts of the 19th-century Enlightenment movement was to protect children from the exploitation of such work, which led in turn to the privatization of the home and the seclusion of women from what came to be considered the men's world of work. Later, other legislation, protecting women who had to work, also turned into rules to keep women out of "men's jobs" as much as possible. Social policy meant to correct one evil often creates new evils. The significance of women's employment during the 1960s and 1970s was its new meaning, not its existence.

It is worth noting that the labor-force participation rates of White women now approximate the rates for Black women, which historically have always been high (Turner & McCaffrey, 1974). The dramatic increase in labor-force participation among married mothers of preschoolers—from 13% in 1960 to 30% in 1970 to 45% in 1980 (see Figure 6-2)—highlights changing expectations. Child-rearing norms, buttressed by lack of child-care facilities, still make employment more difficult for this group, however.

During the second half of the 19th century, few married women in the United States worked outside their homes. In 1893, only 5% did so, and these were mainly from the slum districts—Blacks and immigrants. Between 1900 and 1969, the percentage of all adult women working outside their homes more than doubled—from 20% to 42% of the adult female population (Sheppard, 1971). By 1980, more than half of all adult women were working (Women's Bureau, 1980), and women constituted 43% of the total work force.

In 1948, although it was customary for unmarried women to have jobs, only 22% of married women did. A generation later, in 1980, nearly 40% of married women had jobs, and the percentage of married women employed exceeded for the first time that of widowed, separated, or divorced women. In 1980, 60% of all working women were married (U.S. Department of Labor, Women's Bureau, 1980).

The needs of World War II brought many married women into the factories and offices, but this was only temporary. After the war, it was again considered inappropriate for them to work outside their homes unless their

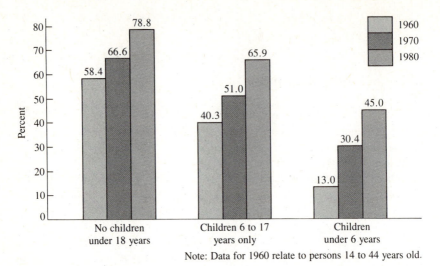

Note: Data for 1960 relate to persons 14 to 44 years old.

Figure 6-2. Labor-force participation rates for married women 16 to 44 years old with husband present, by presence and age of children: 1960, 1970, and 1980. (Source: U.S. Department of Commerce, Bureau of the Census, *Census Population Reports,* January 1982, p. 30.)

families needed the money. Three million women left the labor force in the two years between April 1945 and April 1947 (U.S. Department of Labor, Women's Bureau, 1969). It was a teacher shortage, caused by the growing number of children in the population—the "baby boom"—that first drew married women back to work (Helson, 1972); others followed rapidly.

Some women who are about to retire or who have already retired have worked all their adult lives at full-time jobs. These women have generally had the same anxieties and financial pressures as their male counterparts. For example, a study of women workers in a garment factory in Bayonne, New Jersey, found that 61% were 50 or older and had worked in the same factory since their youth (Goodman, 1978). Their greatest concern was that the factory might close, and they felt the most important function of government was to provide jobs.

Both income (husband's) and education are related to women's employment. Women whose husbands are very rich or very poor are not as likely to be employed as those whose husbands are in the middle-income bracket. On the other hand, the more education women have, the more likely they are to work. It is easier to understand why wives of wealthy men do not work than why wives of very poor men don't. In part, the latter are likely to hold very traditional values, to have few job skills, and to have many children.

The more a woman is likely to earn, the more likely she is to be employed (Fischer, Carlton-Ford, & Briles, 1979). Not surprisingly, the longer a woman is employed and the more satisfaction she gets from her job, the more committed she is to it (Haller & Rosenmayr, 1971). Daughters of women who were employed during their youth are more likely to work and also to combine jobs and families. Although, as a general rule, men are likely to encourage traditional femininity in their daughters, high-status fathers tend to encourage achievement, particularly for oldest girls or when there are no sons (Hoffman, 1974). Middle-aged women executives today are mostly first-born children of successful fathers and nonworking mothers. They felt that their fathers encouraged them to achieve, both in school and after (Henning & Jardim, 1976).

Some women hold jobs for the first time in middle age. Others return to jobs similar to those they held before or during their early years of marriage. In 1966, the U.S. Labor Department forecast that by 1980 at least 60% of all women 45 to 54 years old would be working. In fact, this peak was reached two years earlier than predicted.

Although an impressive number and proportion of American women are working, the other side of the picture is the kinds of work they do and the kinds of prestige and status they have. As shown in Table 6-2, women are clustered into a few job categories relative to men. More than one-third are clerical workers, compared with only 6% of men. While women are equal to men in professional and technical work, they are far below them in managerial positions. An interesting finding from a longitudinal study of employed women between 30 and 44 is that their wages are more predictable from their educational level, occupational status, and work experience than are those of men (Parnes, Shea, Spitz, Zeller, & Associates, 1970). In other words, they are more likely to be paid strictly by the rules than are men.

Kanter (1977) points out that, although women populate corporations, they almost never run them. As of 1970, men constituted 96% of all managers and administrators earning more than $15,000 a year. In three-fourths of the companies, women held less than 2% of the middle-management jobs, and in three-fourths of the companies, they held none of the top-management jobs. The few women scientists tended to be concentrated in a few fields and in the lower echelons of these fields. Furthermore, women generally moved into scientific careers only after being divorced.

Years ago, only single women were career women. This picture has not changed completely. By their mid-20s, those women who have not married are likely to be either professional women—or, three times as many of them, clerical workers. Thus, there is a bimodal distribution of working single women— one age group being young and uneducated, and the other group being older and better educated (Donelson & Gullahorn, 1977). Women are usually shunted to the "emotional," people-handling jobs and are kept far away from the power.

Finally, women returning to jobs and careers after their children are grown usually find it hard to catch up. They have to go back to where they

Table 6-2. Occupational distribution in the United States, 1910–1981

Occupational Class	Percent of Men						Percent of Women					
	1910	1930	1950	1960	1970	1981	1910	1930	1950	1960	1970	1981
Professional and technical	3.1	4.0	6.4	10.7	14.0	15.9	9.2	13.6	10.0	12.2	14.5	17.0
Managers, proprietors, and officials	7.9	9.0	12.9	13.4	14.2	14.6	1.6	2.2	5.7	5.0	4.5	7.4
Clerical	9.2[a]	12.8[a]	7.2	7.1	7.1	6.1	13.9[a]	28.8[a]	26.2	29.8	34.5	34.7
Sales			5.7	6.1	5.6	6.3			8.3	7.6	7.0	6.8
Craftsmen and foremen	14.5	16.4	17.7	18.7	20.1	20.7	1.2	0.8	1.1	1.0	1.1	1.9
Service workers, including private household workers	2.0	2.7	6.4	6.6	6.7	8.9	24.9	21.6	22.0	24.6	21.6	19.4
Farmers and farm managers	19.9	15.2	9.4	6.4	3.2	3.9[b]	3.5	2.5	1.5	0.5	0.3	1.3[b]
Farm laborers	14.0	9.5	5.3	3.5	1.9		16.4	5.4	5.5	3.9	1.5	
Operatives (semiskilled)	11.2	14.4	20.8	19.4	19.6	11.1	27.9	23.7	19.1	15.0	14.5	9.7
Nonfarm laborers (unskilled)	18.2	16.1	8.1	8.1	7.3	7.1	1.4	1.5	0.5	0.4	0.5	1.2
Number employed (millions)	29.5	37.9	42.2	44.5	49.0	57.4	7.8	10.7	17.5	22.2	29.7	43.0

[a]Clerical and Sales are combined.
[b]Farmers and farm laborers

Source: U.S. Department of Commerce, Bureau of the Census, *Statistical Abstract of the United States, 1982/83* (103rd ed.), Table 651, p. 388.

left off 10 or 15 years before; the men in their cohorts, meanwhile, have been developing expertise and status all that time. Thus, women go back to the level of a younger age cohort, their skills are rusty, their information outdated, and their status anomalous. Women of a younger age cohort, who did not "drop out" for family involvement, may not be as far along as their male age mates, but they, too, overshadow the returning older women.

The kinds of work women do vary with age, education, race, where they grew up, and where they live (Sheppard, 1971). For instance, White women have more white-collar jobs than do Black women. They are also likely to earn more, although this depends on city size and age. Young Black women in big cities are less likely to be domestics than are older Black women or younger Black women in small cities. Generally, older women seem to be more polarized in income and job status than younger women, regardless of size of city and race. Older women who are not top earners are likely to be at the bottom of the range; they are not spread as evenly over the income range as are younger women. However, even those women who are top earners are not likely to earn as much as average-earning men. On the average, women earn 60% of what men do in comparable jobs.

Choices and Options

People differ greatly in the ways they find a suitable occupation for themselves. Some are forced into the job market long before they finish high school or have enough education or training for the work they would like to do. Others apparently stumble into the job market, unconcerned about preparation, either because they don't understand how important it is or because they consider it irrelevant to success in life. Still others plan their careers very carefully and persist in acquiring the necessary education and preparation in the face of economic hardship. In general, the higher the social status of the family they come from, the more people are able to and likely to plan a career, or at least the general outlines of one.

Entry into the work world has become increasingly difficult over the last few generations, partly because there are more types of jobs from which to choose and less information about each job on which to base a choice. Because of the increasingly complex nature of many jobs, training has also become longer and more expensive. We tend to believe that freedom of choice is important. Therefore, adolescents feel great responsibility for choosing well. Consequences can be serious. (Compare this choice with the woman's on entering marriage, discussed in Chapter 5.) Our options can also be many or few, depending on the state of the economy and our position in it. During economic depressions, the most elaborately trained workers are lucky to find any job. Even in times of economic abundance, many untrained people and those with outdated skills cannot choose. There is no point to vocational choice unless there is a range of available jobs. Older people, women, and Blacks all have difficulty in finding work commensurate with their education, in getting the same pay as others doing the same work, and in holding on to jobs when they do get them.

A 1977 review of existing practices (U.S. Commission on Civil Rights, 1977) shows age discrimination in federal retraining and reemployment programs. The only factor slightly more important than age is education (but most older workers also have little education). Older workers are less successful in finding new jobs, and they receive lower wages when they do, even though there are no age differences in the numbers applying to employment services. It may take many years before new legislation removes these more subtle age-discrimination situations.

Racial inequality has been so long taken for granted, and its effects have been so pervasive in our country, that, in spite of affirmative-action legislation, several generations may pass before it can disappear. Employment figures still show racial differences in rates of unemployment, and wage differentials are probably comparable. Whether the new cohort of young advantaged Blacks is the first wave of a sweeping tide or a short-lived historical event cannot be judged.

Wage improvements have affected Black men much more than Black women. Among Black couples in which both husband and wife are employed, the husbands earn more than their wives for the same kind of work, just as with White couples.

On the whole, career preferences of Black and White women students are similar, but many more Black women expect to work full time than do White women (54% of Blacks versus 16% of Whites). Tangri (1972) found that University of Michigan students whose mothers had careers were more likely to plan on having careers themselves. Because more Black women than White can be said to hold dual careers, their daughters would be more likely to adopt such a pattern. (The Rapoports, in a 1969 study, use the term **dual career** to describe all women who are responsible for both outside jobs and homes.)

Poor women have long worked away from home—in the homes of others, in factories, in the streets. Therefore, poor families who "better themselves" take pride in the wives' being able to restrict themselves to "feminine" activities. Many working women, as in the Bayonne garment factory studied by Goodman, would not mind staying home. However, men with equivalent monotonous, difficult jobs are also happy to stop working if they have enough money to do something more to their liking. For many traditional men whose mothers had to work during their sons' childhoods, the ability to support wives and raise them to housewife status is an important sign of success. Middle-class families have usually had a different history. Only the educated woman, who is more able than the less-educated to find an interesting, challenging, and rewarding job, can feel superior to "just a housewife."

A comparison between women and men in the general clerical categories of the company that Kanter studied showed, first, that men had higher expectations of advancement and wanted to advance and, second, that women had fewer supports for advancement. Table 6-3 shows the unequal number of men and women in the clerical ranks: 88 women to 23 men. Compare this with Table 6-2. Furthermore, the women were largely lower-level clerical workers or junior secretaries—dead-end jobs. The men were accounting clerks—jobs that were on the ladder to management. The men were younger, had worked fewer years, and had already had supervisory experience. In the lower half of the table are shown ratings of amount of encouragement: the higher the number, the more the support. The men had significantly more help in ascending the career ladder than the women had. When they were asked to rate possible outcomes of promotion on desirability and likelihood, the men saw such outcomes as both desirable and likely; the women saw them as desirable but unlikely. It is no surprise that women, on the whole, were less committed to their jobs than were men. Like the AT&T executives who found themselves at a dead end, most women who work in corporations turn to other sources of gratification—friendships and outside interests.

Because women in large organizations—and small ones, too—do

Table 6-3. Situations reflecting opportunity differences for men and women at one company

	Men (N = 23)	Women (N = 88)	
Proportion under 25 years old	44%	30%	
Proportion with the company less than 5 years	65%	40%	
Proportion who have *ever* held a supervisory position	57%	20%	
Mean rating on scale of 1–9[a] of Amount of encouragement received from superiors to improve	7.62	6.20	$p<.05$
Amount of encouragement received from superiors to advance	7.18	6.32	$p<.05$
Amount of company awareness of one's contributions	7.15	6.10	$p<.05$

[a]Larger number indicates greater amount.
Note: Figures reported with the permission of G. Homall (1974).
Source: Kanter, 1977.

not have explicit power, they can only advance through the help of others, particularly men. Those few women who have made it to top executive positions stressed the essential roles that male sponsors played in their rise (Henning & Jardim, 1976). Women's relative lack of power as bosses—when they get to be bosses—is associated with their tendency to be rules-minded, authoritarian, nagging, and conservative. The vicious circle is demonstrated by the responses of 1000 male and 900 female executives, one-fifth of whom said, in 1965, that they would feel uncomfortable working for women. And 51% of the men said that women are temperamentally unfit for management positions (Kanter, 1977).

Women trying to make it up the business ladder are one category of "new woman." Women physicians and college presidents represent two different kinds of "new women." Lillian Cartwright and her colleagues (for example, Cartwright & Schmuckler, 1982) have been following these unusual women over a period of years. Almost all the presidents followed a set career trajectory: tenured faculty, faculty chair, and then dean. They thus came up through the ranks, like corporation executives, and power was slowly granted them. Like corporation executives, therefore, they probably needed mentors along the way. Physicians, however, are much more individualistic, or at least follow less defined pathways. They do not have to dominate others, and others do not have to give them power.

One of the women interviewed by Baruch, Barnett, and Rivers (1983) said, "I think men basically choose their successors, and they choose someone who's basically like them. Very few men can make the abstraction that a woman is like them. She starts with one strike against her" (p. 135). These authors note that the high-prestige women they studied did not follow any one path to success. Some went from college to job to career as most men do. Others started late and hurried to catch up. The unique position of the married woman is discussed later in this chapter.

Personality Correlates

The personal aspect of working is most commonly measured by "job satisfaction." Recent studies, primarily of women workers, have looked more at self-esteem and even feelings of mastery. As noted in Chapter 4, one of the "keynote themes" of the youth of the late 1960s and 1970s was devaluation of work, or at least stress of intrinsic rather than extrinsic aspects of work. A large-scale study at the University of Michigan (Quinn, Staines, & McCullough, 1974) and their later data of 1977 (Quinn & Staines, 1979), found some evidence for the spread of "blue-collar blues and white-collar woes." Table 6-4 shows that about half the workers were less than satisfied in 1973 and even more in 1977.

Table 6-4.   Attitudes toward the job: 1977 versus 1973

Statement	Percent Agreeing	
	1973	*1977*
Very satisfied with the job	52	47
Would prefer a different job	52	60
Job is very much like the job respondent wants	58	53
Would strongly recommend this job to a friend	64	62
Has skills that cannot be used in this job	25	36
Is overeducated for this job	28	32
Very likely will seek another job	14	16
Easy to find a job with similar income and fringe benefits	27	20
There is a shortage of workers with respondent's experience, training, and skills	48	37

Source: Adapted from Quinn and Staines, 1979.

Being jobless and poor rarely breeds satisfaction. The primary objective of jobs for most people is income. Only when workers feel they are earning enough money do they look for more intrinsic rewards. The lower the position of workers in the occupational hierarchy—skilled, manual, and below—the more they are likely to be motivated by extrinsic factors such as pay and job security. It is usually higher-status or higher-paid workers—business, professional, and white-collar—who value the more intrinsic qualities of achievement, recognition, responsibility, and self-fulfillment (Crites, 1969).

Most jobs are satisfying in some ways and not in others. Some factors contribute to satisfaction (the positive end) such as achievement and recognition, while others contribute more to dissatisfaction (the negative end) such as company-policy manipulations and working conditions (Herzberg, Mausner, & Snyderman, 1959). In general, good working conditions by themselves are not likely to make a job highly desirable, although bad working conditions will make it very undesirable.

Although high achievement motivation, defined as a desire for recognition of accomplishment, was not associated with particular jobs for younger men, it was correlated with jobs of high prestige among older men. It may be that psychological factors such as motivation have more predictive power on job behavior over the long run than they do in the early work years. Generally, though, Veroff and Feld's (1970) findings (and those of others, such as Voydanoff, 1977) show that motives have less relevance to the work *satisfactions* of older men than they do to those of younger men.

As executives get older, they become more and more autonomous and also more aggressive, feeling freer to express hostility. Although the AT&T executives learned more about the business over the years, they did not really improve in their basic management abilities. In some ways, they had reached a plateau at the end of 20 years of work. Most were satisfied with the level they had reached and with their material success. They no longer had the same push toward upward mobility or promotion they had had when they started, even though they enjoyed doing difficult jobs well more than they ever had. The more successful executives—those who had reached higher job levels—differed from the less successful, not in life satisfaction, but in job commitment, forcefulness, and dominance (Bray & Howard, 1983).

Are women who are employed more satisfied with their lives than are full-time housewives? The answer is not clear. Huston-Stein and Higgins-Trenk (1978) reviewed the data from research to that time and concluded that, in general, they are. This seems to be more evident for middle-class women, however, particularly those with fewer children. From national survey data, Wright (1978) concluded that there were no clear differences in satisfaction between working and nonworking women. A third view is that of Baruch and Barnett (Baruch, Barnett, & Rivers, 1983), who found no overall difference, but did find that working women had a higher sense of mastery, while married women were higher in pleasure. They suggest that since working women's satisfaction derives from their own efforts, while nonworking women's derives from their husbands' approval of them, the working women have more control over their fate and may therefore be considered ahead. Their findings are illustrated in Figure 6-3.

An Austrian study of satisfaction with work, marriage, and household activities found that women who worked for intrinsic reasons—because they themselves wanted to—were more satisfied than those who worked in order to help their families (Szinovacz, 1973). Finally, gifted women first studied as children by Lewis Terman, when followed over the years, turned out to be much more satisfied with their lives if they had careers (Sears & Sears, 1978).

Women who are clerical workers are poorly paid, given few possibilities for advancement, allowed little say in what their work will be, and are dissatisfied. Their consequent high degree of stress is indicated by the fact that, in a recent study (Haynes & Feinleib, 1980) while working women as a whole showed no higher rate of heart disease than housewives, women employed in clerical and sales occupations did. Their coronary-disease rates were twice those of other women.

Figure 6-4, based on a study at Columbia University, shows the components of job stress along two axes: psychological demand and decision control. The jobs in the lower right corner, which have low decision control and high psychological demand, have been found to be associated with high psychological strain and greater risk of cardiovascular disease. This chart does not include office clerical workers, but presumably they would be close to sales clerks (female). It is much better for one's health to be a secondary school teacher or even a sales clerk (male) than a cashier or telephone operator. Findings from their national study, however, led Veroff, Douvan, and Kulka

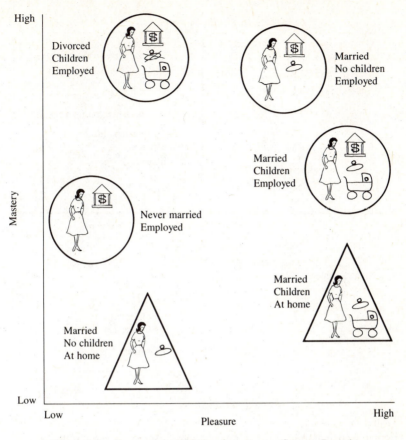

Figure 6-3. Sources of well-being for women. (Source: Baruch, Barnett, and Rivers, 1983, p. 37.)

(1981) to conclude that just the fact of working for pay contributes to people's—particularly women's—feelings of resourcefulness to such an extent that it can compensate for many problems on the job.

Conflicts between Work and Family Life

An analysis of the Quality of Employment Survey (Pleck, Staines, & Lang, 1980) shows that one-third of men and women who are currently married and have children under 18 living at home report moderate or severe interference between job and family life. Surprisingly, there are no sex differences in these reports: men report as much conflict as women. The three most common responses are "excessive work time," "schedule conflicts," and

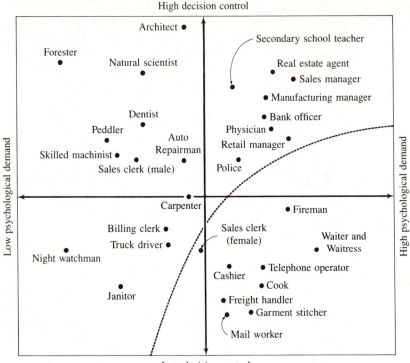

High decision control

Architect ●

Secondary school teacher

Forester
●

Natural scientist
●

Real estate agent
●   ● Sales manager

● Manufacturing manager

Dentist
●

● Bank officer

Peddler
●

Auto
Repairman

Physician ●

Retail manager

Skilled machinist ●   ●   ●

Sales clerk (male)

Police

Carpenter

● Fireman

Billing clerk ●

Truck driver ●

Sales clerk
(female)

Waiter and
● Waitress

Night watchman
●

Cashier
●

● Telephone operator

Janitor
●

● Cook

● Freight handler

● Garment stitcher

Mail worker

Low decision control

Low psychological demand

High psychological demand

Figure 6-4.   Components of stress. (Source: Nelson, 1983.)

"fatigue and irritability." Men report more "excessive work time," though, and women more "schedule conflicts." In an earlier survey, Quinn and his associates (1974) reported lowest job and marital satisfaction for both men and women when their children were preschoolers.

Weingarten and Daniels (1978) have been examining ways in which couples coordinate work and family roles. They distinguish between sequential and simultaneous patterns. In sequential patterns, women first have children and then work, or first work and then have children. In simultaneous patterns, child rearing and work occur at the same time. The presence of young children while both parents are struggling to establish their separate careers seems to produce the most stress, so that either sequential pattern is easier than a simultaneous one. The study of women executives by Henning and Jardim (1976) shows the advantages, for women intent on success, of delaying marriage and childbearing. It helps marital relations if the husbands are able to reach a middle level of success before parenting starts. Although most research shows no increase in men's participation in household work after the birth of children or after the women return to work (Pleck, Staines, & Lang, 1980), at least there may be greater economic security.

Figure 6-5 shows women's rate of employment in relation to the birth of their first child. The rate of employment drops precipitously during the months of pregnancy, coming close to zero for women with less than a high school education, and only slightly higher for more educated women. The more educated women, however, are more likely to be employed before the birth and more likely to return to work during the baby's first year. Mothers of preschool children still tend to be employed less frequently than mothers of older children, even though the percentage of working mothers has gone up over the years for both groups, as was seen in Figure 6-2.

Not only is a mother's education a predictor of her employment during her child's first months and years, but so is her early sex-role socialization (Katz, 1975). Women who had been raised to expect more than becoming a wife and mother coped more effectively with conflicts between their family and work roles and tended to be more satisfied with their lives. A recent study of employed mothers (Kaplan, 1983) that focused upon stress found that most of the respondents managed their double job well. Only those mothers who were not currently married felt both overload and conflict, and even those problems were less if they had a good job that provided enough money for

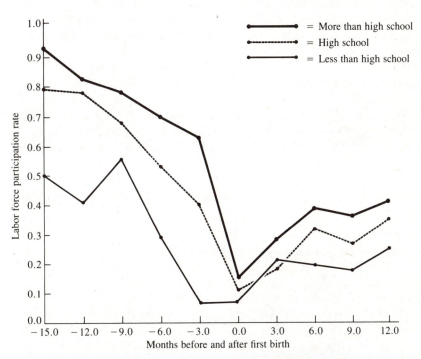

Figure 6-5.   Mean labor-force participation rate by months before and after first birth by education. (Source: McLaughlin and Micklin, 1983, Figure 2.)

adequate help at home. One of the conclusions of Baruch, Barnett, and Rivers (1983), in fact, is that "marriage and children do not guarantee well-being for a woman. Being without a man or being childless does not guarantee depression and misery" (p. 14).

Job Mobility

Parnes, Nestel, and Andresani (1972) found that about one-fifth of the men who were employed in 1966 changed employers over the next three years. More than three-fifths of these changes were voluntary, not the result of being laid off. Furthermore, these changes were concentrated among a minority of highly mobile individuals.

More recent data show the mobility rate of employed people moving into new occupations at 8.7% per year. The marked relation between mobility and age is shown in Table 6-5. More than a third of young workers changed jobs, only a quarter of those in their 20s did, and fewer and fewer at older ages until only 3% of men over 45 did (Arbeiter, 1979).

In their middle years, Black and White men show differences in rates of voluntary job change. Whites drop from 12% to 9% of all job moves between the 45–49 age range and the 55–59 age range, while their involuntary changes remain at a constant 6% or 7%. Blacks show less age-related variation in voluntary change but increase in involuntary changes—from 5% to 8%—as they get older (Arbeiter, 1979). Middle-aged men—both Blacks and Whites—prefer to stick to their jobs, but Black men are more vulnerable to being fired. The exception is men with 20 or more years of service, who increase in voluntary changes, opting for early retirement and subsequently changing to new or part-time jobs. More blue-collar workers show this pattern. Almost half the White men in the construction industry who were surveyed in 1966 were with different employers in 1969. In general, mobility is related to wages. Those whose hourly rates were less than $2 an hour (in 1969) were almost three times as likely to make voluntary job changes as those earning

Table 6-5. Occupational mobility rate for men in 1975

Age	Rate
18–19	37.3%
20–24	24.9
25–34	12.4
35–44	6.2
45–54	3.5

Source: Arbeiter, 1979 after Byrne, 1975.

more. Having a pension works in the opposite direction: it tends to decrease mobility.

Hill's three-generation data (Hill et al., 1970) show a steady increase in job mobility from the oldest to the youngest generation. The grandfathers were apt to have still been on their first jobs during the first decade of their marriage (and they did not marry before they were about 25). Almost half of their sons were on their second jobs by the second year of their marriage, and 40% were in at least their fourth jobs after ten years of marriage. Their fathers had taken their whole lifetimes to go through this many jobs. During the year these families were observed, the grandchildren showed the most job mobility of all. Almost 60% had changed jobs; of the men, 76% had. The greatest mobility was shown among men in semiskilled and minor clerical jobs, suggesting that the lowest job satisfaction occurs in these categories, which is consistent with findings in all other studies. In all three generations, job change was associated with periods of prosperity. It did not seem to be associated with individual planning; overall, little planning was reported. Therefore, to a large extent, changes could be attributed to opportunity more than to motive.

Unemployment

A large part of the January 1983 issue of the *APA Monitor* (Turkington, 1983) was devoted to the effects of unemployment, underlining the widespread disaster, both economic and psychological, of a depression. Figure 6-6 shows that the unemployment rate in 1982 was the highest in a decade. Recent research documents a variety of reactions to job loss, depending on social class, race, sex, and age. One of the staff writers, Carol Turkington, cited the observations of Judson Stone and his colleagues, who studied unemployed workers in Detroit and Chicago. White-collar workers, Stone concluded, felt betrayed. Blue-collar workers felt that tradition had been broken— traditions of their fathers and grandfathers who had worked in the mills or factories that were now closed to them. A study in Youngstown, Ohio, by Buss and Redburn reported that Blacks suffered more than Whites in every United States economic downturn. Their feeling of victimization increased over the four years of the study.

Like Blacks and other discriminated-against groups, women are the last hired and the first fired. Women between 30 and 50 are particularly disadvantaged. Whereas the cohort before them moved back into the job market once their child-rearing responsibilities were diminished, today's post-child-rearing women find that there are no jobs for them. In general, the move into traditionally male jobs has been cut off. Once women lose their jobs, they are even less likely than men in the same job category to find comparable new jobs. Instead, they are shunted into more marginal and unskilled work.

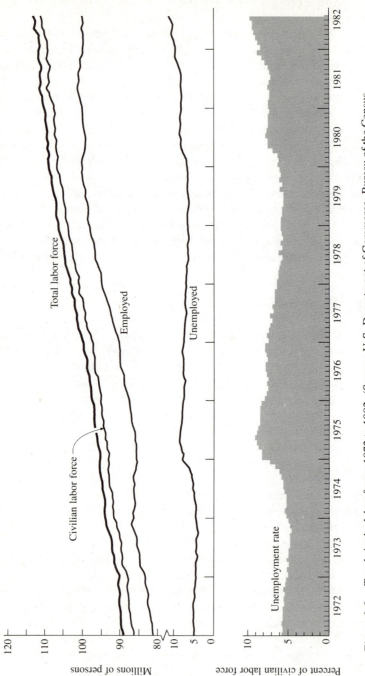

Figure 6-6. Trends in the labor force: 1972 to 1982. (Source: U.S. Department of Commerce, Bureau of the Census. Statistical Abstract of the United States (103rd ed.), Figure 13.2, p. 374.

Youth, particularly Black youth, show increased negative self-expression, more illegal activity, and more pregnancies (among women), according to studies by William Kornblum cited by staff writer Kathleen Fisher. Fisher reports that data from the Bureau of Labor Statistics show unemployment increasing 24% during 1982 for people aged 55 to 64, compared with 11% for the total work force. Furthermore, older workers who lose their jobs remain unemployed longer—23% longer than other workers—and face salary cuts of $500 for each year of age if they do find a new job. Those over 60 are three times as likely as younger workers to become discouraged and retire prematurely with no pension or medical benefits just when they need them most. The protection of seniority and recall rights present in earlier economic recessions has been lost. To make matters worse, older workers are less likely to move because their homes have been paid for and their children are in school or, if older, live nearby with their grandchildren. Their children, in fact, may also be unemployed, confronting families with double and triple burdens.

Sheppard and Belitsky (*The Job Hunt,* 1966) studied 309 male blue-collar workers looking for jobs. Older workers waited longer than younger ones in starting their job hunts and used fewer job-seeking techniques. But even if they used as many techniques and started as soon as younger workers, their job-finding success was lower. They were referred to fewer jobs by the employment service, and they got fewer jobs of those they were referred to.

Considering the consequences of technological change for manpower obsolescence, there are two possibilities for displaced workers. One path is followed by many older men, who reclassify themselves as early retirees. The other path is followed by those who prepare for new careers. So far, our socialization does not prepare people to think of a lifetime of multiple careers, although Toffler (1970) thinks we should be moving in this direction. For one thing, there are institutional obstacles, such as pension plans, seniority rules, and early-retirement programs, that militate against making any kind of change if one doesn't have to. When Sheppard and Belitsky (1966) interviewed 140 workers in Pennsylvania, only 49 (35%) were interested in second careers. Belbin and Belbin (1968) found that most adults they tried to recruit avoided entering retraining programs. They were more willing to accept job downgrading than to train for new jobs. When a group of 115 unemployed middle-aged managers and engineers in Los Angeles were interviewed (Dyer, 1972), most were not interested in new careers, although half did consider using their current skills in self-employment.

Multiple careers may be related to personal development and creativity if they include opportunities for acquiring new perspectives. It may be that there is an optimal duration for any one pursuit. After 15 years, for instance, a person may have "drawn out" all the "juice" from one activity but may start a whole new cycle of creativity by shifting to a different arena.

Some of the dramatic productivity of women who return to careers after a period spent in child rearing suggests that regular switching of arenas of achievement may encourage cognitive and creative development in many people.

Leisure

The increased number of retired people in our society today has pushed the topic of leisure into prominence. If people are not nominally working, may we ask whether they are *leisuring*? Most of today's retirees have not been socialized for leisure in any sense and thus can be considered pioneers in this domain. They are exploring for themselves what they want to do, or what they can do, and they are also leading the way for younger cohorts. At the same time, a historical trend toward devaluation of the work ethic may be making the youngest adult cohorts more ready to accept leisure than are their parents and grandparents.

Robinson (1979) points out that as a nation we are singularly inept in leisure, prey to artificial and commercial purveyors of recreation that often leaves us bored or dissatisfied. The market has caught on to the vast possibilities of this ineptness and has come forth with all kinds of mechanized, routinized, and packaged "recreation." At the same time, many adult educators have spread the idea that we are facing longer periods of nonwork time and that it behooves us to learn "leisure skills." This last statement is misleading, though, in implying a general increase in time for leisure. It is true that men's work years have shortened as they enter the labor market later and retire earlier, but so far the number of hours worked per day has not changed since 1948 for nonstudent males (Owen, 1976). The apparent shortening of working time is an artifact of the number of part-time workers who are students or housewives. Thus, the working man's available time for leisure is limited, although it is not as restricted as that of the employed woman's.

Figure 6-7 shows a sequence of leisure activities in terms of expressive involvement. It is assumed that solitude, resting, and sleeping demand very little involvement or feeling, while sexual activity, drug experiences, and highly competitive games demand almost total personal involvement. To bring this table up to date, computer self-education might be added to the Medium list and video games to the Medium-low category.

Gordon et al. (1976) interviewed Houston adults over the age of 20 about their leisure activities. The study was carried out in 1969–1970, using a stratified sample of 1441 people, balanced by sex, ethnicity, and occupational status. The age patterns they found for frequency of different activities are shown in Figures 6-8, 6-9, and 6-10. Activities that decreased from age 20 to age 94 (cross-sectionally) are shown in Figure 6-8; those that remained at

Intensity	Forms of Leisure Activity
Very high	*Sensual Transcendence* Sexual activity Psychoactive chemical use Ecstatic religious experience Aggression, "action" (physical fighting, defense or attack, verbal fighting) Highly competitive games and sports Intense and rhythmic dancing
Medium high	*Creativity* Creative activities (artistic, literary, musical, and so on) Nurturance, altruism Serious discussion, analysis Embellishment of instrumental (art or play in work)
Medium	*Developmental* Physical exercise and individual sports Cognitive acquisition (serious reading, disciplined learning) Beauty appreciation, attendance at cultural events (galleries, museums, and so on) Organizational participation (clubs, interest groups) Sightseeing, travel Special learning games and toys
Medium low	*Diversion* Socializing, entertaining Spectator sports Games, toys of most kinds, play Light conversation Hobbies Reading Passive entertainment (as in mass-media usage)
Very low	*Relaxation* Solitude Quiet resting Sleeping

Figure 6-7. Qualitatively varying forms of leisure activity (expressive primacy in personal activity), according to intensity of expressive involvement. (Adapted from Gordon, Gaitz, and Scott, 1976.)

relatively the same level are shown in Figure 6-9; and those that increased are shown in Figure 6-10.

In general, there were lower levels at older ages in the more vigorous activities and those that required going out of the home, although there were also lower levels of reading and cultural production. The Duke study, in contrast, found that reading was significantly greater among older than among

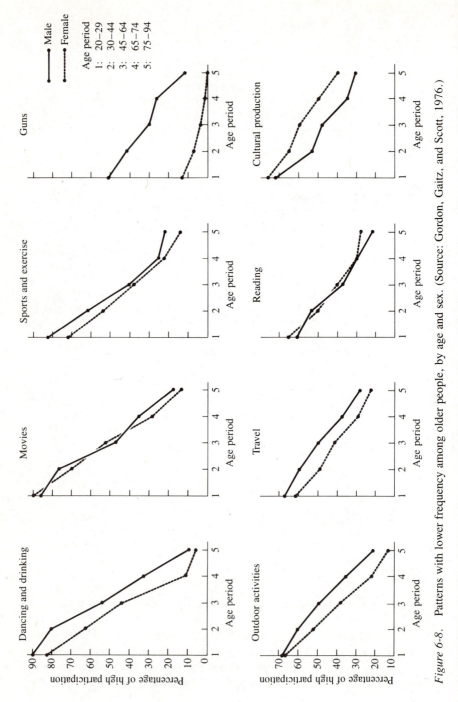

Figure 6-8. Patterns with lower frequency among older people, by age and sex. (Source: Gordon, Gaitz, and Scott, 1976.)

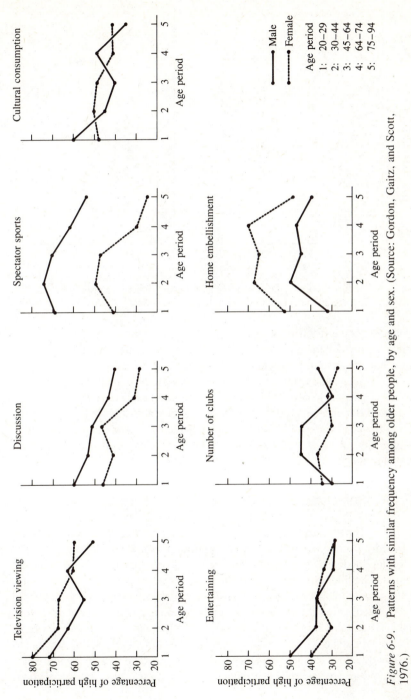

Figure 6-9. Patterns with similar frequency among older people, by age and sex. (Source: Gordon, Gaitz, and Scott, 1976.)

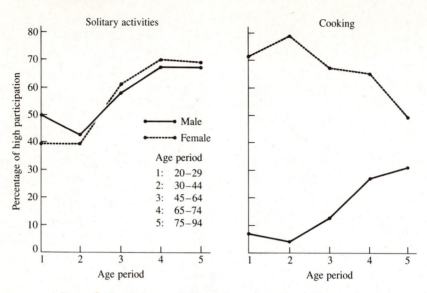

Figure 6-10.   Patterns with higher frequency among older people, by age and sex. (Source: Gordon, Gaitz, and Scott, 1976.)

younger people (Pfeiffer & Davis, 1971). Some of these age differences are undoubtedly due to aging, but others, such as for reading, could be attributed to cohort or group differences in education.

Social and community activities tended to be of equivalent frequency at all ages among Houston respondents, and Pfeiffer and Davis similarly reported no age differences in church attendance. Solitary activities and cooking were more frequent among older people, although there is a clear sex/age difference. Older women cook less than younger women; older men cook more than younger men.

Summary

Three kinds of development in working fit the different possibilities offered by jobs. Where little or no opportunity for selection and choice of working mode exists, as is true for most jobs, development can be measured only by settling into some kind of income-producing position and accommodating to its demands. Where possibilities for movement along a socially recognized ladder are available, as in most bureaucratic positions, development is measured by external criteria such as title, salary, and positional labels. Where workers have options for decisions about how to work and are able to be creative, they can develop along a pathway of increasing complexity. Since these options are variously distributed according to sex, race, and social class, not to mention economic and historical conditions, there are understandably sex, race, social-class, and cohort differences in kinds of job development.

Women in general earn less than men in equivalent positions, tend to be clustered into a restricted set of occupations, and, because they usually retain family responsibilities, have a more irregular time pattern of employment. Whether or not they are employed at all is often contingent upon their husband's income and their own education, although not in a straight-line fashion. To the extent that Black workers and older cohorts have not had the opportunities to start out and move up in more desirable occupations, they are likely to fit into the first definition of development mentioned above. Older workers of all categories face powerful age biases in job evaluation, promotion, job maintenance, job choice, and rehiring. There seems to have been a secular trend over the past few decades away from stereotyped sex-role preferences for activities, with men becoming more interested in family and recreation, and women more interested in jobs. However, more men than women are still interested primarily in their jobs, and more women primarily in their families.

Matching of individual characteristics and job characteristics is associated with greater job satisfaction and lower job mobility. Jobs that permit more autonomy produce less stress and are thus associated with better health. While leisure activities might be expected to fit personality requirements better than job activities, since presumably they offer more choice, inexperience in handling leisure by work-oriented cohorts often leads to work- and achievement-oriented leisure pursuits. Unemployment cannot be equated with leisure nor, for most people, can retirement. Given the prevailing limited options, we may never know what potential development in arenas other than jobs might be.

Epilogue

Maybe

One perspective on age is that to be young is to be fresh, lively, eager, quick to learn; to be mature is to be done, complete, sedate, tired. From this point of view, only the distraught young would think positively about growing up, and most of the mature would think longingly about being young. But consider a different perspective. To be young is to be unripe, unfinished, raw, awkward, unskilled, inept; to be mature is to be ready, whole, adept, wise. How inevitable are our glorification of youth and our shame about having lived many years?

In this book, I have reviewed the too often meager information about age changes during the adult years. Most of it is based on cross-sectional research—comparisons between people of different ages studied at the same point in time—and thus perhaps more representative of cohort or generational differences than of changes that come with age. Nevertheless, it can be said that physical deterioration is neither universal nor inevitable, and that development is at least possible in intelligence, in personality, in social relations, and in productive endeavors.

How long we are "programmed" to live is probably genetically predetermined, but more and more of us are likely to live out our span of years—unless, of course, world conditions get worse. Because of medical advances, fewer infants fail to grow up and fewer young adults die from disease. If we apply what we have learned about nutrition, exercise, and balancing our rhythm of living, we can prolong vigor and health. It may become possible to restrict senescence or terminal deterioration to only a brief period at the end of our allotted span of years.

However, staying the same for many years could be boring, even if it were possible in a rapidly changing world. It is probably fortunate that we have to learn to adapt to changes we had not anticipated. By integrating the new with the old, the person we have been with the person we have become, we achieve a sense of continuity of self. We need to understand what is happening so that it makes sense to us, just as we need to be able to feel some predictability in or control over the events of our life.

The intellectual demands of youth are different from those of later adulthood. In youth, it is important to be able to assimilate quickly. Most of what young people see or experience is new to them. They have only a short past to provide clues. As people accumulate more experience, their intellectual functioning changes. In youth, intelligence is relatively fluid. Speed of processing new information is high. As time goes on, if the environment stays the same, speed seems to give way to a "filling in" or "rounding out" process. Qualitative changes may take place in learning and creativity, but neither learning nor creativity need to stop. Overall, general intelligence can remain constant well into the period we call old age. Old dogs can learn new tricks. What is more, they can make decisions about which new tricks are worth learning.

Most heroes tend to be heroes of youth. They win apparently unwinnable victories over insurmountable odds by quick wits and brute strength. But dotted through the history of mankind are a handful of heroes more suitable for longer lives: the heroes of wisdom, of continued creativity in living, of movement toward a promised land, of integrating past and present to suggest a better future. As more of us live out more of our promised life, we may produce more heroes and models for the mature years.

The sweet smile shared by parents and infants when they look into each other's eyes is echoed by the looks exchanged by confident lovers. Early parent/infant attachment must develop into the complex human interrelationships of later life, and perhaps the elementary relationship serves as a template for later ones. The study of dyadic and group relationships from a life-span point of view may open up vistas for human attachment that we cannot even imagine now. Longer lives may be accompanied not by stagnation or deprivation of love and friendship but by transformations of old patterns into richer new ones.

So far in the history of the human species, there has been no time or place where people have had optimal conditions for developing throughout their life. It is therefore impossible to say with confidence that we know the limits of human development. The best is yet to be—maybe.

References

Adams, B. N. (1968). *Kinship in an urban setting*. Chicago: Markham.

Adams, B. N. (1979). Mate selection in the United States: A theoretical summarization. In W. Burr, R. Hill, I. Nye, & I. Reis (Eds.), *Contemporary theories about the family: Vol. 1. Research-based theories* (p. 259–267). New York: Free Press.

Ainsworth, M. D. (1969). Object relations, dependency, and attachment: A theoretical review of the infant-mother relationship. *Child Development, 40,* 969–1025.

Aldous, J. (1978). *Family careers: Developmental change in families*. New York: Wiley.

Aldrich, D. (1974, October). *Familism and the prestige of the aged in two societies*. Paper presented at the meeting of the Gerontological Society, Portland, OR.

Allan, G. (1977). Sibling solidarity. *Journal of Marriage and the Family, 39,* 177–184.

Alston, J. P., & Dudley, C. J. (1973). Age, occupation, and life satisfaction. *Gerontologist, 13,* 58–61.

Anderson, B. J., & Standley, K. A. (1976, September). *A methodology for observation of the childbirth environment*. Paper presented at the meeting of the American Psychological Association, Washington, DC.

Anderson, J. E. (1957). Dynamics of development: Systems in process. In D. Harris (Ed.), *The concept of development: An issue in the study of human behavior* (pp. 25–48). Minneapolis: University of Minnesota Press.

Anderson, S. A., Russell, C. S., & Schumm, W. R. (1983). Perceived marital quality and family life-cycle categories: A further analysis. *Journal of Marriage and the Family, 45,* 127–140.

Angres, S. (1975). *Intergenerational relations and value congruence between young adults and their mothers*. Unpublished doctoral dissertation, U. of Chicago.

Arbeiter, S. (1979). Mid-life career change. *AAHE* (American Association for Higher Education) Bulletin, *32*(2), 1, 11–12.

Arenberg, D. (1974). A longitudinal study of problem solving in adults. *Journal of Gerontology, 29,* 650–658.

Arenberg, D. (1982). Estimates of age changes on the Benton Visual Retention Test. *Journal of Gerontology, 37*(1), 87–90.

Arenberg, D., & Robertson-Tchabo, E. (1977). Learning and aging. In J. E. Birren & K. W. Schaie (Eds.), *Handbook of the psychology of aging* (pp. 421–449). New York: Van Nostrand Reinhold.

Babchuck, N., & Booth, A. (1969). Voluntary association membership: A longitudinal analysis. *American Sociological Review, 34,* 31–45.

Bahrick, H. P., Bahrick, P. O., & Wittlinger, R. P. (1975). Fifty years of memory for names and faces: A cross-sectional approach. *Journal of Experimental Psychology: General, 104,* 54–75.

Baltes, P.B. (1979). Life-span developmental psychology: Some converging observations on history and theory. In P. B. Baltes & O. G. Brim, Jr. (Eds.), *Life-span development and behavior (Vol. 2),* 256–280. New York: Academic Press.

Bandura, A. (1969). Social-learning theory of identificatory processes. In D. A. Goslin (Ed.), *Handbook of socialization theory and research,* 213–262. Chicago: Rand-McNally.

Barber, C. E. (1978, November). *Gender differences in experiencing the transition to the empty nest: Reports of middle-aged women and men.* Paper presented at the meeting of the Gerontological Society, Dallas.

Bardwick, J. (1971). *Psychology of women.* New York: Harper & Row.

Bart, P. B. (1970, November-December). Mother Portnoy's complaints. *Trans-Action,* pp. 69–74.

Bartell, G. (1971). *Group sex.* New York: Wyden.

Baruch, G. K., & Barnett, R. C. (1980). On the well-being of adult women. In L. A. Bond & J. C. Rosen (Eds.), *Competence and coping during adulthood.* Hanover, NH: University Press of New England.

Baruch, G. K., Barnett, R. C., & Rivers, C. (1983). *Lifeprints: New patterns of love and work for today's woman.* New York: McGraw-Hill.

Baruch, R. (1966). The interruption and resumption of women's careers. *Harvard Studies in Career Development, 50* (whole issue).

Bastida, E. (1978, November). *Family integration in later life among Hispanic Americans.* Paper presented at the meeting of the Gerontological Society, Dallas.

Bayley, N. (1968). Behavioral correlates of mental growth: Birth to 36 years. *American Psychologist, 23,* 1–10.

Beauvoir, S. de. (1953). *The second sex.* New York: Knopf.

Becker, H. S. (1951). The professional dance musician and his audience. *American Journal of Sociology, 58,* 136–144.

Becker, H. S., Geer, B., Hughes, E., and Strauss, A. L. (1961). *Boys in white: Student culture in medical school.* Chicago: University of Chicago Press.

Becker, H. S., & Strauss, A. L. (1956). Careers, personality, and adult socialization. *American Journal of Sociology, 62,* 253–263.

Becker, W. C. (1964). Consequences of differential kinds of parental discipline. In M. L. Hoffman (Ed.), *Review of child development research (Vol. 1),* 169–208. New York: Russell Sage Foundation.

Belbin, E., & Belbin, R. M. (1968). New careers in middle age. In B. L. Neugarten (Ed.), *Middle age and aging,* 341–346. Chicago: University of Chicago Press.

Bell, I. P. (1970, November-December). The double standard. *Trans-Action,* pp. 23–27.

Benedek, T. (1959). Sexual functions in women and their disturbance. In S. Arieti (Ed.), *American handbook of psychiatry.* New York: Basic Books.

Bengtson, V. L., & Black, K. D. (1973). Intergenerational relations and continuities in socialization. In P. B. Baltes & K. W. Schaie (Eds.), *Life-span developmental psychology: Personality and socialization,* 208–234. New York: Academic Press.

Bengtson, V. L., Kasschau, P., & Ragan, P. K. (1977). The impact of social structure on aging individuals. In J. E. Birren & K. W. Schaie (Eds.), *Handbook of the psychology of aging*, 327–354. New York: Van Nostrand Reinhold.

Bengston, V. L., & Starr, J. M. (1975). Contrasts and consensus: A generational analysis of youth in the 1970s. In R. Havighurst (Ed.), *Youth: The 74th yearbook of the National Society for the Study of Education* (Pt. 1), 224–266. Chicago: University of Chicago Press.

Bengtson, V. L., & Troll, L. E. (1978). Youth and their parents: Feedback and inter-generational influence in socialization. In R. Lerner & G. Spanier (Eds.), *Child influences on marital and family interaction*, 215–240. New York: Academic Press.

Bergman, M., Blumenfeld, V. G., Cascardo, D., Dash, B., Levitt, H., & Margulies, M. K. (1976). Age-related decrement in hearing for speech: Sampling and longitudinal studies. *Journal of Gerontology, 31*, 533–538.

Bernard, J. (1973). *The future of marriage*. New York: Bantam Books.

Billings, A. G., & Moos, R. H. (1981). The role of coping responses and social resources in attenuating the stress of life events. *Journal of Behavioral Medicine, 4*, 139–157.

Birren, J. E. (Ed.). (1964). *Relations of development and aging*. Springfield, IL: Charles C. Thomas.

Birren, J. E. (1969). Age and decision strategies. In A. T. Welford & J. E. Birren (Eds.), *Interdisciplinary topics in gerontology* (Vol. 4) (pp. 23–36). Basel: Karger.

Birren, J. E., & Renner, V. J. (1977). Research on the psychology of aging: Principles and experimentation. In J. E. Birren & K. W. Schaie (Eds.), *Handbook of the psychology of aging* (3–39). New York: Van Nostrand Reinhold.

Bischof, L. J. (1969). *Adult psychology*. New York: Harper & Row.

Block, E. (1953). A quantitative morphological investigation of the follicular system in newborn female infants. *Acta Anatomica, 17*, 201–206.

Block, J. (1971). *Lives through time*. Berkeley, CA: Bancroft.

Blood, R. O., Jr., & Wolfe, D. M. (1960). *Husbands and wives: The dynamics of married living*. New York: Free Press.

Borland, D. C. (1979, November). An investigation of the empty nest syndrome among parents of different marital status catagories: Evidence from national surveys. Paper presented at the meeting of the Gerontological Society, Washington, DC.

Bornstein, P. E., Clayton, P. J., Halikas, J. A., Maurice, W. L., & Robbins, E. (1973). The depression of widowhood after thirteen months. *British Journal of Psychiatry, 122*, 561–566.

Bortner, R., & Hultsch, D. (1976). *Subjective deprivation: Characteristics of groups demonstrating different patterns of subjective deprivation*. Unpublished manuscript, College of Human Development, Pennsylvania State University.

Bossard, J. H., & Boll, E. (1956). *The large family,* Philadelphia: University of Pennsylvania Press.

Bott, E. (1971). *Family and social network: Roles, norms, and external relationships in ordinary urban families*. New York: Free Press.

Botwinick, J. (1965). Theories of antecedent conditions of speed of response. In A. T. Welford & J. E. Birren (Eds.), *Behavior, aging, and the nervous system*, 67–87. Springfield, IL: Charles C. Thomas.

Botwinick, J. (1966). Cautiousness in advanced age. *Journal of Gerontology, 21*, 347.

Botwinick, J. (1967). *Cognitive processes in maturity and old age*. New York: Springer.

Botwinick, J., & Storandt, M. (1974). *Memory, related functions and age*. Springfield, IL: Charles C. Thomas.

Botwinick, J., & Thompson, L. W. (1968). Age differences in reaction time: An artifact? *Gerontologist, 8*, 25–28.

Bowlby, J. (1969). *Attachments*. New York: Basic Books.

Bradley, R. H., & Webb, R. (1976). Age-related differences in locus of control orientation in three behavioral domains. *Human Development, 19*, 49–55.

Bray, D. W., Campbell, R. J., & Grant, D. L. (1974). *Formative years in business: A long-term study of managerial lives*. New York: Wiley.

Bray, D. W., & Howard, A. (1983). The AT&T longitudinal studies of managers. In K. W. Schaie, (Ed.). *Longitudinal studies of adult psychological development* (pp. 226–312). New York: Guilford Press.

Brim, O. G., Jr. (1977). Theories of the male mid-life crisis. In N. Schlossberg & A. D. Entine (Eds.), *Counseling adults*. Monterey, CA: Brooks/Cole.

Brim, O. G., Jr., & Kagan, J. (1980). Constancy and change: A view of the issues. In O. G. Brim, Jr., & J. Kagan (Eds.), *Constancy and change in human development*. Cambridge, MA: Harvard University Press.

Broadbent, D. E., & Heron, A. (1962). Effects of a subsidiary task on performance involving immediate memory by younger and older men. *British Journal of Psychology, 53*, 189–198.

Brooks, J., & Lewis, M. (1981). Infant Perception: Responses to pictures of parents and strangers *Developmental Psychology, 17*, 647–654.

Brown, A. S. (1974). Satisfying relationships for the elderly and their patterns of disengagement. *Gerontologist, 14*, 258–262.

Browning, R. (1961). Rabbi Ben Ezra. In O. Williams (Ed.), *The centennial edition of F. T. Palgreave's The golden treasury of the best songs and lyrical poems*. New York: Mentor Books. (Original work published 1864)

Büchi, E. C. (1950). Anderung der Körperform beim erwachsenen Menschen, eine Untersuchung nach der Individual-Methode. *Anthropoligische Forschungen* (Vol. 1). Vienna: Anthropologische Gesellshaft.

Buhler, C. (1972). In W. R. Looft (Ed.), The course of human life as a psychological problem. In Looft, W. (Ed.) *Developmental psychology: A book of readings* (pp. 68–84). Hinsdale, IL: Dryden Press.

Butler, R. N. (1967). Creativity in later life. In S. Levin & R. J. Kahana (Eds.), *Psychodynamic studies on aging: Creativity, reminiscing, and dying*. New York: International Universities Press.

Butler, R. N., & Lewis, M. (1976). *Sex after sixty: A guide for men and women for their later years*. New York: Harper & Row.

Byrne, D. (1966). *An introduction to personality*. Englewood Cliffs, NJ: Prentice-Hall.

Bytheway, W. R. (1981). The variation with age of age differences in marriage. *Journal of Marriage and the Family, 43*, 923–927.

Campbell, A., Converse, P. E., & Rodgers, W. L. (1976). *The quality of American life: Perceptions, evaluation, and satisfaction*. New York: Russell Sage Foundation.

Canestrari, R. E., Jr. (1963). Paced and self-paced learning in young and elderly adults. *Journal of Gerontology, 18*, 165–168.

Cantor, M. (1977, May). *The extent and intensity of the informal support system among New York inner city elderly: Is ethnicity a factor?* Paper presented at Hunter College School of Social Work.

Cartwright, L. K., & Schmuckler, J. M. (1982, August). *Women college presidents and women physicians*. Paper presented at the meeting of the American Psychological Association, Washington, DC.

Cattell, R. B. (1963). Theory of fluid and crystallized intelligence: A critical experiment. *Journal of Educational Psychology, 54,* 1–22.

Charness, N. (1981). Search in chess: Age and skill differences. *Journal of Experimental Psychology, Human Perception and Performance, 7,* 467–476.

Chiriboga, D. A. (1979, November). *Marital separation in early and late life: A comparison.* Paper presented at the meeting of the Gerontological Society, Washington, DC.

Chown, S. M. (1961). Age and the rigidities. *Journal of Gerontology, 16,* 353–362.

Christenson, C. V., & Gagnon, J. H. (1965). Sexual behavior in a group of older women. *Journal of Gerontology, 20,* 351–356.

Cicirelli, V. (1979). *Social services for the elderly in relation to the kin network.* Report to the National Retired Teachers Association/American Association of Retired Persons, Andrus Foundation, Washington, DC.

Cicirelli, V. (1980a). A comparison of college women's feelings toward their siblings and parents. *Journal of Marriage and the Family, 42,* (1), 111–120.

Cicirelli, V. (1980b). Sibling relationships in adulthood: A life span perspective. In L. Poon (Ed.), *Aging in the 1980s,* pp. 455–462. Washington, DC: American Psychological Association.

Clark, A. L., & Wallin, P. (1965). Women's sexual responsiveness and the duration and quality of their marriages. *American Journal of Sociology, 71,* 187–196.

Clark, M. (1969). Cultural values and dependency in later life. In R. A. Kalish (Ed.), *The dependencies of old people,* pp. 59–72. Ann Arbor: University of Michigan, Institute of Gerontology.

Clausen, J. A. (1972). The life course of individuals. In M. W. Riley, M. Johnson, & A. Foner (Eds.), *The sociology of age stratification,* pp. 457–514. New York: Russell Sage Foundation.

Cohler, B. (1979, January 29). Close-knit ethnic ties can heighten stress in older women. *Behavior Today,* pp. 3–4.

Cohler, B., & Grunebaum, H. U. (1981). *Mothers, grandmothers, and daughters.* New York: Wiley.

Collins, G. R. (1964). Changes in optimal level of complexity as a function of age. *Dissertation Abstracts, 24,* 5538.

Comalli, P. E., Jr. (1962, October). *Differential effects of context on perception in young and aged groups.* Paper presented at the meeting of the Gerontological Society, Miami Beach.

Comalli, P. E. Jr. (1965). Cognitive functioning in a group of 80-to 90-year-old men. *Journal of Gerontology, 20,* (1), 14–17.

Comalli, P. E., Jr. (1970). Life-span changes in visual perception. In L. R. Goulet & P. B. Baltes (Eds.), *Life-span developmental psychology: Research and theory* (pp. 211–227). New York: Academic Press.

Comalli, P. E., Jr., Wapner, S., & Werner, H. (1959). Perception of verticality in middle and old age. *Journal of Psychology, 47,* 259–266.

Condran, J. C., & Bode, J. G. (1982). Rashomon, working wives, and family division of labor: Middletown, 1980. *Journal of Marriage and the Family, 44,* 421–426.

Constantine, L. L., & Constantine, J. M. (1973). *Group marriage.* New York: Collier Books.

Coombs, R. H., & Kenkel, W. F. (1966). Sex differences in dating aspirations and satisfaction with computer-selected partners. *Journal of Marriage and the Family, 28,* 62–66.

Costa, P., & McCrae, R. R. (1976). Age differences in personality structure: A cluster analytic approach. *Journal of Gerontology, 31*, 564–570.

Craik, F. I. M. (1977). Age differences in human memory. In J. E. Birren & K. W. Schaie (Eds.), *Handbook of the psychology of aging* (pp. 384–420). New York: Van Nostrand Reinhold.

Craik, F. I. M., & Masani, P. A. (1969). Age and intelligence differences in coding and retrieval of word lists. *British Journal of Psychology, 60*, 315–319.

Crites, J. (1969). *Vocational psychology.* New York: McGraw-Hill.

Cropley, A. J. (1969). Creativity, intelligence and intellectual style. *Australian Journal of Education, 13*, 3–7.

Crosson, C. W., & Robertson-Tchabo, E. A. (1983). Age and preference for complexity among manifestly creative women. *Human Development, 26*, 149–155.

Crowley, J. E., Levitin, T. E., & Quinn, R. P. (1973, October). Seven deadly half-truths about women. *Psychology Today,* pp. 94–96.

Csikszentmihalyi, M., Graef, R., & Larson, R. (1979, August). *Age differences in the quality of subjective experience.* Paper presented at the meeting of the American Psychological Association, San Francisco.

Cuber, J. F., & Harroff, P. B. (1963). The more total view: Relationships among men and women of the upper middle class. *Marriage and Family Living, 25*, 140–145.

Cumming, E., & Henry, W. (1961). *Growing old: The process of disengagement.* New York: Basic Books.

Datan, N., Antonovsky, A., & Maoz, B. (1981). *A time to reap.* Baltimore, MD: Johns Hopkins University Press.

Davies, A. D. M., & Laytham, G. W. H. (1964). Perception of verticality in adult life. *British Journal of Psychology, 55*, 315–320.

Death of the family. (1983, January 17). *Newsweek,* pp. 26–28.

De Lissovoy, V. (1973). High school marriages: A longitudinal study. *Journal of Marriage and the Family, 35*, 245–255.

Dennis, W. (1966). Age and creative productivity. *Journal of Gerontology, 21*, 1–8.

de Vries, H. A. (1975). Physiology of exercise and aging. In D. S. Woodruff & J. E. Birren (Eds.), *Aging: Scientific perspectives and social issues* (pp. 257–278). New York: Van Nostrand.

Dingle, J. (1973). *The ills of man: Life and death and medicine* (Scientific American Book). San Fransisco: W. H. Freeman.

Dobrof, R., & Litwak, E. (1977). *Maintenance of family ties of long-term care patients: Theory and guide to practice.* Washington, DC: U.S. Government Printing Office.

Doering, C. (1980). The endocrine system. In O. G. Brim, Jr., & J. Kagan (Eds.), *Constancy and change in human development* (pp. 229–271). Cambridge, MA: Harvard University Press.

Donelson, E., & Gullahorn, J. E. (1977). *Women: A psychological perspective.* New York: Wiley.

Douglas, K., & Arenberg, D. (1978). Age changes, cohort differences, and cultural change in the Guilford-Zimmerman Temperament Survey. *Journal of Gerontology, 33*, 737–747.

Douvan, E. (1979, Spring). Differing views on marriage, 1957 to 1976. *Newsletter, Center for Continuing Education for Women* (University of Michigan), pp. 1–2.

Duncan, O. D., Schuman, H., & Duncan, B. (1973). *Social change in a metropolitan community.* New York: Russell Sage Foundation.

Duvall, E. M. (1954). *In-laws pro and con.* New York: Associates Press.

Dyer, L. (1972, November). *Career implications of job displacement in middle-age: Experiences of managers and engineers.* Paper presented at the meeting of the Gerontological Society, San Juan, PR.

Eichorn, D. H. (1973). The Institute of Human Development Studies, Berkeley and Oakland. In L. F. Jarvik, C. Eisdorfer, & J. E. Blum (Eds.), *Intellectual functioning in adults* (pp.1–6). New York: Springer.

Eisdorfer, C. (1968). Arousal and performance: Experiments in verbal learning and a tentative theory. In G. A. Talland (Ed.), *Human aging and behavior* (pp. 146–151). New York: Academic Press.

Eisner, D. A., & Schaie, K. W. (1971). Age changes in response to visual illusions from middle age to old age. *Journal of Gerontology, 26,* 146.

Elder, G. (1974). *Children of the Great Depression.* Chicago: University of Chicago Press.

Elias, M. E., Elias, P. K., & Elias, J. W. (1977). *Basic processes in adult developmental psychology.* St. Louis: C. V. Mosby.

Elkind, D. (1970). *Children and adolescents.* New York: Oxford University Press.

Elo, A. E. (1965). Age changes in master chess performance. *Journal of Gerontology, 20,* 289–299.

Erikson, E. (1950). *Childhood and society.* New York: Norton.

Feldman, H. (1964, August). *Development of the husband-wife relationship.* Research report presented to the Department of Child Development and Family Relationships, New York State College of Home Economics, Cornell University, Ithaca, NY.

Feldman, H. (1971). The effects of children on the family. In A. Michel (Ed.), *Family issues of employed women in Europe and America.* (pp. 107–125). Leiden, The Netherlands: Brill.

Feldman, H. (1981). A comparison of intentional parents and intentionally childless couples. *Journal of Marriage and the Family, 43,* 593–600.

Feldman, S., & Nash, S. (1978). Interest in babies during young adulthood. *Child Development, 49,* 617–622.

Feldman, S., & Nash, S. (1979). Sex differences in responsiveness to babies among mature adults. *Developmental Psychology, 15,* 430–436.

Fischer, J. S., Carlton-Ford, S. L., & Briles, B. J. (1979). *Life-cycle career patterns: A typological approach to female status attainment.* (Tech. Bull. No. 8). University of Alabama, Center for the Study of Aging.

Flavell, J. H. (1970). Cognitive changes in adulthood. In L. R. Goulet & P. B. Baltes (Eds.), *Life-span development psychology* (Vol. 1, pp. 247–253). New York: Academic Press.

Folkman, S., & Lazarus, R. S. (1980). An analysis of coping in a middle-aged community sample. *Journal of Health and Social Behavior, 21,* 219–239.

Fox, G. L. (1975, November). *Before marriage; An assessment of organization and change in the premarital period.* Paper presented at the Merrill-Palmer Conference on Changing Sex Roles and the Family, Detroit.

Fozard, J., Nutall, R. L., & Waugh, N. C. (1972). Age-related differences in mental performance. *Aging and Human Development, 3,* 19–43.

Framo, J. (1979, September). *Family psychology and intimate contexts: Neglected areas in social psychology.* Paper presented at the meeting of the American Psychological Association, New York.

Freedman, D. G. (1965). An ethological approach to the genetic study of human behavior. In S. G. Vandenberg (Ed.), *Methods and goals in human behavior genetics (pp. 141–161). New York: Academic Press.*

Freilich, M. (1964). The natural trends in kinship and complex systems. *American Sociological Review, 29,* 529–540.

Freud, S. (1927). *The ego and the id.* London: Hogarth Press.

Friday, N. (1981). *My mother, myself.* New York: Dell.

Friedan, B. (1963). *The feminine mystique.* New York: W. W. Norton.

Friedmann, E. A., & Havighurst, R. J. (1954). *The meaning of work and retirement.* Chicago: University of Chicago Press.

Froehling, S. (1974). Effects of propranolol on behavioral and physiological measures of elderly males. Unpublished doctoral dissertation, Duke University.

Furstenberg, F. F., Jr., & Crawford, A. G. (1978). Family support: Helping teenage mothers to cope. *Family Planning Perspectives, 10,* 322–333.

Gagné, R. H. (1968). Contributions of learning to human development. *Psychological Review, 75,* 177–191.

Gajo, F. D. (1966). *Adult age differences in the perception of visual illusion.* Unpublished doctoral dissertation, University of Michigan.

Gaylord, S. A., & Marsh, G. R. (1975). Age differences in the speed of a spatial cognitive process. *Journal of Gerontology, 30,* 674–678.

Giambra, L. M. (1973, August). *Daydreaming in males from seventeen to seventy-seven: A preliminary report.* Paper presented at the meeting of the American Psychological Association, Montreal.

Gibbs, J. M. (1979). *The social world of the older widow in the nonmetropolitan community.* Unpublished doctoral dissertation, Kansas State University.

Gilford, R., & Bengtson, V. L. (1979). Measuring marital satisfaction in three generations: Positive and negative dimensions. *Journal of Marriage and Family, 41,* 387–398.

Gilford, R., & Black, D. (1972, December). *The grandchild-grandparent dyad: Ritual or relationship?* Paper presented at the meeting of the Gerontological Society, San Juan, PR.

Gladis, M., & Braun, H. W. (1958). Age differences in transfer and retroaction as a function of intertask response similarity. *Journal of Experimental Psychology, 55,* 25–30.

Glenn, N. D. (1980). Values, attitudes, and beliefs. In O. G. Brim, Jr. & J. Kagan (Eds.), *Constancy and change in human development* (pp.596–640). Cambridge, MA: Harvard University Press.

Glenn, N. D., & Hefner, T. (1972). Further evidence on aging and party identification. *Public Opinion Quarterly, 36,* 31–47.

Glenn, N. D., & McLanahan, S. (1982). Children and marital happiness: A further specification of the relationship. *Journal of Marriage and the Family, 44,* 63–72.

Glick, I. O., Weiss, R. S., & Parkes, C. M. (1974). *The first year of bereavement.* New York: Wiley.

Glick, P. C. (1977). Updating the life cycle of the family. *Journal of Marriage and the Family, 39,* 5–13.

Glick, P. C. (1979, Summer/Fall). Future American families. *Washington Cofo Memo,* pp. 2–5.

Glick, P. C., & Norton, A. J. (1977, October). Marrying, divorcing, and living together in the U.S. today. *Population Bulletin, 32,* 1–53.

Glick, P. C., & Spanier, G. B. (1980). Married and unmarried cohabitation in the United States. *Journal of Marriage and the Family, 42,* 19–31.

Goldstein, A. G., & Chance, J. E. (1965). Effects of practice on sex-related differences in performance on embedded figures. *Psychonomic Science, 3,* 361–362.

Goodman, C. J. (1978). *Growing old in a garment factory: The effects of occupational segregation and runaway shops in working-class women.* Unpublished master's thesis, Rutgers University.

Gordon, C., Gaitz, C. M., & Scott, J., Jr. (1976). Leisure and lives: Personal expressivity across the life span. In R. H. Binstock & E. Shanas (Eds.), *Handbook of aging and the social sciences* (pp. 310–341). New York: Van Nostrand Reinhold.

Gottman, J. M. (1979). *Marital interactions: Experimental investigation.* New York: Academic Press.

Gottschalk, L. P., Kaplan, S., Gleser, G. G., & Winget, C. M. (1962). Variations in magnitude of emotion: A method applied to anxiety and hostility during phases of the menstrual cycle. *Psychosomatic Medicine, 24,* 300–311.

Granick, S., & Friedman, A. S. (1967, February). Uneven decline in mental functions with age. *Geriatric Focus,* p. 3.

Greenberg, M., & Morris, M. (1974). Engrossment: The newborn's impact upon the father. *American Journal of Orthopsychiatry, 44,* 520–531.

Grotevant, H. D. (1976). Family similarities in interests and orientation. *Merrill-Palmer Quarterly, 22,* 61–72.

Gruen, W. (1964). Adult personality: An empirical study of Erickson's theory of ego development. In B. L. Neugarten & Associates (Eds.), *Personality in middle and late life: Empirical studies* (pp. 1–14). New York: Atherton.

Gsell, O. R. (1967). Longitudinal gerontological research over ten years. (Basel Studies, 1955–1965). *Gerontologia Clinica, 9,* 67–80.

Gubrium, J. F. (1975). Being single in old age. *International Journal of Aging and Human Development, 6,* 29–41.

Gutmann, D. (1975). Parenthood: Key to the comparative study of the life cycle. In N. Datan & L. H. Ginsburg (Eds.), *Life-span developmental psychology: Normative life crises* (pp. 167–184). New York: Academic Press.

Guttentag, M., & Secord, P. (1983). *Too many women?* Beverly Hills, CA: Sage.

Haan, N. (1976). Personality organizations of well-functioning younger people and older adults. *International Journal of Aging and Human Development, 7,* 117–127.

Haan, N., & Day, D. (1974). A longitudinal study of change and sameness in personality development, adolescence to later adulthood. *Aging and Human Development, 5,* 11–39.

Hagestad, G. O. (1977). *Role change in adulthood: The transition to the empty nest.* Unpublished manuscript, Committee on Human Development, University of Chicago.

Hagestad, G. O. (1978, August). *Patterns of communication and influence between grandparents and grandchildren in a changing society.* Paper presented at the World Congress of Sociology, Uppsala, Sweden.

Hagestad, G. O. (1981). Problems and promises in the social psychology of intergenerational relations. In R. W. Fogel & J. G. March (Eds.) (p. 11–46), *Stability and change in the family.* New York: Academic Press.

Hagestad, G. O. (1982). Parent and child. In T. Field, A. Huston, H. C. Quay, L. E. Troll, & G. Finley (Eds.), *Human development* (pp. 485–489). New York: Wiley.

Hagestad, G. O. (1983). *Multigenerational families: Socialization, support, and strain.* Paper presented at the International Symposium on Intergenerational Relationships, West Berlin.

Hagestad, G. O., & Snow, R. B. (1977, November). *Young adult offspring as interpersonal resources in middle age*. Paper presented at the meeting of the Gerontological Society, San Fransico.

Hagestad, G. O., & Speicher, J. L. (1981, March). *Grandparents and family influence: Views of three generations*. Paper presented at the meeting of the Society for Research in Child Development, Boston.

Haller, M., & Rosenmayr, L. (1971). The pluridimensionality of work commitment: A study of young married women in different social contexts of occupational and family life. *Human Relations, 24,* 501–518.

Haller, O. (1982). *An investigation of the perceptions of attachment in the mother–adult child dyad*. Unpublished doctoral dissertation, New York University.

Hareven, T. (1976). The last stage: Historical adulthood and old age. *Daedalus, 105* (4), 13–28.

Hareven, T. (1977). Historical changes in the life course and the family: Policy implications. In M. Yinger & S. Cutler (Eds.), *Major social issues: A multidisciplinary view.* New York: Free Press.

Harris, D. (Ed.). (1957). *The concept of development: An issue in the study of human behavior.* Minneapolis: University of Minnesota Press.

Hartup, W. W., & Lempers, J. (1973). A problem in life-span development: The interactional analysis of family attachments. In P. B. Baltes & K. W. Schaie (Eds.), *Life-span developmental psychology: Personality and socialization.* New York: Academic Press.

Havighurst, R. J. (1957). The leisure activities of the middle-aged. *American Journal of Sociology, 63,* 152–162.

Havighurst, R. J. (1953). *Human development and education.* New York: Longmans.

Havighurst, R. J. (1972). *Developmental tasks and education.* New York: David McKay.

Havighurst, R. J. (1982). The world of work. In B. Wolman (Ed.), *Handbook of developmental psychology* (pp. 771–790). Englewood Cliffs, NJ: Prentice-Hall.

Haviland, J., & Myers, J. (1979). *Attribution of affect to faces of different ages.* Unpublished manuscript, Department of Psychology, Rutgers University.

Haynes, S. O., & Feinleib, M. (1980). Women, work and coronary heart disease: Prospective findings from the Framingham heart study. *American Journal of Public Health, 70,* 133–141.

Hays, W. C., & Mindel, C. H. (1973). Extended kinship relations in Black and White families. *Journal of Marriage and the Family, 35,* 51–57.

Heath, D. H. (1978). What meaning and effects does fatherhood have for the maturing of professional men? *Merrill-Palmer Quarterly, 24,* 265–278.

Heins, M., Smock, S., & Stein, M. (1976, October 25). Productivity of women physicians. *Journal of the American Medical Association,* 1961–1964.

Helson, R. (1972). The changing image of the career women. *Journal of Social Issues, 28,*(2), 33–46.

Henning, M., & Jardim, A. (1976). *The managerial woman.* New York: Doubleday.

Henry, W., Sims, J., & Spray, L. (1971). *The fifth profession: Becoming a psychotherapist.* San Francisco: Jossey-Bass.

Herzberg, F., Mausner, B., & Snyderman, B. (1959). *The motivation to work.* New York: Wiley.

Hess, B., & Waring, J. M. (1978). Parent and child in later life: Rethinking the relationship. In R. Lerner & G. B. Spanier (Eds.), *Child influences in marital and family interaction* (pp. 241–274). New York: Academic Press.

Hetherington, E. M., Cox, M., & Cox, R. (1976). Divorced fathers. *Family Coordinator, 25,* 417–428.

Hicks, L. H., & Birren, J. E. (1970). Aging, brain damage, and psychomotor slowing. *Psychological Bulletin, 74,* 377.

Hill, R., Foote, N., Aldous, J., Carlson, R., & Macdonald, R. (1970). *Family development in three generations.* Cambridge, MA: Schenkman.

Hoffman, L. (1974). Effects on child. In L. Hoffman & G. Nye (Eds.), *Working mothers* (pp. 126–166). San Francisco: Jossey-Bass.

Hoffman, L., & Manis, J. (1978). Influences of children on marital interaction and parental satisfactions and dissatisfactions. In R. Lerner & G. B. Spanier (Eds.), *Child influences on marital and family interaction* (pp. 165–214). New York: Academic Press.

Holland, J. L. (1973). *Making vocational choices: A theory of careers.* Englewood Cliffs, NJ: Prentice-Hall.

Honeycutt, J. M., Wilson, C., & Parker, C. (1982). Effects of sex and degrees of happiness on perceived styles of communicating in and out of the marital relationship. *Journal of Marriage and the Family, 44,* 395–406.

Honzik, M. P. (1964). Personality consistency and change: Some comments on papers by Bayley, Macfarlane, Moss and Kagan, and Murphy. *Vita Humana, 7,* 139–142.

Honzik, M. P., & Macfarlane, J. W. (1973). Personality development and intellectual functioning. In L. F. Jarvik, C. Eisdorfer, & J. E. Blum (Eds.), *Intellectual functioning in adults* (pp. 45–58). New York: Springer.

Horn, J. L. (1970). Organization of data on life-span development of human abilities. In L. R. Goulet & P. B. Baltes (Eds.), *Life-span developmental psychology: Research and theory* (pp. 424–467). New York: Academic Press.

Horner, M. S. (1970). Femininity and successful achievement: A basic inconsistency. In J. Bardwick, E. Douvan, M. Horner, & D. Gutmann (Eds.), *Feminine personality and conflict* (pp. 45–74). Monterey, CA: Brooks/Cole.

Howell, F. M., & Frese, W. (1982). Adult role transitions, parental influence, and status aspirations early in the life course. *Journal of Marriage and the Family, 44,* 35–49.

Hoyer, W. J., Labouvie, G. V., & Baltes, P. B. (1973). Modification of response speed and intellectual performance in the elderly. *Human Development, 16,* 233–242.

Huston-Stein, A., & Higgins-Trenk, A. (1978). Development of females from childhood through adulthood: Career and feminine role orientations. In P. B. Baltes (Ed.), *Life-span development and behavior* (Vol. 1, pp. 258–296). New York: Academic Press.

"Ideal weight" for a long life adjusted upward in a survey (1983, March 2). *New York Times,* p. A21.

Ilfield, F. W. (1980). Coping styles of Chicago adults: Description. *Journal of Human Stress, 6,* 2–10.

Inkeles, A. (1968). Society, social structure and child socialization. In J. A. Clausen (Ed.), *Socialization and society.* Boston: Little, Brown.

Ivey, M. E., & Bardwick, J. M. (1968). Patterns of affective fluctuation in the menstrual cycle. *Psychosomatic Medicine, 30,* 336–345.

Izard, C. (1971). *The face of emotion.* New York: Appleton-Century-Crofts.

Jackson, J. J. (1977). Older Black women. In L. E. Troll, J. Israel, & K. Israel (Eds.), *Looking ahead: A women's guide to the problems and joys of growing older* (pp. 149–156). Englewood Cliffs, NJ: Prentice-Hall.

Jackobson, R. (1962). Why "Momma" and "Poppa". In *Selected writings of Roman Jakobson.* The Hague. Mouton.

Jerome, E. A. (1962). Decay of heuristic processes in the aged. In C. Tibbitts & W. Donahue (Eds.), *Social and psychological aspects of aging*. New York: Columbia University Press.

Jones, E. (1953). *Freud*. New York: Basic Books.

Jones, H. E., & Conrad, H. S. (1933). The growth and decline of intelligence: A study of a homogeneous group between the ages of ten and sixty. *Genetic Psychology Monographs, 13,* 223–298.

Jung, C. (1971). The stages of life. (R. F. C. Hill, Trans.). In J. Campbell (Ed.), *The portable Jung*. New York: Viking. (Original work published 1930.)

Kagan, J., & Moss, H. A. (1962). *Birth to maturity: A study in psychological development*. New York: Wiley.

Kahana, B., & Kahana, E. (1970). Grandparenthood from the perspective of the developing grandchild. *Developmental Psychology, 3,* 98–105.

Kangas, J., & Bradway, K. (1971). Intelligence at middle age: A thirty-eight year follow-up. *Developmental Psychology, 5,* 333–337.

Kanter, R. M. (1977). *Men and women of the corporation*. New York: Basic Books.

Kaplan, E. (1983). *Work-family stress: Its nature, prevalence, causes, and consequences among full-time employed women with children*. Unpublished doctoral dissertation, Rutgers University.

Kastenbaum, R., & Symonds, D. (1977). Those endearing young charms: Fifty years later. In L. E. Troll, J. Israel, & K. Israel (Eds.), *Looking ahead: A women's guide to the problems and joys of growing older* (pp. 196–206). Englewood Cliffs, NJ: Prentice-Hall.

Katz, M. (1975, August). *Sex role training and coping behavior in a role conflict situation: Homemaking-career conflicts*. Paper presented at the meeting of the American Psychological Association, Chicago.

Kellam, S., Adams, R., Brown, C. H., & Ensminger, M. (1982). The long-term evolution of the family structure of teenage and older mothers. *Journal of Marriage and the Family, 44,* 539–554.

Kelly, E. L. (1955). Consistency of the adult personality. *American Psychologist, 10,* 659–681.

Kent, S. (1976, March). How do we age? *Geriatrics,* pp. 128–134.

Kerckhoff, A. C., & Davis, K. E. (1962). Value consensus and need complementarity in mate selection. *American Sociological Review, 27,* 295–303.

Kimura, D. (1973, September). The asymmetry of the human brain. *Scientific American,* pp. 70–78.

Kinsey, A. C., Pomeroy, W. B., & Martin, C. E. (1948). *Sexual behavior in the human male*. Philadelphia: Saunders.

Kinsey, A. C., Pomeroy, W. B., Martin, C. E., & Gebhard, P. H. (1953). *Sexual behavior in the human female*. Philadelphia: Saunders.

Kitson, G. C., & Sussman, M. B. (1982). Marital complaints, demographic characteristics, and symptoms of mental distress in divorce. *Journal of Marriage and the Family, 44,* 87–102.

Kivnick, H. (1981). Grandparenthood and the mental health of grandparents. *Aging and Society, 1,* 365–391.

Klatsky, S. R. (1972). *Patterns of contact with relatives* (Arnold and Caroline Rose Monograph Series in Sociology). Washington, DC: American Sociological Association.

Klein, D. C., & Ross, A. (1958). Kindergarten entry: A study of role transition. In M. Krugman (Ed.), *Orthopsychiatry and the school*. New York: American Orthopsychiatric Association.

Kohlberg, L. (1973). Continuities in childhood and adult moral development revisited. In P. B. Baltes & K. W. Schaie (Eds.), *Life-span developmental psychology: Personality and socialization* (pp. 180–207). New York: Academic Press.

Kohn, M. L., & Schooler, C. (1979). The reciprocal effects of the substantive complexity of work and intellectual flexibility: A longitudinal assessment. In M. W. Riley (Ed.), *Aging from birth to death: Interdisciplinary perspectives.* Boulder, CO: Westview Press.

Kohn, R. R. (1977). Heart and cardiovascular system. In C. Finch & L. Hayflick (Eds.), *Handbook of the physiology of aging* (pp. 281–317). New York: Van Nostrand Reinhold.

Komarovsky, M. (1964). *Blue-collar marriage*. New York: Random House.

Kuhn, D., Langer, J., Kohlberg, L., & Haan, N. S. (1977). The development of formal operations in logical and moral judgment. *Genetic Psychology Monographs, 95,* 97–188.

Labouvie-Vief, G. (1979, March). *Continuities and discontinuities between childhood and adulthood: Piaget revisited.* Paper presented at the meeting of the Society for Research in Child Development, San Francisco.

Lake, A. (1976, September). Divorcees: The new poor. *McCall's,* pp. 20, 22, 24, 152.

Lamb, M. E. (1978). Influence of the child on marital quality and family interaction during prenatal, perinatal, and infancy periods. In R. Lerner, & G. B. Spanier (Eds.), *Child influences on marital and family interaction: A life-span perspective* (pp. 137–163). New York: Academic Press.

Lamb, M. E., & Lamb, J. E. (1976). The nature and importance of the father-infant relationship. *Family Coordinator, 25,* 379–388.

Laurie, W. F. (1977). Health status of people over 65. *Center Reports on Advances in Research* (Duke University Center for the Study of Aging and Human Development), 1(2), B1.

Lehman, H. C. (1953). *Age and achievement.* Princeton, NJ: Princeton University Press.

Levinson, D. J. (with Darrow, C. N., Klein, E. B., Levinson, M. H., & McKee, B.), (1976). Periods in the development of men: Ages 18 to 45. *Counseling Psychologist, 6,* (1), 21–25.

Levinson, D. J. (with Darrow, C. N., Klein, E. B., Levinson, M. H., & McKee, B.), (1978). *The seasons of a man's life.* New York: Knopf.

Lewis, M., & Brooks, J. (1975). Infants' social perception: A constructivist view. In L. B. Cohen & B. Salapatek (Eds.), *Infant perception: From sensation to cognition* (Vol 2), pp. 101–148. New York: Academic Press.

Lewis, M., & Feiring, C. (1978). The child's social world. In R. Lerner & G. B. Spanier (Eds.), *Child influences on marital and family interaction: A life-span perspective.* New York: Academic Press.

Lewis, R. (1973). Social reaction and the formation of dyads: An interactionist approach to mate selection. *Sociometry, 36,* 409–418.

Libow, L. S. (1974). Interaction of medical, biologic, and behavioral factors on aging, adaptation, and survival: An 11-year longitudinal study. *Geriatrics, 29* (11), 75–88.

Livson, F. B. (1976, October). *Coming together in the middle years: A longitudinal study of sex-role convergence.* Paper presented at the meeting of the Gerontological Society, New York.

Livson, F. B. (1977). Coming out of the closet: Marriage and other crises of middle age. In L. E. Troll, J. Israel, & K. Israel (Eds.), *Looking ahead: A woman's guide to the problems and joys of growing older* (pp. 81–92). Englewood Cliffs, NJ: Prentice-Hall.

Locksley, A. (1982). Social class and marital attitudes and behaviors. *Journal of Marriage and the Family, 44,* 427–440.

Loevinger, J. (1976). *Ego development: Conceptions and theories.* San Francisco: Jossey-Bass.

Lopata, H. Z. (1971). *Occupation: Housewife.* London: Oxford University Press.

Lopata, H. Z. (1973). *Widowhood in an American city.* Cambridge, MA: Schenkman.

Lorge, I. (1936). The influence of the test upon the nature of mental decline as a function of old age. *Journal of Educational Psychology, 27,* 100–110.

Lowenthal, M. F., Thurnher, M. T., & Chiriboga, D. (1975). *Four stages of life.* San Francisco: Jossey-Bass.

Luck, P. W., & Heiss, J. (1972). Social determinants of self-esteem in adult males. *Sociology and Social Research, 57,* 69–84.

Luckey, E. B. (1961). Perceptual congruence of self and family concepts as related to marital interaction. *Sociometry, 24,* 234–250.

Lurie, E. E. (1972). *Role scope and social participation.* Unpublished paper no. 10A, 11, University of California, Human Development Program, San Francisco.

Maas, H., & Kuypers, J. A. (1974). *From thirty to seventy: A forty-year longitudinal study of adult life styles and personality.* San Francisco: Jossey-Bass.

Maccoby, E. E., & Jacklin, C. N. (1974). *The psychology of sex differences.* Stanford, CA: Stanford University Press.

Macklin, E. D. (1978). Nonmarital heterosexual cohabitation. *Marriage and Family Review, 1,* (March-April), 1–12.

Marini, M. M. (1981). Measuring the effects of the timing of marriage and first birth. *Journal of Marriage and the Family, 43,* 19–26.

Markman, H. J. (1981). Prediction of marital distress: A five-year follow-up. *Journal of Consulting and Clinical Psychology, 49,* 760–762.

Masters, W. H., & Johnson, V. E. (1966). *Human sexual response.* Boston: Little, Brown.

Masters, W. H., & Johnson, V. E. (1968). Human sexual response: The aging female and male. In B. Neugarten (Ed.), *Middle age and aging.* Chicago: University of Chicago Press.

Masters, W. H., & Johnson, V. E. (1974). Emotional poverty: A marriage crisis of the middle years. In *Proceedings of the Second National Congress on the Quality of Life: The Middle Years.* Acton, MA: Publishing Sciences Group.

McClintock, M. K. (1971). Menstrual synchrony and suppression. *Nature, 37,* 571–605.

McCrae, R. R. (1982). Age differences in the use of coping mechanisms. *Journal of Gerontology, 37,* 454–460.

McLaughlin, S. D., & Micklin, M. (1983). The timing of the first birth and changes in personal efficacy. *Journal of Marriage and the Family, 45,* 47–55.

Mead, G. H. (1934). *Mind, self, and society.* Chicago: University of Chicago Press.

Meyerowitz, J. H., & Feldman, H. (1967). Transitions to parenthood. In I. E. Cohen (Ed.), *Family structure, dynamics, and therapy* (pp. 78–84). New York: American Psychiatric Association.

Mischel, W. (1968). *Personality and assessment.* New York: Wiley.

Mischel, W. (1979, September). *Looking for personality.* Paper presented at the meeting of the American Psychological Association, New York.

Mitchell, G. (1969). Paternalistic behavior in primates. *Psychological Bulletin, 71,* 399–417.

Money, J., & Erhardt, A. A. (1972). *Man and woman, boy and girl: Differentiation and dimorphism of gender identity from conception to maturity.* Baltimore: Johns Hopkins Press.

Monge, R. H. (1975). Structure of the self-concept from adolescence through old age. *Experimental Aging Research, 1,* 281–291.

Moos, R. (1968). The development of a menstrual stress questionnaire. *Psychosomatic Medicine, 30,* 853–867.

Moss, H. A., & Susman, E. J. (1980). Longitudinal study of personality development. In O. G. Brim, Jr., & Kagan, J. (Eds.), *Constancy and change in human development* (pp. 530–595).

Mullener, N., & Laird, J. D. (1971). Some developmental changes in the organization of self-evaluations. *Developmental Psychology, 5,* 233–236.

Murray, J. (1973). Family structure in the pre-retirement years. *Social Security Bulletin, 36*(10), 25–44.

Murstein, B. I. (1972). Person perception and courtship progress among premarital couples. *Journal of Marriage and the Family, 34,* 621–626.

Mussen, P. H., & Jones, M. C. (1957). Self-conceptions, motivations, and interpersonal attitudes of late-and early-maturing boys. *Child Development, 28,* 243–256.

Nagle, J.J. (1984). *Heredity and human affairs.* St. Louis: C.V. Mosby.

Nehrke, M. F. (1971, October). *Age, sex, and educational difference in logical judgements.* Paper presented at the meeting of the Gerontological Society, Houston.

Nelson, B. (1983, April 3). Bosses face less risk than the bossed. *New York Times,* p. E 16.

Neugarten, B. L. (Ed.). (1968). *Middle age and aging.* Chicago: University of Chicago Press.

Neugarten, B. L. (1973). Personality change in late life: A developmental perspective. In C. Eisdorfer & M. Powell-Lawton (Eds.), *The psychology of adult development and aging.* (pp. 311–338). Washington, DC: American Psychological Association.

Neugarten, B. L. (1977). Personality and aging. In J. E. Birren & K. W. Schaie (Eds.), *Handbook of the psychology of aging* (pp. 626–649). New York: Van Nostrand Reinhold.

Neugarten, B. L., & Gutmann, D. L. (1964). Age-sex roles and personality in middle age: A thematic apperception study. In B. L. Neugarten & Associates (Eds.), *Personality in middle and late life: Empirical studies* (pp. 44–90). New York: Atherton

Neugarten, B. L., Moore, J. W., & Lowe, J. C. (1965). Age norms, age constraints, and adult socialization. *American Journal of Sociology, 70,* 710–717.

Neugarten, B. L., & Weinstein, K. K. (1964). The changing American grandparent. *Journal of Marriage and the Family, 26,* 199–204.

Noberini, M., & Neugarten, B. L. (1975, October). *A follow-up study of adaptation in middle-aged women.* Paper presented at the meeting of the Gerontological Society, Louisville, KY.

Norton, A. J., & Glick, P. C. (1976). Marital instability: Past, present, and future. *Journal of Social Issues, 32*(1), 6–7.

Novak, E. R. (1970). Ovulation after fifty. *Obstetrical Gynecology, 36,* 903–910.

Nowak, C. A. (1976, March). *Youthfulness, attractiveness and the midlife women: An analysis of the appearance signal in adult development.* Paper presented at the meeting of the Midwestern Psychological Association, Chicago.

Nunn, C. Z., Crockett, H. J., Jr., & Williams, J. A., Jr. (1978). *Tolerance for nonconformity.* San Francisco: Jossey-Bass.

Nydegger, C. N. (1973, November). *Late and early fathers.* Paper presented at the meeting of the Gerontological Society, Miami Beach.

Nydegger, C. N., & Mitteness, L. (1979). Transitions in fatherhood. *Generations, 4,* 14–15.

Obrist, W. D., Henry, C. E., & Justiss, W. A. (1961). A longitudinal study of EEG in old age. *Excerpta medica* (International Congress Series), *37,* 180–181.

O'Leary, V. (1977). *Toward understanding women.* Monterey, CA: Brooks/Cole.

Owen, J. D. (1976, August). Work weeks and leisure: An analysis of trends, 1948–1975. *Monthly Labor Review,* pp. 3–8.

Palmer, R. D. (1968). Psychological factors in visual acuity. *Proceedings, of the 97th Annual Convention of the American Psychological Association, 10,* 539–560.

Palmore, E. (1969). Physical, mental, and social factors in predicting longevity. *Gerontologist, 9,* 103–108.

Paris, B. L., & Luckey, E. B. (1966). A longitudinal study in marital satisfaction. *Sociological and Social Research, 50,* 212–222.

Parke, R. D., & O'Leary, S. (1975). Father-mother-infant interaction in the newborn period: Some findings, some observations, and some unresolved issues. In K. F. Riegel & J. Meacham (Eds.), *The developing individual in a changing world: Vol. 2. Social and environmental issues* (pp. 653–663). The Hague: Mouton.

Parke, R. D., & Sawin, D. B. (1975, April). *Infant characteristics and behavior as elicitors of maternal and paternal responsivity.* Paper presented at the meeting of the Society for Research in Child Development, Denver.

Parkes, C. M. (1964). Effects of bereavement on physical and mental health: A study of the medical records of widows. *British Medical Journal, 2,* 274–279.

Parnes, H. S., Nestel, G., & Andresani, P. (1972). *The pre-retirement years: A longitudinal study of the labor market experience of men.* (Vol. 3). Columbus: Ohio State University, Center for Human Resource Research.

Parnes, H. S., Shea, J. R., Spitz, R. S., Zeller, F., & Associates. (1970). *Dual careers: A longitudinal study of labor market experience of women* (Vol. 1). Columbus: Ohio State University, Center for Human Resource Research. (Also published as Manpower Research Monograph No. 21. Washington, DC: U.S. Government Printing Office.

Parron, E. M. (1978). *An exploratory study of intimacy in golden wedding couples.* Unpublished master's thesis, Rutgers University.

Pearlin, L. I., & Schooler, C. (1978). The structure of coping. *Journal of Health and Social Behavior, 19,* 2–12.

Perlmutter, M. (1978). What is memory aging the aging of? *Developmental Psychology, 14,* 330–335.

Pfeiffer, E., & Davis, G. C. (1971). Use of leisure time in middle life. *Gerontologist, 11,* 187–195.

Pfeiffer, E., & Davis, G. C. (1972). Determinants of sexual behavior in middle and old age. *Journal of the American Geriatric Society, 20,* 151–158.

Piaget, J. (1970). Piaget's theory (G. Gellerier & J. Langer, Trans.). In P. Mussen (Ed.), *Carmichael's manual of child psychology,* (Vol. 1, pp. 703–732). New York: Wiley.

Piaget, J. (1972). Intellectual evolution from adolescence to adulthood. *Human Development, 15,* 1–12.

Pineo, P. C. (1961). Disenchantment in the later years of marriage. *Marriage and Family Living, 23,* 1–12.

Pleck, J. H. (1975, October). *Men's roles in the family: A new look.* Paper presented at the Ford Foundation Conference on Changing Sex Roles and the Family, Detroit.

Pleck, J. H. (1977). The work-family role system. *Social Problems, 24,* 417–427.

Pleck, J. H., Staines, G. L., & Lang, L. (1980, March). Conflicts between work and family life. *Monthly Labor Review,* pp. 29–32.

Powell, D. A., Tkacik, M. F., Buchanan, S. L., & Milligan, W. L. (1976). Cardio-vascular responses elicited by electrical brain stimulation in the rabbit. *Physiology & Behavior, 16,* 227–230.

Quinn, R. P., & Staines, G. L. (1979). *The 1977 Quality of Employment Survey.* Ann Arbor: University of Michigan, Institute for Social Research, Survey Research Center.

Powell, D. A., Buchanan, S., & Milligan, W. (1975, October). *Relationships between learning performance and arousal in aged, versus younger VA patients.* Paper presented at the meeting of the Gerontological Society, Louisville, KY.

Quinn, R. P., Staines, G. L., & McCullough, M. R. (1974). *Job satisfaction: Is there a trend?* (U.S. Department of Labor, Manpower Research Monograph No. 30). Washington, DC: U.S. Government Printing Office.

Rabbit, P. M.A. (1964). Age and time for choice between stimuli and between responses. *Journal of Gerontology, 19,* 307–312.

Rapoport, R., & Rapoport, R. (1969). The dual-career families: A variant pattern and social change. *Human Relations, 22,* 3–30.

Raush, H. L., Barry, W. A., Hertel, R. H., & Swain, M. A. (1974). *Communication, conflict, and marriage.* San Francisco: Jossey-Bass.

Reedy, M. N. (1977). *Age and sex differences in personal needs and the nature of love: A study of happily married young, middle-aged, and older adult couples.* Unpublished doctoral dissertation, University of Southern California.

Reedy, M. N., & Birren, J. E. (1978, November). *How do lovers grow older together? Types of lovers and age.* Paper presented at the meeting of the Gerontological Society, Dallas.

Reichard, S., Livson, F., & Peterson, P. (1962). *Aging and personality.* New York: Wiley.

Riegel, K. F. (1975). Adult life crises: A dialectic interpretation of development. In N. Datan & L. H. Ginsberg (Eds.), *Life-span developmental psychology: Normative life crises* (pp. 99–129). New York: Academic Press.

Riegel, K. F., Riegel, R., & Meyer, G. (1967). Sociopsychological factors of aging: A cohort-sequential analysis. *Human Development, 10,* 27–56.

Robertson, J. F. (1977). Grandmotherhood: A study of role conceptions. *Journal of Marriage and the Family, 39,* 165–174.

Robinson, J. P. (1979, September). *How people feel about how they use their time.* Paper presented at the meeting of the American Psychological Association, New York.

Robson, K. S., & Moss, H. A. (1970). Patterns and determinants of maternal attachment. *Journal of Pediatrics, 77,* 976–985.

Roe, A. (1961). The psychology of the scientist. *Science, 134,* 456–459.

Rosen, J., & Neugarten, B. L. (1960). Ego functions in the middle and later years: A thematic apperception study of normal adults. *Journal of Gerontology, 15,* 62–67.

Rosenberg, G. L., & Anspach, D. F. (1973). Sibling solidarity in the working class. *Journal of Marriage and the Family, 35,* 108–113.

Rosenblatt, P. C. (1974). Behavior in public places: Comparison of couples accompanied and unaccompanied by children. *Journal of Marriage and the Family, 36,* 750–755.

Rosow, I. (1967). *Social integration of the aged.* New York: Free Press.

Rossman, I. (1977). Anatomic and body composition changes with aging. In C. Finch & L. Hayflick (Eds.), *Handbook of the biology of aging.* (pp. 189–221). New York: Van Nostrand Reinhold.

Rothbart, M. K., & Maccoby, E. E. (1966). Parents' differential reactions to sons and daughters. *Journal of Personality and Social Psychology, 4,* 237–243.

Rotter, J. (1966). Generalized expectancies for internal versus external control of reinforcement. *Psychological Monographs,* 80(1, Whole No. 609).

Rovee, C. K., Cohen, R. Y., & Schlapek, W. (1975). Life-span stability in olfactory sensitivity. *Developmental Psychology, 11,* 311–318.

Rubin, L. (1976). *Worlds of pain.* New York: Basic Books.

Russell, C. S. (1974). Transition to parenthood: Problems and gratifications. *Journal of Marriage and the Family, 36,* 244–303.

Ryder, R. G. (1968). Husband-wife dyads versus married strangers. *Family Process, 7,* 232–238.

Salthouse, T. A. (1976a). Does speed of performance change with increased age? In L. W. Poon & J. L. Fozard (Eds.), *Design conference on decision making and aging* (pp. 104–117). Boston, V. A. Geriatric Education and Clinical Center Technical Report 76-01.

Salthouse, T. A. (1976b). Speed and age: Multiple rates of decline. *Experimental Aging Research, 2,* 349–359.

Schaie, K. W. (1958). Rigidity-flexibility and intelligence: A cross-sectional study of the adult life span from 20 to 70 years. *Psychological Monographs, 72,* 1–62.

Schaie, K. W. (1970). A reinterpretation of age-related changes in cognitive structure and functioning. In L. R. Goulet & P. B. Baltes (Eds.), *Life-span developmental psychology: Research and theory.* New York: Academic Press.

Schaie, K. W., Labouvie, G. V., & Buech, B. U. (1973). Generational and cohort-specific differences in adult cognitive functioning: A fourteen-year study of independent samples. *Developmental Psychobiology, 9,* 151–166.

Schmidt, W. H., & Hore, T. (1970). Some nonverbal aspects of communication between mother and preschool child. *Child Development, 41,* 889–896.

Schonfield, D., & Robertson, B. A. (1966). Memory storage and aging. *Canadian Journal of Psychology, 20,* 228–236.

Schonfield, D., & Smith, G. A. (1976). Searching for multiple targets and age. *Educational Gerontology, 1,* 119–129.

Schvanaveldt, J. D., & Ihinger, M. (1979). Sibling relationships in the family. In W. Burr, R. Hill, G. Nye, & I. Reiss, *Contemporary theories about the family* (Vol. 1, pp. 453–467). New York: Free Press.

Scott, F. G. (1962). Family group structure and patterns of social interaction. *American Journal of Sociology, 68,* 214–228.

Sears, P. S., & Sears, R. R. (1978, August). *From childhood to middle age to later maturity: Longitudinal study.* Paper presented at the meeting of the American Psychological Association, Toronto.

Sears, R. R. (1977). Sources of life satisfaction of the Terman gifted men. *American Psychologist, 32,* 119–128.

Shanas, E., Townsend, P., Wedderburn, D., Friis, H., Milhoj, P., & Stehouwer, J. (1968). *Older people in three industrial societies.* New York: Atherton.

Shapiro, E. (1978, August). *Transition to parenthood in adult and family development.* Paper presented at the meeting of the American Psychological Association, Toronto.

Sheehy, G. (1976). *Passages: Predictable crises in adult life.* New York: Dutton.

Sheppard, H. L. (1971). *New perspectives on older workers*. Washington, DC: W. E. Upjohn Institute for Employment Research.

Sheppard, H. L., & Belitsky, A. H. (1966). *The job hunt*. Baltimore: Johns Hopkins Press.

Shmavonian, B. M., & Busse, E. W. (1963). The utilization of psychophysiological techniques in the study of the aged. In R. H. Williams, C. Tibbetts, & W. Donahue (Eds.), *Process of aging: Social and psychological perspectives* (pp. 235–258). New York: Atherton.

Shock, N. W. (1972). Energy metabolism, caloric intake and physical activity of the aging. In L. A. Carlson (Ed.), *Nutrition in old age* (a symposium of the Swedish Nutrition Foundation) (pp. 12–23). Uppsala, Sweden: Almqvist & Wiksell.

Shope, D. F., & Broderick, C. B. (1967). Level of sexual experience and predicted adjustment in marriage. *Journal of Marriage and the Family, 29,* 424–427.

Siegler, I. C. (1978). *Longitudinal patterns in locus of control.* Unpublished manuscript, Duke University.

Siegler, I. C. (1980). The psychology of adult development and aging. In E. W. Busse & D. G. Blazer (Eds.), *The biological and psychological basis of geriatric psychiatry* (pp. 169–221). New York: Van Nostrand Reinhold.

Sigel, I. (1970). The distancing hypothesis: A causal hypothesis for the aquisition of representational thought. In M. R. Jones (Ed.), *Miami Symposium on the Prediction of Behavior, 1968: Effect of early experiences* (pp. 99–118). Coral Gables, FL: University of Miami Press.

Sigusch, V., Schmidt, G., Reinfeld, A., & Wiedemann–Sutor, I. (1970). Psychosexual stimulation: Sex differences. *Journal of Sex Research, 6*(1), 10–24.

Sinnot, J. D. (1975). Everyday thinking and Piagetian operativity in adults. *Human Development, 18,* 430–443.

Skinner, B. F. (1983). Intellectual self-management in old age. *American Psychologist, 38,* 239–244.

Skolnick, A. (1966a). Motivational imagery and behavior over 20 years. *Journal of Consulting Psychology, 30,* 463–478.

Skolnick, A. (1966b). Stability and interrelations of thematic test imagery over 20 years. *Child Development, 37,* 389–396.

Sontag, L. W., Baker, C. T., & Nelson, V. L. (1958). Mental growth and personality development: A longitudinal study. *Monographs of the Society for Research in Child Development, 23,*(68).

Soule, A. B. (1974, August). *The pregnant couple.* Paper presented at the meeting of the American Psychological Association, New Orleans.

Spanier, G. B., & Furstenberg, F. F., Jr. (1982). Remarriage after divorce: A longitudinal analysis of well-being. *Journal of Marriage and the Family, 44,* 709–720.

Spence, D. L., & Lonner, T. D. (1972). *Career set: A resource through transitions and crises.* Unpublished manuscript, Department of Psychology, University of Rhode Island.

Spirduso, W. W. (1975). Reaction and movement time as a function of age and physical activity level. *Journal of Gerontology, 30,* 435–440.

Srole, L., & Fischer, A. (1978, November). *The Midtown Manhattan study: Longitudinal focus on aging genders and life transitions.* Paper presented at the meeting of the Gerontological Society, Dallas.

Staats, S. (1974). Internal versus external locus of control for three age groups. *International Journal of Aging and Human Development, 5,* 7–10.

Staples, R. (1977). *Single and Black in America*. Unpublished manuscript, University of California, Program in Human Development, San Francisco.

Staples, R., & Mirandé, A. (1980). Racial and cultural variations among American families: A decennial review of the literature on minority families. *Journal of Marriage and the Family, 42,* 887–903.

Stein, A. H., & Bailey, M. M. (1973). The socialization of achievement orientation in females. *Psychological Bulletin, 80,* 345–366.

Stein, P. (1978). The lifestyle and life chances of the never-married. *Marriage and Family Review, 1*(4), 1–11.

Stoller, S. A., & Field, T. (1981, April). *A comparison of teenage mother and grandmother behaviors during floor play interactions with their infants.* Paper presented at the meeting of the Society for Research in Child Development, Boston.

Strong, E. K., Jr. (1959). *Changes of interest with age.* Stanford, CA: Stanford University Press.

Surwillo, W. W. (1963). The relation of response time variability to age and the influence of brain wave frequency. *Electroencephalography and Clinical Neurophysiology, 15,* 1029–1032.

Sutton-Smith, B., & Rosenberg, B. G. (1970). *The sibling.* New York: Holt, Rinehart, & Winston.

Switzer, A. (1975). *Achievement motivation in women: A three-year generational study.* Unpublished master's thesis, Wayne State University.

Szalai, A. (Ed.). (1973). *The use of time: Daily activities of urban and suburban populations in twelve countries.* The Hague: Mouton.

Szinovacz, M. E. (1973, August). *Satisfaction with work, marriage and household activities in women blue-collar and white-collar workers.* Paper presented at the meeting of the International Society for the Study of Behavioral Development, University of Michigan, Ann Arbor.

Talbert, G. B. (1977). Aging of the reproductive system. In C. E. Finch & L. Hayflick (Eds.), *Handbook of the biology of aging* (pp. 318–356). New York: Van Nostrand Reinhold.

Tangri, S. S. (1972). Determinants of occupational role innovation among college women. *Journal of Social Issues, 28*(2), 177–199.

Tanner, J. M. (1962). *Growth at adolescence* (2nd ed). Springfield, IL: Charles C. Thomas.

Taylor, C. (1969). Age and achievement of noted pianists. *Proceedings of 77th Annual Convention of the American Psychological Association,* 745–746.

Terkel, S. (1972). *Working.* New York: Random House.

Thackrey, D. (Ed.), in cooperation with L. Pastalan of the Institute of Gerontology. (1975). *Research News* (Division of Research and Development, University of Michigan), *27*(5–6), 5.

Thompson, L. W., & Marsh, G. (1973). Psychological studies of aging. In C. Eisdorfer & M. P. Lawton (Eds.), *The psychology of adult development and aging.* Washington, DC: American Psychological Association.

Thompson, L. W., & Nowlin, J. B. (1973). Relation of increased attention to central and autonomic nervous system states. In L. F. Jarvik, C. Eisdorfer, & J. E. Blum (Eds.), *Intellectual functioning in adults* (pp. 107–123). New York: Springer.

Thornton, A., & Freedman, D. (1979). Changes in the sex role attitudes of women, 1962–1977: Evidence from a panel study. *American Sociological Review, 44,* 831–842.

Timiras, P. S. (1972). *Developmental physiology and aging*. New York: Macmillan.

Tinsley, B. R., & Parke, R. D. (1984). Grandparents as support and socialization agents. In M. Lewis (Ed.), *Beyond the dyad* (pp. 161–194). New York: Plenum.

Tobin, S., & Kulys, R. (1979). The family and services. In C. Eisdorfer (Ed.), *Annual review of gerontology and geriatrics*. New York: Springer.

Toffler, A. (1970). *Future shock*. New York: Random House.

Troll, L. E. (1972). Is parent-child conflict what we mean by the generation gap? *Family Coordinator, 21,* 347–349.

Troll, L. E. (1982). *Continuations: Adult development and aging*. Monterey, CA: Brooks/Cole.

Troll, L. E., & Bengtson, V. L. (1979). Generations in the family. In W. Burr, R. Hill, I. Nye, & I. Reiss (Eds.), *Contemporary theories about the family*. New York: Free Press.

Troll, L. E., & Bengtson, V. L. (1982). Intergenerational relations through the life span. In B. B. Wolman (Ed.), *Handbook of developmental psychology*. Englewood Cliffs, NJ: Prentice-Hall.

Troll, L. E., Miller, S., & Atchley, R. C. (1979). *Families of later life*. Belmont, CA: Wadsworth.

Troll, L. E., Neugarten, B. L., & Kraines, R. (1969). Similarities in values and other personality characteristics in college students and their parents. *Merrill-Palmer Quarterly, 15,* 323–337.

Troll, L. E., & Schwartz, L. (in press). A three-generational analysis of changes in women's achievement motivation and power. In L. S. Auerbach & C. D. Ryff (Eds.), *Social power and dominance in women: Interdisciplinary perspective on women's contexts for exerting control and influence*. Washington, DC: American Association for the Advancement of Science.

Troll, L. E., & Smith, J. (1972, December). *Three-generation lineage changes in cognitive style and value traits*. Paper presented at the meeting of the Gerontological Society, San Juan, PR.

Troll, L. E., & Turner, B. F. (1979). Sex differences in problems of aging. In E. S. Gomberg & V. Franks (Eds.), *Gender and disordered behavior: Sex differences in psychopathology* (pp. 124–158). New York: Brunner/Mazel.

Turkington, C. (1983, January). Special issue on unemployment. *APA Monitor.*

Turner, B. F., & Huyck, M. H. (1982). Gerontologists and their parents: It's not any easier. In L. E. Troll (Ed.), *Elders and their families: Generations* (pp.32–33). San Francisco: Western Gerontological Association.

Turner, B. F., & McCaffrey, J. H. (1974). Socialization and career orientation among Black and White college women. *Journal of Vocational Behavior, 5,* 307–319.

U. S. Commission on Civil Rights. (1977). *The age discrimination study*. Washington, DC: U.S. Government Printing Office.

U.S. Department of Commerce, Bureau of the Census. (1976). *Current population reports: Population characteristics* (Series P-20, No. 297). Washington, DC: U.S. Government Printing Office.

U.S. Department of Commerce, Bureau of the Census. (1981). *Statistical abstracts of the United States. (102nd ed.).*

U.S. Department of Commerce, Bureau of the Census. (1982, January). *Census Population Reports*. Washington, DC: U.S. Government Printing Office.

U.S. Department of Commerce, Bureau of the Census. (1983). *Statistical tables of the United States, 1982/83*. Washington, DC: U.S. Government Printing Office.

U.S. Department of Health, Education, and Welfare, National Center for Health Statistics. (1971). *Health in the late years of life*. Washington, DC: U.S. Government Printing Office.

U.S. Department of Health, Education, and Welfare, National Center for Health Statistics. (1973, June 27). *Monthly Vital Statistics Report*. Washington, DC: U.S. Government Printing Office.

U.S. Department of Health, Education, and Welfare, National Center for Health Statistics. (1977). *Vital Statistics of the United States* (Vol 2). Washington, DC: U.S. Government Printing Office.

U.S. Department of Health, Education, and Welfare, National Center for Health Statistics. (1978). *Current estimates from the Health Interview Survery: United States, 1977*. Vital and Health Statistics, No. 126. Washington, DC: Public Health Service.

U.S. Department of Health, Education, and Welfare, National Center for Health Statistics. (1979). *Vital Statistics of the United States, 1975* (Vol. 2). Washington, DC: U.S. Government Printing Office.

U.S. Department of Labor, Bureau of Labor Statistics. (1982). *Special Labor Force Reports* (Bulletin 2096, Series C 3.134), p. 30. Washington, DC: U.S. Government Printing Office.

U.S. Department of Labor, Women's Bureau. (1969). *Handbook on women workers*. Washington, DC: U.S. Government Printing Office.

U.S. Department of Labor, Women's Bureau. (1980). *Handbook on women workers* (Bulletin 297). Washington, DC: U.S. Government Printing Office.

Vaillant, G. E. (1977). *Adaptation to life*. Boston: Little, Brown.

Veroff, J., Douvan, E., & Kulka, R. A. (1981). *The inner American: A self-portrait from 1957 to 1976*. New York: Basic Books.

Veroff, J., & Feld, S. (1970). *Marriage and work in America: A study of motives and roles*. New York: Van Nostrand Reinhold.

Verwoerdt, A., Pfeiffer, E., & Wang, H. S. (1969). Sexual behavior in senescence: II. Patterns of sexual activity and interest. *Geriatrics, 24*, 137–154.

Voydanoff, P. (1977). An analysis of sources of job satisfaction by age. In National Institute of Mental Health, *Research on the mental health of the aging, 1960 – 1976*. Washington, DC: U.S. Government Printing Office. (RO3 MH 27080)

Walker, A., Thompson, L., & Morgan, C. (1982, October). *Two generations of mothers and daughters: Role status and interdependence*. Paper presented at the meeting of the National Council on Family Relations, Washington, D.C.

Walker, A., & Thompson, L. (1983). Intimacy and intergenerational aid and contact among mothers and daughters. *Journal of Marriage and the Family, 45*, 841–850.

Walker, K. (1970, June). Time spent by husbands in household work. *Family Economics Review*, pp. 8–11.

Walsh, D. A. (1975). Age differences in learning and memory. In D. Woodruff & J. E. Birren (Eds.), *Aging: Scientific perspectives and social issues* (pp. 125–151). New York: Van Nostrand.

Wang, H. S., & Busse, E. W. (1969). EEG of healthy older persons—A longitudinal study: Dominant background activity and occipital rhythm. *Journal of Gerontology, 24*, 419–426.

Wapner, S., Werner, H., & Comalli, P. E., Jr. (1960). Perception of part-whole relationships in middle and old age. *Journal of Gerontology, 15*, 412–415.

Warrington, E. K., & Silberstein, M. (1970). A questionnaire technique for investigating very long-term memory. *Quarterly Journal of Experimental Psychology, 22*, 508–512.

Waugh, N. C., & Norman, D. A. (1965). Primary memory. *Psychological Review, 72*, 89–104.

Weg, R. (1982). Selected characteristics of the aging in the United States: The demography of growing older. In H. Dennis (Ed.), *Preparation for retirement manual* (9th ed.). Los Angeles: University of Southern California, Andrus Gerontology Center.

Weingarten, K., & Daniels, P. (1978, August). *Family/career transitions in women's lives: Report on research in progress*. Paper presented at the meeting of the American Psychological Association, Toronto.

Weiss, R. (1975). The provisions of social relationships. In Z. Rubin (Ed.), *Doing unto others*. Englewood Cliffs, NJ: Prentice-Hall.

Welford, A. T. (1977). Motor performance. In J. E. Birren & K. W. Schaie (Eds.), *Handbook of the psychology of aging*. New York: Van Nostrand Reinhold.

Werner, H. (1948). *Comparative psychology of mental development*. New York: International Universities Press.

Wetherick, N. E. (1964). A comparison of the problem-solving ability of young, middle-aged and old subjects. *Gerontologia, 9*, 164–178.

Wilensky, H. L. (1961). Orderly careers and social participation: The impact of work history on social integration in the middle class. *American Sociological Review, 26*, 521–539.

Wilson, W. C. (1975). The distribution of selected sexual attitudes and behaviors among the adult population of the United States. *Journal of Sex Research, 11*, 46–64.

Winter, W. D., Ferreira, A. J., & Bowers, N. (1973). Decision-making in married and unrelated couples. *Family Process, 12*, 83–94.

Wood, V., & Robertson, J. (1976). The significance of grandparenthood. In J. F. Gubrium (Ed.), *Time, roles, and self in old age*. New York: Human Sciences Press.

Woodruff, D. S. (1975). Relationships between EEG alpha frequency, reaction time, and age: A biofeedback study. *Psychophysiology, 12*, 673–681.

Woodruff, D. S. (1978). Brain activity and development. In P. B. Baltes (Ed.), *Life-span development and behavior* (Vol. 1, pp. 112–181). New York: Academic Press.

Woodruff, D. S., & Birren, J. E. (1972). Age changes and cohort differences in personality. *Developmental Psychology, 6*, 252–259.

Wright, V. D. (1978). Are working women *really* more satisfied? Evidence from several national surveys. *Journal of Marriage and the Family, 40*, 301–313.

Wyly, M. V., & Hulicka, I. M. (1975, August). *Problems and compensations of widowhood: A comparison of age groups*. Paper presented at the meeting of the American Psychological Association, Chicago.

Yarrow, M. R., Waxler, C. Z., & Scott, P. M. (1971). Child effects on adult behavior. *Developmental Psychology, 5*, 300–311.

Zelnick, M., & Kantner, J. F. (1977). Sexual and contraceptive experience of young married women in the United States, 1976 and 1971. *Family Planning Perspectives, 9*, 55–71.

INDEX

Credits

This page constitutes an extension of the copyright page.

Chapter One
17, Figure 1–2: From "A Reinterpretation of Age-Related Changes in Cognitive Structure and Functioning," by K. W. Schaie. In L. R. Goulet and P. B. Baltes (Eds.), *Life-Span Developmental Psychology: Research and Theory.* Copyright © 1970 by Academic Press. Reprinted by permission.

Chapter Two
31. Figure 2–2: From *The Research News,* Division of Research and Development, University of Michigan, by Donald Thackrey (Ed.), November-December, 1975, *27*(5–6), 5. Copyright © 1975 by *The Research News* and Leon Pastalan of the Institute of Gerontology. Reprinted by permission.

Chapter Three
51, Figure 3–2: Reprinted from Larry W. Thompson and John B. Nowlin, "Relation of Increased Attention to Central and Autonomic Nervous System States," p. 144. In Lissy F. Jarvik, Carl Eisdorfer, and June E. Blum, Eds., *Intellectual Functioning in Adults.* Copyright © 1973 by Springer Publishing Company, Inc., New York. Used by permission. **60,** Figure 3–5: From "Fifty Years of Memory for Names and Faces: A Cross-Sectional Approach," by H. P. Bahrick, P. O. Bahrick, and R. Wittlinger. In *Journal of Experimental Psychology: General,* 1975, *104*(1), 54–75. Copyright 1975 by the American Psychological Association. Reprinted by permission. **61,** Table 3–1: From "A Questionnaire Technique for Investigating Very Long-Term Memory," by E. Warrington and M. Silberstein. In *Quarterly Journal of Experimental Psychology,* 1970, *22*(3), 508–512. Copyright © 1970 by Academic Press. Reprinted by permission. **64,** Table 3–2: From "Age and Creative Productivity," by W. Dennis. Reprinted by permission of the *Journal of Gerontology,* 1966, *21*(1), 1–8. **67,** Figure 3–6: From "Generational and Cohort–Specific Differences in Adult Cognitive Functioning: A Fourteen-Year Study of Independent Samples," by K. W. Schaie, G. V. Labouvie, and B. Beuch. In *Developmental Psychology,* 1973, *9*(2), 18. Copyright 1973 by the American Psychological Association. Reprinted by permission. **69,** Figure 3–7: From "Organization of Data on Life-Span Development of Human Abilities," by J. Horn. In L. R. Goulet and P. B. Baltes (Eds.), *Life-Span Developmental Psychology: Research and Theory.* Copyright © 1970 by Academic Press. Reprinted by permission.

Chapter Four
80 and 81, Tables 4–1 and 4–2: From *The Inner American:A Self-Portrait from 1957–1976,* by J. Veroff, E. Douvan and R. A. Kukla. © 1981 by Basic Books, Inc., Publishers. Reprinted by permission of the publisher. **85,** Figure 4–3: From *Adaptation to Life,* by G. E. Vaillant. Copyright © 1977 by George E. Vaillant. By permission of Little, Brown and Company. **91,** Figure 4–4: Reprinted by permission of the author and editors of *Experimental Aging Research,* 1975, *1*(2), 281–291. From "Structure of the Self-Concept from Adolescence through Old Age," by R. Monge. Copyright Beech Hill Enterprises, Inc. **99,** Tables 4–5 and 4–6: From "The Midtown Manhattan Study: Longitudinal Focus on Aging Genders and Life Transitions," by L. Srole and A. Fischer. Paper presented at the meeting of the Gerontological Society, Dallas, 1978. **100,** Table 4–7: Reprinted from *Children of the Great Depression,* by G. Elder, by permission of The University of Chicago Press, copyright 1974.

Chapter Five
111, Figure 5–1: From *Early and Middle Adulthood,* by L. E. Troll. Copyright © 1975 by Wadsworth Publishing Company, Inc. Reprinted by permission of Brooks/Cole Publishing Company, Monterey, California 93940. **133,** Table 5–2: From *Family Development in Three Generations,* by R. Hill, N. Foote, J. Aldous, R. Carlson, and R. Macdonald. Copyright © 1970 by Schenkman Publishing Company. Reprinted by permission.

Chapter Six
162, Figure 6–1: Reprinted from *Children of the Great Depression,* by G. Elder, by permission of The University of Chicago Press, copyright 1974. **163,** Table 6–1: Adapted from *The Inner American: A Self-Portrait from 1957–1976,* by Joseph Veroff, Elizabeth Douvan, and Richard A. Kulka. © 1981 by Basic Books, Inc., Publishers. Reprinted by permission of the publisher. **179,** Figure 6–3: Adapted from *Lifeprints: New Patterns of Love And Work for Today's Woman,* by G. K. Baruch, R. C. Barnett, and C. Rivers. Copyright © 1983 by McGraw-Hill Company. Reprinted by permission. **180,** Figure 6–4: Adapted from "Bosses Face Less Risk than the Bossed," by B. Nelson, April 3, 1983. Copyright © 1983 by The New York Times Company. Reprinted by permission. **181,** Figure 6–5: From "The Timing of the First Birth and Changes in Personal Efficacy," by S. D. McLaughlin and J. Micklin. In *Journal of Marriage and the Family, 45,* 1983, pp. 47–55. Reprinted by permission.